GROWING UP ENLIGHTENED

How Maharishi School
of the Age of Enlightenment
is Awakening the
Creative Genius of Students
and Creating Heaven on Earth

•

SANFORD I. NIDICH, ED.D.
RANDI JEANNE NIDICH, ED.D.

MAHARISHI INTERNATIONAL UNIVERSITY PRESS

Library of Congress Catalog Card Number: 90–61520
ISBN 0–923569–03–0

Maharishi International University Press, Fairfield Iowa, U.S.A.

To His Holiness Maharishi Mahesh Yogi,
whose Science and Technology of the Unified Field
is transforming the trends of time —
developing higher states of consciousness within the individual
and creating a permanent state of world peace and
Heaven on Earth for all the world's family.

C O N T E N T S

CHAPTER FOUR   59

**Connecting All Knowledge to the Self:
Teaching the Academic Disciplines in Light of
Maharishi's Science of Creative Intelligence**

CHAPTER FIVE   83

**Excellence in Education:
Gaining the Fruit of All Knowledge**

CHAPTER SIX   101

**Social Development:
Action in Accord With All the Laws of Nature**

CHAPTER SEVEN   **123**

School Climate:
Producing a Coherent Collective Consciousness
Within the School

CHAPTER EIGHT   **141**

The Technology for Creating World Peace:
Maharishi's Transcendental Meditation (TM)
and TM-Sidhi Program

CHAPTER NINE   **157**

Maharishi International University:
Higher Education for Higher Consciousness

A C K N O W L E D G M E N T S

THIS BOOK WAS THE CULMINATION OF THE EFFORTS OF many people who are dedicated to improving the quality of education throughout the world. We wish to express our deepest gratitude to Susan Shatkin, Blair Butterfield, Craig Pearson, and Toni Alazraki for their wonderful job in editing the book.

We would also like to express our appreciation to Dr. Bevan Morris, Dr. Susan Dillbeck, Dr. Geoffrey Wells, and Dr. James Karpin for their continual encouragement of this project and for their review of the manuscript. We wish to thank Dr. Vinton Tompkins for his research on the rise of world peace, which we used in Chapter 8, and for his timely comments.

This book would not have been possible without the cooperation of the Directors of Maharishi School of the Age of Enlightenment, Dr. Robin Rowe and Dennis Rowe, and all the administrators, teachers, parents, and students at Maharishi School.

Many people helped us collect and analyze the research data, including Dr. Fred Travis, Maxwell Rainforth, John Zanath, Catharine Cole, Sharon Prathar, and Patrick Moulin. We express our appreciation to the late Dr. Lawrence Kohlberg and to Dr. Ann Higgins of Harvard University for inspiring us to research moral development and school climate and for sharing their Just Community School data with us.

We also wish to thank Dr. Katharine Borman and Dr. Patricia O'Reilly of the University of Cincinnati, Dr. Ronald Zigler, Sheila and Stephen Terry, Alex Stolley, Marjorie and Randall Wood, Charles Edwards, and our parents, Frances and Louis Nidich and Doris and Stanley Finkel, for their encouragement and support.

Our thanks to Robert Oates for the main title of the book, to Shepley Hansen for the book and cover design, to Bob Stone for his photographs, to Lee and Anna Fergusson, Sue Ruby, and Mac Muehlman for their help in completing the book, and to all the staff at MIU Press for their time and energy.

P R E F A C E

EDUCATION IS ONCE AGAIN AT THE FOREFRONT OF NA-
tional attention. In its 1983 report, the National Commission on Excellence in Education concluded that "our nation is at risk." The commission cited compelling statistics showing that our schools are not doing the job we expect of
them: twenty-three million American adults are functionally il-
literate by the simplest tests of everyday reading, writing, and
comprehension; nearly 40 percent of all 17-year-olds cannot draw
inferences from written material; and over 60 percent cannot
solve a mathematics problem requiring several steps.[1]

Since this initial report, we have seen an upsurge of interest
in improving our nation's schools among parents, educators, and
legislators. But this renewed interest has not solved the problems: a report recently issued by the Secretary of Education emphasizes that our schools are still at risk.[2]

Countless articles and books have dramatized the failure of
the schools. A major report by Dr. Ernest Boyer, president of the
Carnegie Foundation for the Advancement of Teaching, stated:
"A deep erosion of confidence in our schools, coupled with dis-
turbing evidence that at least some of the skepticism is justified,
has made revitalizing the American high school an urgent matter."[3] National interest is so high that education is rapidly becoming the number one domestic issue among politicians and voters.

The last time there was such a strong interest in improving
American education was in the 1960s. During this period, there
was a demand for more "open," less structured approaches to
schooling and a de-emphasis on traditional, text-book learning,
to allow freer expression of the students' creativity. Schools offered more elective courses catering to the immediate interests
of students, and substantially reduced the number of academic
courses required for graduation.[4]

Throughout the past century, education has repeatedly swung
back and forth between more traditional and more open approaches.

Today, education is once again emphasizing more traditional approaches to gaining knowledge — for example, studying the great books and memorizing facts and information.[5] Unfortunately, history has shown that neither the more structured, content-oriented approaches nor the more open approaches have been able to develop the full creative potential of the student and create a prosperous and harmonious world, free from conflict and suffering.

The need for a new approach to education is clear. This book presents a new and effective approach, one that delivers to students the "fruit of all knowledge" — the ability to fulfill one's own desires without making mistakes or causing suffering to others. This new approach is called Maharishi's Unified Field Based Education. It upholds the study of the traditional academic disciplines while providing something even more central to education — the development of consciousness, the basis of the student's intelligence.

Every teacher knows that students display different levels of intelligence. Some students grasp new material without difficulty, while others never seem to grasp it at all. At the foundation of Maharishi's system of education is the discovery that intelligence can be increased through the development of consciousness. Maharishi's Unified Field Based Education provides the missing element in education — a simple and effective means for awakening the full value of consciousness in each student. In this way, Unified Field Based Education supplies the key which unlocks every student's ability to learn.[6]

We are presenting in this book a case study of Maharishi School of the Age of Enlightenment in Fairfield, Iowa, to give parents, educators, and students in colleges of education a concrete understanding of how Maharishi's Unified Field Based Education affects student intellectual and social development. To this end, we have spent the past five years conducting extensive interviews with the students, teachers, administrators, and parents of Maharishi School. We have spent hundreds of hours with our teams of graduate students observing classes and administering numerous surveys and tests to students and teachers from kindergarten through 12th grade.

The following summarizes some of the more striking research findings which will be discussed in more detail in the book:

• Both new and continuing Lower and Middle School students

showed significant improvement in academic achievement within a year's time, as assessed by the Iowa Tests of Basic Skills (ITBS) — a standardized measure of educational performance administered nationally to elementary and middle school students. The students improved significantly in overall academic achievement, reading, mathematics, language, and work-study skills. New students were at about grade level when they entered Maharishi School.

• New Upper School students showed significant improvement in academic achievement within a one-year period, as measured by the Iowa Tests of Educational Development (ITED), administered nationally to assess educational performance at the secondary level. Significant increases were found in overall academic achievement, reading, quantitative thinking, social studies, and knowledge of literary materials.

• Upper School classes have consistently scored at or near the 99th percentile nationally on overall academic achievement, as measured by the ITED.

• New students throughout the school showed significant improvement in IQ over a one-year period. Lower School students also exhibited a higher level of cognitive performance than students from similar backgrounds who were not enrolled in a unified field based school.

• Lower and Middle school students showed significantly higher levels of creative thinking than student controls.

• Upper School students reported a high degree of self-concept. One hundred percent of the students surveyed said they are happy, feel good most of the time, can make up their own mind about things, and are able to do schoolwork at least as well as most other students. Ninety-six percent said they are easy to like and are popular with students their own age.

• Upper School students showed a high level of social development, as measured by the Moral Atmosphere Interview developed by researchers at Harvard University. When compared to students from special alternative schools on the East Coast designed to promote moral development, students at Maharishi School exhibited significantly higher levels of "prosocial behavior norms" for caring, keeping agreements, not stealing, and restitution. Overall, the responses of Maharishi School students expressed values in favor of the harmony and growth of all students in the school.

• Over the past three years, Upper School students have won more than 100 awards in regional, state, and international science fair competitions. Students have also won awards in computer science, history, speech, poetry, acting, and music competitions at the district, regional, state, and national levels.

• Eighty-four percent of Maharishi School graduates have enrolled in accredited post-secondary institutions. The list of schools students have been accepted to includes Harvard University, New York University, Carleton College, Grinnell College, the University of Iowa, and Washington University in St. Louis.

Maharishi School of the Age of Enlightenment is named for its founder, Maharishi Mahesh Yogi, who is known and respected as the greatest scientist and teacher in the field of consciousness. With the inauguration of his worldwide Transcendental Meditation movement in 1957, Maharishi embarked on a historic endeavor to spiritually regenerate the whole of mankind through the knowledge and experience of higher states of consciousness. Thirty years later, Maharishi's teachings have been endorsed and implemented by leaders and institutions in all areas of society worldwide.[7]

Today, the signs are clear that Maharishi's goal is being achieved; with the rise of coherence in world consciousness, the trend of human life has changed from continued suffering and unhappiness to growing peace and fulfillment. Thus, the name "Maharishi" stands as an inspiration to all students at Maharishi School of the Age of Enlightenment to achieve greatness in their lives.

The Age of Enlightenment was inaugurated by Maharishi on January 12, 1975, on the basis of scientific research indicating that as little as one percent of a population practicing his Transcendental Meditation technique produces significant improvements in the quality of life of the whole society. With this discovery, Maharishi was inspired to proclaim the dawning of a new time of peace, prosperity, and happiness for the whole world. Maharishi's unified field based system of education, described in this book, is one of the principal means for perpetuating the Age of Enlightenment for generations to come. Maharishi School of the Age of Enlightenment is therefore aptly named for its role in creating fully educated individuals who promote progress and fulfillment in every area of society.

Maharishi School of the Age of Enlightenment in Fairfield, Iowa, is just one of many schools throughout the world providing Maharishi's Unified Field Based Education. Maharishi Schools have also been established in Washington, DC, Austin, Texas, Canada, Holland, and Great Britain. Courses in Maharishi's unified field based knowledge have been taught in high schools in the U.S. and Canada, as well as in many institutions of higher learning throughout the United States.

We hope you enjoy reading this book. We encourage parents and educators to introduce this new and important knowledge in your schools to help your children develop their full intellectual and creative potential. By developing the full potential of every student through ideal education, we can contribute to a better future for all mankind and create a world free from problems, mistakes and suffering — a Heaven on Earth.

Sanford I. Nidich, Ed.D.
Randi Jeanne Nidich, Ed.D.
Fairfield, Iowa
December, 1989

C H A P T E R   O N E

Introduction to Unified Field Based Education

THIS BOOK IS ABOUT A SCHOOL THAT IS BRINGING A NEW meaning to the term "excellence in education." It is about a school in which the children are happy, intelligent, creative, caring, and kind. It is about teachers and administrators who are enthusiastic about education and who share a bright vision for the future of their students.

This book is about children whose parents moved hundreds and even thousands of miles to a small southeastern Iowa community so they could obtain the best education offered anywhere in the United States. It is about a system of education that is helping to create a permanent state of world peace and Heaven on Earth.

This book is about Maharishi School of the Age of Enlightenment, located on the campus of Maharishi International University (MIU) in Fairfield, Iowa. Maharishi School began in 1974 as a small elementary school for children of the MIU faculty and staff. In 1981, the school expanded to include the Middle and Upper School grade levels. Since then, enrollment has increased by about 20 to 25 percent each year, and the school now has over 600 students from preschool through 12th grades. It is currently accredited by the Iowa Department of Education and the Independent Schools Association of the Central States.[1]

Maharishi School of the Age of Enlightenment is a success story. Hundreds of visitors from all over the world have come to visit and observe its remarkable quality of education. Newspapers across the country have run articles on the students' high level of academic achievement. Research papers have been presented at

■ Maharishi School of the Age of Enlightenment is a private, nonsectarian school, accredited by the Iowa Department of Education and the Independent Schools Association of the Central States. Due to the rapidly expanding enrollment, a new Lower School building was recently constructed.

professional education association meetings describing the holistic development of the students.

In many ways, Maharishi School appears to be like other accredited, nonreligious, private schools throughout the country. The school has a permanent physical facility — two three-story buildings, one for the Lower School, and one for the Middle and Upper Schools. Throughout their schooling, students take courses in all the major disciplines, including English, science, mathematics, social studies, computer science, and foreign languages. Textbooks and lectures by teachers are the major methods for presenting knowledge. Students wear uniforms and are expected to be punctual and regular in their attendance. And there is a strong community of parents that sustains the functioning of the school. On the surface, Maharishi School resembles hundreds of schools that take a conservative and structured approach to learning.

But the real basis of the school's success is more subtle. Unlike other schools, Maharishi School provides a way to develop the most important aspect of the educational process — the awareness, or consciousness, of the student.

Maharishi School of the Age of Enlightenment has been established at a time of great need in education. The statistics mentioned in the Preface on the level of achievement in education today by no means delineate the full extent of the current problems. Maharishi Mahesh Yogi, founder of Maharishi School of the Age of Enlightenment and Maharishi International University, points out that the widespread problems in schools today arise from their emphasis on the outer objects of knowledge without a corresponding emphasis on developing the subjective side of the educational process, the full mental potential and creativity of the student. Maharishi explains:

> Whatever education has been and whatever it is today, it does not develop the full man. If we look into the process of gaining knowledge, we find there are two sides to knowledge — the object [the object of knowledge], and the subject of knowledge [the knower]. What the present system of education provides is the knowledge of the object; what it misses is the knowledge of the subject. Without the full knowledge of the knower, when the knower is in ignorance about himself, the whole structure of knowledge is as if baseless. And baseless knowledge can only be non-fulfilling.[2]

It has been our experience that both public and private schools predominantly emphasize the objective knowledge of the academic disciplines and their related skill areas, without providing any systematic means to develop the subjective side of the educational process. Development of the students' inner potential is left more or less to chance, with the assumption that they will somehow become mature, well-rounded human beings as a result of exposure to the standard curriculum. Lack of attention to developing the knower makes learning meaningless and irrelevant to the students' lives. Lack of relevancy leads to a lack of motivation to learn, which in turn produces a substandard level of academic performance and problems with social behavior. The students find that they are simply not growing — not making use of their full creative potential.

This book presents a solution to the academic and social behavior problems encountered by both private and public schools across the country. The solution comes from a new system of education that provides the holistic knowledge and direct experience of the unified field of all the laws of nature — the source of all energy, intelligence, and creativity in nature and in human life. This is the element that has been missing in education so far.

This new educational approach is called Maharishi's Unified Field Based Education. This new system integrates the familiar objective approach to gaining knowledge, in which students study the content of the traditional disciplines, with a

Unified Field Based Education provides the holistic knowledge and direct experience of the unified field of all the laws of nature — the source of all energy, intelligence, and creativity in nature and in human life.

subjective approach that systematically unfolds the students' full inner potential. Central to this new system of education is the practice of Maharishi's Transcendental Meditation technique, a simple, natural, effortless mental technique that directly enlivens the unified field of all the laws of nature in the students' awareness.

In the remainder of this chapter, we will explain the key elements of Unified Field Based Education.

The Unified Field of All the Laws of Nature

What does it mean to say that a system of education "enlivens the unified field of all the laws of nature" in the student's awareness? First, let's consider what the unified field is. Then we can see later in this chapter how the knowledge of the unified field of natural law can be used in education to promote the holistic development of the student.

According to Maharishi, a complete description of the unified field of all the laws of nature has always been available in the texts of the ancient Vedic literature. However, this most fundamental field of life has only recently been glimpsed and described in scientific terms by modern theoretical physics.

Since the time of Einstein, physicists have searched for a theory that would explain all the various forms and phenomena in the universe as emerging from one fundamental, underlying field.

Since the time of Einstein, physicists have searched for a theory that would explain all the various forms and phenomena in the universe as emerging from one fundamental, underlying field. Until recently, it was assumed that all the diverse expressions of natural law arose from four fundamental forces — electromagnetic, strong, weak, and gravitational. The electromagnetic field is responsible for electricity, light, telecommunications capabilities, and indeed most of what we ordinarily experience through our senses. The weak force is responsible for radioactivity, the strong force for nuclear energy, and gravity for the orbits of the planets and for literally keeping our feet on the ground.

In the past two decades, however, advancements in high-energy physics have led to a progressively more unified understanding of these fundamental forces (see Figure 1). Beginning in 1967, physicists developed theories that unified the weak and electromagnetic forces. These theories brought a new understanding that these two fields emerge from one field — the electro-weak field — which exists at a more fundamental level of

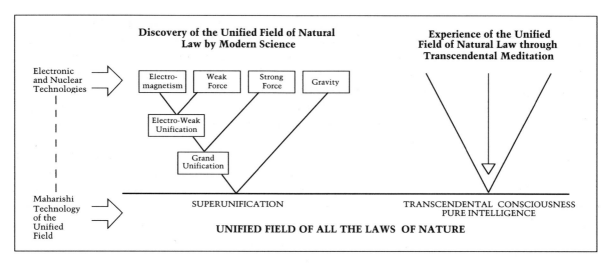

natural law. Later, others postulated "grand unified theories" that applied the same principle to unify the electro-weak and strong forces. With each level of unification, physicists have discovered deeper, more universal levels of natural law, leading to the knowledge that all the force and matter fields are ultimately united within one "supersymmetric" unified field.[3]

The unified field is located at the Planck scale, the most fundamental time and distance scale in nature. Because it is the fountainhead of natural law, the unified field is the most concentrated field of intelligence in nature — a field of *pure intelligence*.[4]

Physics also describes the unified field as having the property of self-interaction.[5] Interacting entirely within itself, the unified field of natural law creates all the diversified levels of natural law, including everything we see around us — from the cells in our bodies to the oceans, mountains, stars, and all the huge galaxies that comprise our physical universe.

Leading physicists today are beginning to realize the intimate relationship between the unified field and consciousness. Dr. John S. Hagelin, Professor of Physics at MIU and former researcher at the European Laboratory for Particle Physics (CERN) and Stanford Linear Accelerator Center, explains that recent advances in unified field theories provide significant evidence that the unified field and consciousness are not separate entities, but are one and the same. Dr. Hagelin asserts: "There is a detailed

■ Figure 1. Recently, modern physics has glimpsed the unified field of all the laws of nature. The individual can gain access to the unified field of natural law, the field of transcendental consciousness, through the practice of the Transcendental Meditation technique — the Maharishi Technology of the Unified Field.

Maharishi explains that the self-interacting nature of the unified field, glimpsed by modern physics, identifies the unified field as the self-referral state of consciousness — the state of transcendental consciousness.

structural correspondence between the unified field of modern theoretical physics and the field of pure, self-interacting consciousness. When we examine the properties of the unified field in detail, we discover all the properties of pure consciousness described in Maharishi's Vedic Science."[6]

According to Maharishi, "Since ancient times the unified field has been described by Vedic Science, the complete science of consciousness, as the field of pure consciousness, the field of infinite energy, creativity, and intelligence underlying man and nature."[7] Maharishi explains that the self-interacting nature of the unified field, glimpsed by modern theoretical physics, identifies the unified field as the self-referral state of consciousness — the state of transcendental (pure) consciousness:

> The knowledge of the unified field has been discovered by modern science during just the last few months and years, but the complete knowledge of the unified field has always been available in the Vedic literature. Today quantum physics is peeping into the details of the unified field and is locating its three-in-one structure. This is precisely the three-in-one structure of the self-referral state of consciousness. This structure is very simple to understand. The awareness is open to itself, and therefore the awareness knows itself. Because the awareness knows itself it is the knower, it is the known, and it is the process of knowing. This is the state of pure intelligence, wide-awake in its own nature and completely self-referral. This is pure consciousness, transcendental consciousness.[8]

According to Maharishi, self-referral consciousness is that unified state of nature's functioning that interacts within itself to create the infinite diversity of the universe. Knowledge of self-referral consciousness, Maharishi says, is that one knowledge whereby the entire field of creation could be handled. It is like handling the root of a tree and thereby handling all aspects of the tree — all the different branches, leaves, and flowers.

Through the applied technology of Maharishi's Vedic Science, Transcendental Meditation, it is very simple for the conscious mind to identify itself with the self-referral state of consciousness, the unified field of natural law. As Maharishi explains, this self-referral state is the unified state of knower, known, and process of knowing — or of subjectivity, objectivity, and their relationship.

From this level, one has the ability to know anything, do anything, and accomplish anything. Maharishi explains:

> In the self-referral consciousness of everyone is the total potential of all knowledge. The goal of all education is that the total potential of knowledge should be enlivened in the awareness of the student. This means that three values of the student's awareness — subjectivity, objectivity, and their relationship — are integrated. This Vedic Science, the science of pure knowledge, delivers the fruit of all knowledge in everyone's self-referral consciousness. In simple words, the fruit of all knowledge should mean the ability to know anything, do anything, and achieve anything.[9]

The knowledge and experience of the unified field provided by Maharishi's Vedic Science and its applied technology, Transcendental Meditation, form the basis for a new approach to education — one that delivers the fruit of all knowledge to every student while the tree of knowledge is still growing. Through this new approach — Maharishi's Unified Field Based Education — students grow in the ability to be at home with everything while they are still in the process of learning.

Unified Field Based Education

Maharishi's Unified Field Based Education includes three components that systematically enliven the unified field of all the laws of nature in the awareness of the student.

At Maharishi School, students first practice the Transcendental Meditation technique, through which they directly experience the unified field in their own simplest state of awareness (please see Figure 1). Then, for one period each day, they study the principles of Maharishi's Science of Creative Intelligence (SCI). SCI is the new integrated science that links modern science with Maharishi's Vedic Science — it therefore brings out the complete knowledge of consciousness and its relationship to all modern fields of knowledge. And finally, Unified Field Based Education includes teaching methods that connect the knowledge of each academic subject to the unified field of natural law — the field of pure consciousness.

By employing these three components of Unified Field Based Education every day, Maharishi School has been successful in

In the self-referral consciousness of everyone is the total potential of all knowledge.
— **Maharishi**

Studies have found that practicing TM for only a few minutes twice a day produces benefits in all areas of life — it unfolds mental potential, strengthens physical health, and improves social behavior.

promoting holistic student development. An introduction to each component follows.

Maharishi's Transcendental Meditation Program

The practice of Maharishi's Transcendental Meditation (TM) technique is the heart of this new integrated system of education. During the past 20 years, over 500 scientific research studies conducted in 125 institutions world-wide have shown the beneficial effects of Transcendental Meditation for the individual and society. These studies have found that practicing TM for only a few minutes twice a day produces benefits in all areas of life — it unfolds mental potential, strengthens physical health, and improves social behavior. The scientific studies on TM have revealed a wide range of benefits for education, including:

- improved academic achievement
- increased intelligence and creativity
- improved memory and learning ability
- increased energy and alertness
- improved concentration and ability to focus
- reduced stress and anxiety
- improved moral reasoning ability and social behavior
- reduced usage of drugs, alcohol, and cigarettes
- increased happiness and self-confidence
- improved self-esteem and self-concept
- increased self-actualization[10]

How can a purely mental procedure give rise to such diverse benefits? TM is a simple, natural, effortless mental technique that enlivens the vast reservoir of intelligence, creativity, and energy — the field of pure consciousness — deep within the mind of every student. Just as watering the root of a tree brings nourishment to all the branches and flowers, diving deep within the mind through the practice of TM enriches all areas of the student's life.

Maharishi's Transcendental Meditation program is easy to learn and does not involve any change in one's beliefs or lifestyle. It is practiced by people from every culture and from all walks of life. TM is practiced with eyes closed, sitting comfortably in a chair, for 10 to 20 minutes twice each day.

All students, teachers, and administrators at Maharishi School practice TM twice daily as part of their daily schedule.

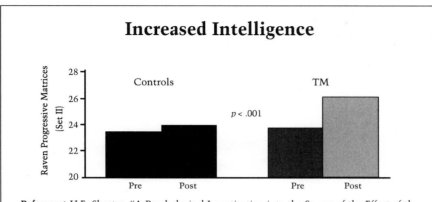

Increased Intelligence

Reference: H.E. Shecter, "A Psychological Investigation into the Source of the Effect of the Transcendental Meditation Technique" (Ph.D. diss., York Univ.), *Dissertation Abstracts International* 38, 7-B (1978): 3372–3373.

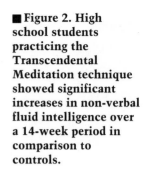

■ Figure 2. High school students practicing the Transcendental Meditation technique showed significant increases in non-verbal fluid intelligence over a 14-week period in comparison to controls.

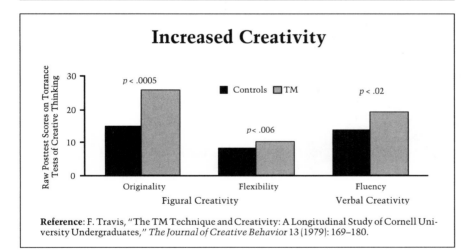

Increased Creativity

Reference: F. Travis, "The TM Technique and Creativity: A Longitudinal Study of Cornell University Undergraduates," *The Journal of Creative Behavior* 13 (1979): 169–180.

■ Figure 3. College students who learned the Transcendental Meditation technique exhibited higher levels of creative thinking ability over a five-month period compared to nonmeditating students.

Students report that the practice makes their mind sharper, releases stress and anxiety, and makes them more creative and energetic. Alison, a 12th-grade student, says: "TM is a wonderful technique. It enables you to settle down and become strong within yourself. It also helps to give you the energy, intelligence, and ability to succeed at whatever you do. Since beginning TM, I have achieved many of the goals I set for myself, including that of becoming a successful high school student."[11]

During the Transcendental Meditation technique the mind

■ Research has found that the practice of Maharishi's Transcendental Meditation technique makes students more creative, intelligent, and energetic.

settles down and becomes completely calm and collected, much as the choppy surface of an ocean settles down and becomes calm. The mind remains fully awake, experiencing its own essential nature, without reference to anything outside itself. As we mentioned earlier, Maharishi calls this self-referral state "pure consciousness" or "transcendental consciousness" — the simplest form of human awareness, in which consciousness knows itself. Maharishi explains that when the conscious mind identifies itself with the field of pure consciousness through Transcendental Meditation, "human awareness is open to its own full potential, the infinite potential of nature's intelligence."[12]

Children four through nine years of age learn the Children's TM technique, suited to their level of neurophysiological development and practiced for a shorter period of time.

In Chapter Two we describe the older students' experiences of the unified field of natural law during their practice of TM, and the younger students' experiences with the Children's TM technique. We also examine in more detail how Transcendental Meditation program unfolds students' full potential.

In addition to Transcendental Meditation, beginning in the Middle School the students may begin to learn the more advanced TM-Sidhi program. Most of the teachers and administrators also practice this program. Maharishi's TM-Sidhi program greatly enhances the benefits of TM and accelerates the development of higher states of consciousness through increased mind-body coordination. The practice of the TM and TM-Sidhi program benefits society as well. A number of studies in the past 15 years have shown that sufficiently large groups practicing this program together in one place produce measurable positive changes in quality of life indicators. The TM-Sidhi program and its effects are discussed in greater detail in Chapter Eight.

Maharishi's Science of Creative Intelligence

In 1970, Maharishi formulated the knowledge of the unified field of natural law contained in the ancient Vedic literature into a new science of consciousness — the Science of Creative Intelligence (SCI). Maharishi has said: "In the Science of Creative Intelligence, we now have a new science of age-old life. We call it new because it provides a new name for the eternal reality of life."[13] In the Science of Creative Intelligence, Maharishi gives expression to the timeless principles of nature's functioning in a language uniquely appropriate to our age.

The Science of Creative Intelligence has two aspects, theoretical and practical. The theoretical aspect of SCI gives complete intellectual understanding of the field of pure intelligence, the unified field of natural law, both from the detailed descriptions of the great sages of the Vedic tradition — including Maharishi himself — and from the knowledge of modern academic disciplines. SCI unifies all knowledge by connecting all streams of knowledge to their source in the field of pure intelligence. In doing so, SCI connects the main conclusions about the structure and functioning of natural law from modern science to those of Maharishi's Vedic Science.

Transcendental Meditation is the applied technology of Maharishi's Vedic Science, and thus it is also considered the "laboratory component" of SCI, because SCI uses this technology to give direct experience of the field of pure intelligence, the unified field of natural law. Because of the intimate connection of theory and practice, both aspects are taught to students at Maharishi School as part of their study of SCI. According to Maharishi, the two aspects of SCI — theoretical and practical, understanding and experience — are both necessary for full knowledge and complete development of creative intelligence in the student's life.

At Maharishi School, SCI is studied as a subject in its own right from kindergarten through 12th grades. The students learn SCI with reference to simple "principles and qualities of creative intelligence." For example, these principles include "The

In the Science of Creative Intelligence, Maharishi gives expression to the timeless principles of nature's functioning in a language uniquely appropriate to our age.

By studying the principles and qualities of SCI, and by experiencing them growing in their own lives through the practice of Transcendental Meditation, students increasingly perceive their own lives in terms of all possibilities rather than in terms of restricting limitations.

nature of life is to grow," "Order is present everywhere," and "The whole is more than the sum of its parts." The qualities of creative intelligence include "intelligence," "creativity," "stability," "adaptability," "orderliness," and "integration."

These universal principles and qualities of creative intelligence are found expressed in nature, in the lives of great men and women, and in the life of the student. By studying the principles and qualities of creative intelligence in different avenues of life, and by experiencing them growing in their own lives through the practice of Transcendental Meditation, students increasingly perceive their own lives in terms of all possibilities rather than in terms of restricting limitations. In Chapter Three, we discuss the study of SCI in terms of student development and give examples of elementary and secondary level SCI lessons at Maharishi School.

Teaching the Academic Disciplines in Light of Maharishi's Science of Creative Intelligence

Maharishi's Science of Creative Intelligence brings out universal principles and qualities that can also be located within each academic discipline. SCI provides a comprehensive framework for interrelating all the academic disciplines and connecting them to the life of the student.

SCI-based teaching methods are used in all the academic subjects on the secondary level to connect the lessons of every discipline to the source of the discipline, the unified field of natural law. These methods include the use of specially designed instructional charts. The most graphic of all the charts are called Unified Field Charts. These charts conceptually map the entire discipline, from its most abstract levels to its most applied levels, and show how the whole discipline emerges from the unified field of all the laws of nature, which students experience during their practice of the Transcendental Meditation technique.

In Chapter Four we give examples of how these SCI-based instructional charts are used at Maharishi School. Chapters Five and Six describe research documenting the effects of Unified Field Based Education on student academic and social development at Maharishi School. Chapter Seven discusses how Unified Field Based Education promotes a positive school climate.

In Chapter Eight we present Maharishi's Transcendental

■ **Maharishi's unified field based education promotes both academic and social development. During their classroom activities, students exhibit a high degree of enthusiasm, cooperation, and receptivity to knowledge.**

Meditation technique and the TM-Sidhi program in terms of their value in promoting world peace. In Chapter Nine we focus on Unified Field Based Education on the post-secondary level as it is implemented at Maharishi International University. And Chapter Ten discusses the importance and timeliness of applying Maharishi's Vedic Science to create Heaven on Earth.

As you will see in the following pages, the Maharishi Unified Field Based Integrated System of Education holds tremendous promise for the field of education. Since the time of Plato, great educators and philosophers have held the lofty goal that education should produce self-realized, enlightened individuals — that is, people who have the ability to fulfill their own aspirations and at the same time promote the continual progress and well-being of society.

Plato stated, "If you ask what is the good of education, the answer is easy — that education makes good men, and that good men act nobly." With reference to the knowledge imparted by education and its results in the lives of students, he stated that "there is a perfection which all knowledge ought to reach, and which our pupils ought to attain." Today, after 2000 years, these

ideals remain essentially unchanged. Abraham Maslow wrote
that "the goal of education . . . is ultimately the self-actualization
of a person, the becoming fully human, the development of the
fullest height that the human species can stand up to. . . . "[14]

Our research indicates that these long-sought goals are now
an attainable reality through Unified Field Based Education,
which can be easily incorporated into any traditional curriculum. As we shall see, in Maharishi Schools of the Age of Enlightenment, students are rapidly developing their full creative
potential and helping to create a permanent state of world peace
and Heaven on Earth.

C H A P T E R   T W O

Maharishi's Transcendental Meditation Program: Developing the Full Potential of the Knower

In Transcendental Meditation, the conscious mind comes to a state of self-referral awareness, which is the simplest form of human awareness where consciousness is open to itself. This self-referral state of consciousness is the ground state of all the laws of nature — the unified field of natural law.

The supersymmetric unified field theories of physics have glimpsed this state of unity, which, in its own self-interacting dynamics, expresses itself as diversified forms and phenomena in creation.

The complete knowledge of the unified field of natural law is available in Vedic Science, which provides the technology for human consciousness to harness the total creative potential of natural law. Through the practice of Transcendental Meditation, the conscious mind identifies itself with the unified field, and human awareness is open to its own full potential, the infinite potential of nature's intelligence.[1]   — *Maharishi*

THE 20 STUDENTS IN ROD MAGOON'S 10TH-GRADE CLASS sit comfortably in their chairs, close their eyes, and begin to practice Maharishi's Transcendental Meditation (TM) technique. After a few minutes, they open their eyes. They smile. They stretch. The students' faces look brighter, more alert . . . and also more relaxed.

They all affirm that their practice was easy and effortless. Gary, one of the students, comments, "During the TM technique, I usually begin with a busy and cluttered mind. My mind becomes gradually clearer and I experience a state of deep silence. A very relaxed feeling accompanies this experience. Due to TM, I feel more energetic and alert throughout the day." Another student, Debby, says, "I experience such relaxation during meditation. Afterwards I have peace of mind, and I feel pleasant and good."

What happens during a session of TM that brings such immediate and beneficial results? Let's look into the mechanics of what takes place in the mind and body of the student. Every day, during those few minutes of TM practice, the students in Mr. Magoon's class experience a unique state of consciousness. In a natural, effortless way, their minds settle down to a rested, silent, yet fully awake state of awareness. This is the state of transcendental consciousness, or pure consciousness — completely silent, yet fully awake within itself.

But what takes place in the mind is not the whole story. Accompanying the subjective experience of refinement of awareness are subtle yet profound changes in the student's physiology. An impressive array of scientific research has found a great many positive physiological changes. For example, respiration, heart rate, and oxygen consumption markedly decrease, indicating a state of deep physical rest. Plasma cortisol and arterial blood lactate, chemicals associated with stress, also substantially decrease. There are also increases in EEG coherence between

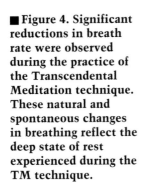

■ Figure 4. Significant reductions in breath rate were observed during the practice of the Transcendental Meditation technique. These natural and spontaneous changes in breathing reflect the deep state of rest experienced during the TM technique.

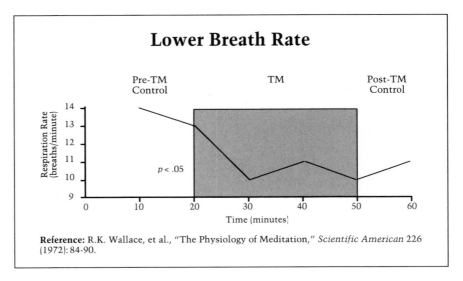

Lower Breath Rate

Reference: R.K. Wallace, et al., "The Physiology of Meditation," *Scientific American* 226 (1972): 84-90.

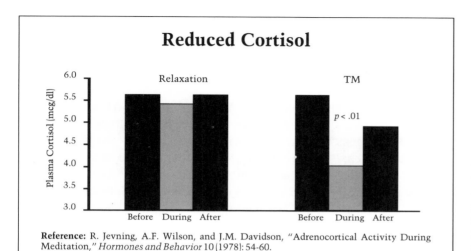

Reduced Cortisol

Reference: R. Jevning, A.F. Wilson, and J.M. Davidson, "Adrenocortical Activity During Meditation," *Hormones and Behavior* 10 (1978): 54-60.

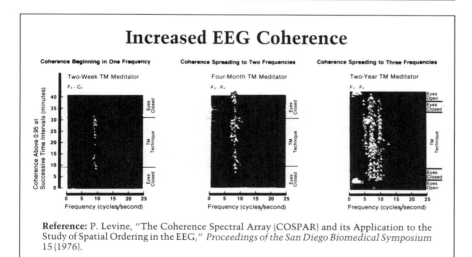

Increased EEG Coherence

Reference: P. Levine, "The Coherence Spectral Array (COSPAR) and its Application to the Study of Spatial Ordering in the EEG," *Proceedings of the San Diego Biomedical Symposium* 15 (1976).

■ **Figure 5.** Significantly lower levels of cortisol — a hormone found in large concentrations in the blood stream during stress — were found in people practicing the Transcendental Meditation technique compared to controls just resting with eyes closed. Lower cortisol levels during the TM technique indicate a state of deep rest that is deeper than ordinary relaxation.

■ **Figure 6.** EEG coherence, which shows the long-range spatial ordering of the brain waves, increases between and within the cerebral hemispheres during the Transcendental Meditation technique. Greater brain-wave coherence, along with the many other physiological changes produced during the practice of the TM technique, indicate a unique style of neurophysiological functioning — a state of restful alertness.

the left and right hemispheres of the brain, and in alpha power throughout the brain, indicating greater orderliness of brain functioning and increased alertness. The charts on these pages illustrate some of these findings.

Why is this a unique state of consciousness? We have known for some time that each of the three ordinary states of consciousness we commonly experience — sleeping, dreaming, and waking — has its own distinct physiological style of functioning. Nearly 20 years ago at UCLA, Dr. Robert Keith Wallace discovered that the individual can, through the practice of Transcendental Meditation, experience a fourth major state of consciousness, which is qualitatively different from the other three states. Dr. Wallace was the first to characterize this state as "restful alertness"; this seemingly paradoxical phrase conveys both the deep physiological rest and extreme alertness produced during TM.[2] Carol, a student in the 9th grade, states: "During meditation, I feel silence, and there is a sense of quiet yet vibrating energy."

The starting point for education at Maharishi School is the development of the consciousness of the knower — the student.

The starting point for education at Maharishi School is the development of the consciousness of the knower — the student. At Maharishi School, every student age 10 and over begins the school day with the practice of Maharishi's Transcendental Meditation technique. This simple, natural, effortless procedure for expanding the conscious capacity of the mind spontaneously results in students becoming more alert and more receptive to knowledge.

In an address to the American Association for Higher Education, Maharishi Mahesh Yogi, founder of the Transcendental Meditation program, explained:

> Of the two points of reference, the knower and the knowledge, the first point of reference is very important. The knowledge is as the knower is. When the mind is dull, when the knower is sleepy, the knowledge is something different from what it is when one is awake, fresh in the morning. Perception is different, understanding is different, emotions are different. Knowledge is different in different states of consciousness.[3]

Maharishi's insight into the process of education has been verified repeatedly by classroom teachers all across the country. How many teachers have complained that their students are very tired on Friday afternoons — or for that matter, most afternoons — and as a result can't keep their attention on the lesson? There is no doubt in any teacher's mind that the starting point of classroom instruction is the quality of attention of the students. When the students are tired and sleepy, motivation drops, receptivity drops, comprehension drops. Yet schools today continue to focus almost exclusively on the content being transmitted to the students with little attempt to develop the alertness and quality of the consciousness of the knower, the recipient of the knowledge.

■ At Maharishi School, every student age 10 and over begins the day with the practice of Maharishi's Transcendental Meditation technique.

It has been estimated that we use only a small portion of our mental potential.[4] How can we develop the rest of our mental potential? According to Maharishi, the total potential of the mind resides in transcendental pure consciousness, that stillness of mind from which all thoughts arise. Contacting the source of thought twice a day through Transcendental Meditation enlivens the full potential of the knower. Maharishi explains:

> Thoughts are the waves of creativity, waves of creative intelligence. They translate into action and all performances. But pure consciousness is where all inspiration, all understanding, all emotions, and thoughts arise. If this field is open to one's awareness, then the knower rises to his full potential and then rises to gain knowledge . . . The direct experience of pure consciousness has remained untouched in the field of education. Some aspects of philosophy or psychology seem to guess about it, but haven't provided the total knowledge of it. It is the first hand experience of the field of pure consciousness during the practice of the Transcendental Meditation technique that awakens the knower and thereby makes the knowledge lively.[5]

"When I am more rested, I am more alert and clearer in school. I have done well in school because of my practice of the TM technique."
— 11th-grade student

When the consciousness of the student is developed, school becomes more of a joy and more learning takes place. Kathy, an 11th-grade student at Maharishi School, comments: "When I am more rested, I am more alert and clearer in school. I have done well in school because of my practice of the TM technique. I no longer want to just memorize material and go through the steps of going through school; I find that I really enjoy thinking about the knowledge deeply and enjoy being in school with my friends and teachers. There is a growing confidence that I own knowledge on the level of the Self."

Susan, a 7th grader, says, "Due to Transcendental Meditation, you learn more and feel better about yourself. I think I have gained a lot of knowledge since I learned TM two months ago."

Kim, a 10th grade student, commented on her personal growth as a result of practicing TM: "At my other school, we were wild. At Maharishi School we are more calm and mature. I feel more self-confident and mature by going to Maharishi School. We do our TM program two times a day which brings us to a more subtle level of awareness. This school is full of so much bliss and happiness with the help of meditation."

Ann, another 10th grader, adds: "It's amazing how much you can improve yourself and how much happier you are when you are doing the TM program regularly with all the other students at Maharishi School." Other students say that they have become friendlier, more caring, more flexible in their thinking, more creative, more self-confident, and happier as a result of practicing the TM technique together in school.

The children under 10 years of age have their own special Children's TM technique, which they also practice together at the beginning of the school day. The technique is designed to strengthen their nervous systems; it gives them the experience of the more orderly and blissful aspects of their nature, and helps them to focus in class. The children notice good effects during their practice and in their activity afterwards. Following are some of the younger children's comments about their practice of the Children's TM technique at Maharishi School:

Grade 1: • I feel great. I feel happy. I feel good. I feel nice. I feel loving. (Johnny)

• I feel peaceful, happy, love, enlightened, more rested. (Sally)

Grade 2: • I feel silent waves of love and waves of happiness. (Allan)
• I feel very intelligent inside. (Bobby)

Grade 3: • I feel happy. I feel like I just achieved something very, very wonderful. I feel fulfilled with peace and fulfillment throughout the whole day. (Arlene)
• I feel like I just did something really good, like I just did something for my mom or dad and they gave me a big hug. (Laura)
• I feel happy when I meditate. It is fun, too. It makes me learn better every day. (Allan)

Teachers at Maharishi School have noticed a vast difference between the quality of student learning at Maharishi School and

■ As a result of practicing the Children's TM technique, children at Maharishi School become more blissful and focused in class.

"**The students at Maharishi School are the most exceptional I have ever taught in my 24 years of teaching. With their ability to focus on class-room instruction, they learn things the first time."**
— **Co-principal of Lower School**

schools where they taught previously. Roxie Teague, Co-principal of Maharishi Lower School and a master teacher, has taught at both the UCLA laboratory school and the Stanford Elementary School. She says, "The students at Maharishi School are the most exceptional I have ever taught in my 24 years of teaching. With their ability to focus on classroom instruction, they learn things the first time. They can work on fine details without losing the big picture, which makes them highly creative in writing stories, poetry, and plays."

Rod Magoon finds the students at Maharishi School much happier than those he taught at other private schools: "They are more intelligent and creative, and they have a greater thirst for knowledge." Adds George Balf, former principal of the Lower School, "When you see these children, you can see in their eyes their brightness and clarity. They are happy children. They have a zest for knowledge. It's not just that they follow a dress code and belong to a strong, supportive community; it is the practice of Transcendental Meditation that is principally contributing to the success of the school."

Pure Consciousness, the Unified Field, as the Most Fundamental Level of the Knower

Maharishi's paradigm of education emphasizes knowledge of the knower. But in this paradigm, "the knower" refers to more than just the personality and the physical body. Like the tip of an iceberg, these are only the most expressed levels of the knower, whose complete nature encompasses the total range of life. The most fundamental level of the knower is the unbounded field of pure consciousness which, as we saw in the previous chapter, is the unified field of natural law, the foundation of existence in the universe. The unified field — the fundamental, unified state of the knower — gives rise, through its own self-interacting dynamics, to all the diversified levels of the knower, including the ego, feelings, intellect, mind, and senses.

The most expressed level of the knower is the senses; the active, thinking level is the mind; the level of discriminative processes is the intellect; the level of feelings comprises the subtlest aspect of the emotions; and the most subtle, integrative level of functioning is the ego.

In the absence of this knowledge that the unified field of natural law is the basis of all the different levels of the individual, contemporary psychologists have been able to adopt only a fragmented approach to human development. Humanistic psychologists, including Carl Rogers, have emphasized the feeling and ego levels of the personality, while cognitive psychologists such as Jean Piaget have mainly investigated the functioning of the intellect. Some psychologists — B.F. Skinner, for example — have disregarded the discriminative faculties of the mind altogether and have encouraged educators to look only to the outer level of behavior to promote student development.

These fragmented approaches have left teachers with a potpourri of inadequate methods for promoting students' growth. Because of this, education today has not been successful in developing the student's inner potential, and has turned its attention to merely transmitting content.

Maharishi's Transcendental Meditation program provides the field of education with one universal method for developing the student's full potential. By handling the most fundamental level of human life, the unified field of natural law, through the practice of the TM technique, all aspects of the student develop — ego, feelings, intellect, mind, and senses. Maharishi explains:

> The entire range of expression of creative intelligence [is] from that universal, unbounded, eternal [unified field] to the individual ego, to feelings, to the thinking ability, and to the senses. The value of creative intelligence is appreciated on all these different levels. And when that universal value of life which we experience at the source of thought during meditation is appreciated on the basis of one's own personal experience, we find that the ego, the emotions, the intellect, the mind, the senses all begin to breathe a richer life. We experience greater comprehension and richer, sharper perception. Activity is strengthened, resulting in greater achievement and a higher level of fulfillment.[6]

Figure 7 illustrates Maharishi's explanation of the levels of the knower, and summarizes findings of scientific research conducted over the past 20 years showing that the repeated experience of the unified field during TM spontaneously promotes the development of each level.[7] For example, the TM technique increases alertness,

By handling the most fundamental level of human life, the unified field of natural law, through the practice of the TM technique, all aspects of the student develop — ego, feelings, intellect, mind, and senses.

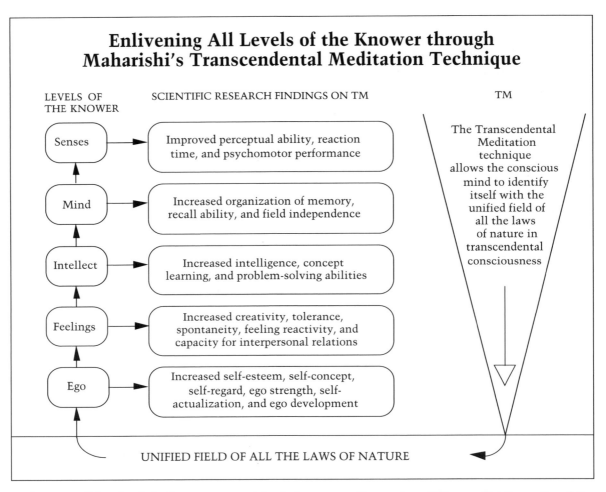

Enlivening All Levels of the Knower through Maharishi's Transcendental Meditation Technique

LEVELS OF THE KNOWER   SCIENTIFIC RESEARCH FINDINGS ON TM   TM

Senses → Improved perceptual ability, reaction time, and psychomotor performance

Mind → Increased organization of memory, recall ability, and field independence

Intellect → Increased intelligence, concept learning, and problem-solving abilities

Feelings → Increased creativity, tolerance, spontaneity, feeling reactivity, and capacity for interpersonal relations

Ego → Increased self-esteem, self-concept, self-regard, ego strength, self-actualization, and ego development

The Transcendental Meditation technique allows the conscious mind to identify itself with the unified field of all the laws of nature in transcendental consciousness

UNIFIED FIELD OF ALL THE LAWS OF NATURE

■ Figure 7: All levels of the knower are enriched when one enlivens the self-interacting dynamics of the unified field of natural law through the practice of the Transcendental Meditation technique. The left side of the figure illustrates the levels of the knower arising from the unified field. The middle section summarizes the research findings on the Transcendental Meditation technique in relation to the levels of the knower. The right side illustrates the process of transcending during the practice of TM.

perceptual ability, reaction time, and psychomotor performance — these are all evidence of improvement on the level of the *senses*. Studies showing increased organization of memory, recall ability, and field independence indicate that the *mind* is strengthened as well. Research demonstrating increased intelligence and problem-solving ability as a result of practicing TM indicates that the repeated experience of the unified field develops the *intellect*.

Feelings are also enriched, as shown by findings on increased creativity, tolerance, feeling reactivity, capacity for warm interpersonal relations, and spontaneity. The research also shows increased self-actualizing abilities, self-regard, self-concept, self-esteem, ego strength, and ego development — all of which indicate that the experience of the unified field promotes *ego* development.

Enlivening All the Qualities of the Unified Field in the Student's Awareness

The essential nature of the mind is not a *tabula rasa*, or blank slate, as Locke postulated; nor is the mind simply a repository for suppressed desires, as Freud believed. Rather, as Maharishi explains, the mind in its essential nature is pure consciousness, the unified field of natural law — an unbounded, lively field of all possibilities, with an abundance of beautiful, innate qualities waiting to be actualized.

Maharishi has identified specific qualities of pure consciousness. Among these, three important qualities are *self-referral*, *self-sufficiency*, and *infinite dynamism*. The experiences of TM meditators and the extensive scientific research on the results of the practice show that these qualities are enlivened in the consciousness of the individual during Transcendental Meditation and are then reflected in thinking and behavior afterwards.

For example, growing *self-referral* is indicated by a sense of greater self-knowledge, increased calm and happiness, and a feeling that all aspects of life are being nourished from within. Increased *self-sufficiency* is seen by greater stability in one's self, feelings, thoughts, and behavior, feelings of increased strength and health, and decreased dependence on drugs and other life-damaging habits. Increased *dynamism* is experienced as increased mental clarity, the growth of new abilities, more effortless accomplishments, improved interpersonal relations, and more practical, effective behavior.[8]

We saw in Chapter One that physics has recently glimpsed the unified field of all the laws of nature, described in the Vedic literature as the field of pure consciousness. According to physics, the unified field is a dynamic field of pure potentiality. MIU's Dr.

As Maharishi explains, the mind in its essential nature is pure consciousness, the unified field of natural law — an unbounded, lively field of all possibilities, with an abundance of beautiful, innate qualities waiting to be actualized.

John Hagelin analyzed the mathematical equations describing the unified field and derived from them 25 of its principal qualities:

- *All Possibilities*
- *Freedom*
- *Unboundedness*
- *Self-Sufficiency*
- *Bliss*
- *Integrating*
- *Invincibility*
- *Perfect Balance*
- *Fully Awake Within Itself*
- *Total Potential of Natural Law*
- *Simplicity*
- *Nourishing*
- *Unmanifest*
- *Harmonizing*
- *Self-Referral*
- *Infinite Correlation*
- *Infinite Dynamism*
- *Infinite Silence*
- *Pure Knowledge*
- *Infinite Organizing Power*
- *Infinite Creativity*
- *Purifying*
- *Evolutionary*
- *Perfect Orderliness*
- *Immortality*

Maharishi emphasizes that these qualities of the unified field are the qualities of the mind in the state of pure consciousness, the simplest and most fundamental state of human awareness. When the mind transcends during TM and experiences pure consciousness, it becomes enlivened with all these qualities, which are then expressed dynamically in the student's activity. The growth of these qualities in the life of the student is the key factor responsible for the immense success that students at Maharishi School are having in their educational careers.

Following are excerpts from experiences of students in grades 4 through 12, illustrating how these qualities of the unified field are actualized during their practice of TM.

Bliss

When I meditate, I am happy and glowing. Sometimes I get a very profound feeling, like I am floating on a cloud.
(Arnie, Grade 6)
I feel enlightened and filled with happiness and love. I feel like a person who will be happy for the rest of her life.
(Hannah, Grade 8)

Infinite Creativity	I feel more creative. Inside of me, I feel more calm and relaxed. I feel like I can do anything. (Jim, Grade 4)
Freedom	I feel very light and happy when I meditate. I feel like a bird soaring free and high with no boundaries. (Ned, Grade 8)
Harmonizing	During meditation, I feel very rested and peaceful. When I come out, I feel better than I did before and I am nicer to people. (Karen, Grade 5)
Infinite Silence	When I'm meditating, I start to feel silent and still. (Tom, Grade 6) During meditation I experience a deep silence and serenity. After meditation I always feel settled. (Bill, Grade 7)
Unboundedness	It usually feels like you're submerging into a deep ocean of quietness and peacefulness. It is unlike any kind of rest or sleep that one experiences if one is not practicing the TM technique. Once in a while, when I've submerged into the quietness, my body becomes one with everything. (Gail, Grade 10)
Infinite Correlation	During meditation, I experience . . . a feeling of wholeness with everything around me. (Arthur, Grade 8) When I meditate, I feel a wholeness within myself and the world around me. (Jay, Grade 12)
Perfect Orderliness	I feel relaxed, peaceful. It is neat because my mind gets cleared instantly. (Jesse, Grade 4)
Purifying	I get a very good feeling of inner fulfillment

when I meditate, and it seems to wash my troubles away. (Samantha, Grade 11)

Infinite Dynamism During my practice of Transcendental Meditation, I feel extremely relaxed. I also experience a feeling of complete rejuvenation, as if I were a battery being recharged. I also experience a diving feeling as if my awareness was going deeper and deeper into a very quiet but active field. (Robert, Grade 12)

Most educators would agree that the 25 qualities of the unified field are those they would like to see developed in their students. Who wouldn't want their students to be more wide awake, self-sufficient, and creative in class, and to have more orderly thinking and greater organizing power to accomplish things? Until now, education has had no systematic means for promoting students' holistic development. By enlivening all the qualities of the unified field in the student's awareness, Maharishi's unified field based system of education gives educators, for the first time, a way to promote the full development of the knower.

Dori Jackson, an elementary teacher at Maharishi School, comments on the development of the qualities of the unified field in the lives of her students:

Everybody wants to know how these students are different. I don't think that they are different in some unusual sense from other students. I think they are just more normal. They are what children are supposed to be. They are indeed quite wonderful and show extraordinary abilities to be creative and get along with others. They merely exhibit the same qualities that we want all the children of the world to exhibit every day. Here at our school, all of the children are just given the opportunity to continually grow in the qualities of the unified field. These beautiful qualities of creativity, intelligence, harmony, bliss, unboundedness, and purity become more and more enlivened in the students at every grade level. There is no limit to what our students will be able to accomplish in their lives. Anxiety, suffering, and unhappiness are not normal aspects of life; they merely result from not having a means of educating students to make use of their full creative potential.

Richard Beall, principal of the Upper School, adds: "All of these qualities of the unified field become enlivened through the students' practice of TM. It is apparent to all the teachers and administrators at Maharishi School that the growth taking place within our students is structured from inside, from within their own consciousness."

Basing an entire system of education on the development of consciousness has unique implications for the students' daily activity. The students are actually growing each day — in happiness, in maturity, and in their intellectual capabilities. This growth is seen not only in the outer, tangible aspects of their academic and social development, which have been measured by standardized test scores and causal-comparative research — but also in the more subtle realm of the quality of consciousness which they bring to their daily activity. Two Maharishi School students describe their experiences:

[In TM] I have very deep experiences, and I feel rested afterwards. I experience the liveliness of the unified field even when I am not practicing the Transcendental Meditation program. I [also] experience more refined perception during activity. (Debby, 10th grade).

My experience has been that of happiness, bliss, and the feeling of strength and energy during my practice. In activity I am more blissful and seem to have a lot of energy and calmness. (Noah, 9th grade).

■ The students grow each day — in happiness, maturity and intellectual capability. This growth takes place from inside, within their own consciousness.

These expressions show how natural the development of consciousness is. According to Maharishi, there is an endpoint to human development, which is known as enlightenment. In this

There is an end-point to human development, which is known as enlightenment. In this highly developed state of life, one lives in complete happiness and perfect health, with the total potential of natural law supporting every thought and action.

highly developed state of life, one lives in complete happiness and perfect health, with the total potential of natural law supporting every thought and action. This is the meaning of "the fruit of all knowledge," which enables one to know anything, do anything, and accomplish anything. Enlightenment is an immensely practical state of life.

The Seven States of Consciousness

Maharishi's Science of Creative Intelligence describes seven states of consciousness. These seven states consist of the three we are familiar with — sleeping, dreaming, and waking — the fourth state, transcendental consciousness, and three further states of consciousness that result from the integration of transcendental consciousness with daily activity.

Because transcendental consciousness is the experience of one's own unbounded, inner nature, it is referred to as the "Self," to distinguish this state from the localized value of the self ordinarily experienced in waking consciousness. According to Maharishi, the fifth state of consciousness — "cosmic consciousness" — arises when transcendental consciousness is permanently maintained along with waking, dreaming, and sleeping states. In this state of consciousness, one's own unbounded Self is never lost in the face of changing activity.

Maharishi explains how cosmic consciousness naturally develops through the regular practice of TM:

> Through daily practice of meditation, the possibility exists of establishing in our life the coexistence of the fourth state and any of the other three. The character of the state of the nervous system thus created would be neither just that of the waking state nor just that of the fourth state, but rather, it would be a combination of both.... Through a technique of making use of the very natural tendency of life [TM], we slip into the reality of the fourth state of consciousness and discover that it is unbounded....
>
> In the beginning, because the system is not used to that style of functioning, after meditation the system returns to its usual, habitual style of functioning.... But because it is such a beautiful, restful state, unbounded and fulfilling, very quickly the system starts to gain the habit of returning to that state. After some time of alternating that fourth state with the other

three, the nervous system becomes habituated to maintaining that style of awareness. . . . Then that state of awareness is maintained even during waking, dreaming, and sleeping. All the jerks and jolts of activity during waking, the rest of the night, or the delusive nature of dreams, all this is not able to overthrow the reality of the fourth state of consciousness; it is forever maintained. . . .

The characteristic of the fifth state is the coexistence of awareness of the unbounded along with awareness of boundaries. . . . The pure awareness which was hidden by the influence of the waking state before starting meditation comes to be experienced consciously by the mind, and the mind maintains this state of unbounded awareness even when experiencing the boundaries of objects of perception.[9]

Once cosmic consciousness is established, the sixth and seventh states develop. The sixth state of consciousness is called "God consciousness." At this stage of human development the outer environment is perceived in its most refined, glorified sense; one appreciates most profoundly the intelligence, harmony, and grandeur of creation.

Maharishi explains how the state of God consciousness develops through the refinement of perception:

When unbounded awareness starts to coexist with awareness of boundaries, our comprehension of the boundaries and what lies outside them becomes more complete. . . . With such an unrestricted, unbounded awareness, we are able to penetrate into the deeper values of perception. Our perception becomes more refined. We would naturally imagine a state in which the finest perception would be possible, so that the finest relative value of the object of experience would become apparent to our perception.

Before gaining that state, this finest value is hidden from view because our vision falls only on the surface of the object. . . . However, when the unbounded awareness becomes established on the level of the conscious mind — we have seen that this is the fifth state of consciousness — then the perception naturally begins to appreciate deeper values of the object, until perception is so refined that the finest relative is capable of being perceived on the gross, surface level.[10]

Finally, the seventh state of consciousness, unity consciousness, dawns when the objects of perception are experienced in

The pinnacle of the development of consciousness, unity consciousness, dawns when the objects of perception are experienced in their infinite, unbounded value, as expressions of one's own Self.

their infinite, unbounded value, as expressions of one's own Self. Maharishi explains that at this level of consciousness the gulf between the knower and the known has been bridged and complete knowledge of the unified state of knower, process of knowing, and known has been gained. Maharishi describes the characteristics of this fully-developed state of human consciousness — unity consciousness — as follows:

> This seventh state of consciousness could very well be called the unified state of consciousness because in that state, the ultimate value of the object, infinite and unmanifest, is made lively when the conscious mind, being lively in the value of unbounded awareness, falls on the object. The object is cognized in terms of the pure subjective value of unbounded, unmanifest awareness. . . . In this unified state of consciousness, the experiencer and the object of experience have both been brought to the same level of infinite value and this encompasses the entire phenomenon of perception and action as well. The gulf between the knower and the object of his knowing has been bridged. When the unbounded perceiver is able to cognize the object in its total reality, cognizing the infinite value of the object, which was hitherto unseen, then the perception can be called total or of supreme value. In this state, the full value of knowledge has been gained, and we can finally speak of complete knowledge.[11]

In the 30 years that Maharishi has been teaching Transcendental Meditation, there have been many hundreds of thousands of experiences of higher states of consciousness. Experiences of higher states of consciousness — transcendental consciousness, cosmic consciousness, God consciousness, and unity consciousness — are also described in detail in the ancient Vedic literature. The following examples, reported by individuals practicing Maharishi's Transcendental Meditation program for several years, show how naturally and spontaneously these higher states of consciousness arise, and how they transform the quality of life of the individual:

> Boundless infinitude, beautiful bliss, total silence. In activity a powerful silent wholeness rests on the surface of everything. A beautiful softness connects and interfuses all I see. (S.B., California)

> The cumulative effects . . . have been most profound for me in the field of action. It is here that I feel is the real test of higher

states of consciousness and here that I most practically appreciate the benefits of Transcendental Meditation. . . .

I noticed an ever-increasing evenness, balance, and concrete smoothness developing. . . . I noticed much less resistance, both on a physical level and in terms of fulfilment of desires. . . . I felt so in tune with nature, that virtually every desire has been consummated very quickly.

This of course gives rise to a feeling of great self-sufficiency and power, a feeling of being able to achieve great things in life with very little effort. But, at the same time as I felt my power and inner strength increase, I also noticed a totally new feeling of softness and sweetness develop. There were days when I felt my heart melting as if I could take everything in creation into myself and cherish it with the greatest love. Often I would have long periods of the day when everything I saw seemed to be glowing with divine radiance. . . .

I noticed especially that along with a comfort and deep at-home feeling in activity, my alertness and perception became very, very sharp and clear, very acute. I noticed details more and also perceived connections between things more. But, at the same time, I also was not overshadowed by my environment. . . . (J.B., Ontario, Canada)[12]

Because experiences of higher states of consciousness are natural to life, they may be glimpsed by anyone at any time. William James and Abraham Maslow, for example, studied such experiences in the lives of contemporary Western authors and scientists. However, while many people in our Western culture have had glimpses of higher states of consciousness, they had no systematic means for eliciting these experiences regularly or maintaining them permanently. Thus enlightenment — in which transcendental consciousness is permanently maintained, even during dynamic activity — has long been assumed to be a far-off goal, attainable only through long and arduous procedures by a few privileged souls living in seclusion in remote areas of the world.

Through Maharishi's Transcendental Meditation technique, anyone can have the regular, effortless, natural experience of transcendental consciousness. Through the regular alternation of this experience with daily activity, it is possible for anyone not only to "glimpse" the reality of higher states of consciousness, but to quickly rise to full enlightenment in a completely natural and spontaneous way and live in unity consciousness, the highest state of human development.

From the age of 10, students at Maharishi School experience the unified field, or transcendental consciousness, as part of their daily schedule. This experience is the heart of the unique system of education at Maharishi School of the Age of Enlightenment. In the next chapter we will see how the Maharishi School curriculum also provides intellectual understanding of the development of higher states of consciousness, which naturally complements the students' personal experiences and stabilizes their growth to enlightenment.

"The personal development of the student is the most important goal at Maharishi School," comments George Balf. "Personal development for us means students growing in the direction of enlightenment, which means being in tune with all the laws of nature so that individuals don't make mistakes and are successful in everything they do. Developing the consciousness of the student is the basis for academic, social, and vocational development."

Dale Monson, former principal of the Middle School, underscores the practicality of the students' growth of consciousness: "Even though our main goal of education is to produce enlightened students, we're finding that the students are also achieving great heights academically due to the fact that they are experiencing the state of transcendental consciousness, the unified field, twice a day. The students become much more orderly and intelligent in their thinking. The development of enlightenment through the practice of the Transcendental Meditation program is something very practical."

Having described the value of the direct experience of the unified field through Maharishi's Transcendental Meditation program in this chapter, Chapters Three and Four explore how the theoretical knowledge of the unified field is integrated into the curriculum. Chapters Five and Six show just how practical is this experience of growing enlightenment, examining the scientific research on the rapid academic and social progress of the students at Maharishi School.

CHAPTER THREE

Maharishi's Science of Creative Intelligence: Perceiving, Developing, and Living the Fullness of Life

The Science of Creative Intelligence brings to light and examines those principles which uphold the development of creative intelligence in nature and in the personal life of the student. When these principles are sufficiently understood and the student appreciates the mechanics of growth of his physiology and psychology, the reality of evolution becomes a joyful and intimate experience. As the student comes to understand the mechanics of evolution, he grows in the inspiration to perform all actions to hasten his evolution.[1]   —*Maharishi*

Here, they care about you. Since they care about you so much, they teach us SCI. It's fun. It's more special, because it's the science of *creative intelligence*. It makes you feel good about yourself. It makes you smart. Everyone feels smart — you feel almost perfect. We study it after meditation. That's when we have our fullest knowledge. When you finish meditation, you're ready to start your day. You're happy. SCI helps you get along with other people because you're happy all day.
    —*Andrea, 5th grader at Maharishi School*

A T FIRST GLANCE, KATHLEEN TACHET'S 3RD-GRADE CLASSroom on the second floor at Maharishi School resembles elementary school classrooms throughout the country. A large American flag stands next to the blackboard; her desk faces rows of small chairs and desks. At the back of the room are shelves crowded with the books, toys, and crayons used by the children in the course of a day. Decorating the walls are collages of pictures cut out from magazines, drawings and paintings by the students, and rows of colorful charts and posters.

On the wall is a picture by one of the children, Ellen, of a seed sprouting in stages to become a tree. Neatly printed letters spell out its caption, "The nature of life is to grow." The other pictures also have captions expressing simple principles: "Rest and activity are the steps of progress," "Every action has a reaction," "The whole is contained in every part," and "The world is as we are." Here, the uniqueness of this 3rd-grade classroom begins to become apparent: in this class students learn about Maharishi's Science of Creative Intelligence (SCI), the cornerstone of the curriculum at Maharishi School of the Age of Enlightenment.

Each day at Maharishi School of the Age of Enlightenment begins with the knowledge that ensures the students' full development.

Maharishi's Science of Creative Intelligence has both a theoretical and a practical aspect. The theoretical aspect gives complete knowledge of the field of pure intelligence — the unified field of natural law — from the perspectives of both Maharishi's Vedic Science and the modern academic disciplines. The practical aspect — the "laboratory" component of SCI — is the Transcendental Meditation technique, a systematic means for students to experience the field of pure intelligence and bring greater energy, intelligence, and happiness into their daily life.

The faculty of Maharishi International University and Maharishi School of the Age of Enlightenment have worked with Maharishi to develop SCI curricula for the elementary, secondary, and post-secondary levels — from kindergarten through Ph.D. In this chapter, we'll discuss how SCI is studied as a subject in its own right and why it is such a vital part of the learning experience for the students at Maharishi School. Then, in the next chapter, we'll explore how SCI illuminates the study of the standard academic subjects.

Each day at Maharishi School of the Age of Enlightenment begins with the knowledge that ensures the students' full development. When they arrive, the students sit with their teachers in the classroom to practice the Transcendental Meditation technique and experience the expanded awareness and profound silence of the field of pure intelligence within their own minds. (The children under 10 practice the Children's TM technique, described in Chapter Two). Then they study SCI — the principles of creative intelligence that uphold growth and progress in nature and in human life.[2]

Overview of the SCI Curriculum

The SCI curriculum unfolds in a sequence of themes. As the themes develop, the students' awareness expands to encompass the entire range of life. At the core of the curriculum are the 16 principles of SCI — these are the foundation for the study of SCI through all the elementary and secondary years. The students first learn about these fundamental principles in Grade 1; these same principles are also studied in higher grades.

Dr. Susan Dillbeck, Chairperson of the MIU Department of Education and an international expert in Maharishi's Unified Field Based education, explains the study of the Science of Creative Intelligence: "These simple but profound principles are laws of nature. They express, in language that students can easily understand, how intelligence unfolds in the universe — the natural laws that govern and maintain the orderly evolution of life, for example: Rest and activity are the steps of progress, Life is found in layers, Knowledge is gained from inside and outside, Opposites are found together."

In the SCI curriculum for grades 1 to 12, specific principles and qualities are studied at each grade level. The curriculum is structured in three-year segments, each focusing on a particular main theme. Students approach the theme from different angles during the three years, as their understanding of the principles matures and their experience of the field of pure intelligence deepens.

The careful structure of the SCI curriculum reveals its fundamental purpose. "Maharishi has explained that our teaching of SCI aims at inculcating in the children the understanding that there is something deep within the surface of everything," says Dr. Robin Rowe, Academic Director of Maharishi School. According to Maharishi, this helps the students grow in inquisitiveness and awareness of the most basic values of life, eventually leading them to the laws of nature in all the different fields of knowledge. The students grow in the awareness that the deeper the level of natural law from which they function, the greater the achievement and fulfillment they gain through their action.[3] Maharishi further explains that for complete fulfillment, thinking and action must be spontaneously in tune with the unified field of all the laws of nature, which is the total potential of natural law.

SCI principles express, in language that students can easily understand, the laws of nature that govern and maintain the orderly evolution of life.

The fulfillment of inquiry for the children is in knowing the reality that lies beyond the surface of their perception.

The SCI curriculum helps the children to appreciate, in Maharishi's words, "the more fundamental values of life from where their whole life can be organized and made fulfilled." Maharishi has said that the fulfillment of inquiry for the children is in knowing the reality that lies beyond the surface of their perception. With the growth of this knowledge their hearts never become cramped. They enjoy fulfillment and the growth of creativity.[4]

Very young children first locate the principles in their own lives at home and at school, in the lives of people they know, and in nature. As they grow older and their awareness of the world broadens, the students discover these principles in the lives of local and national heroes and great men and women, in community life, the nation, and the world. They see how creative intelligence is expressed in myths, in the sciences, arts, and humanities, and eventually, in the 12th grade, in 24 academic disciplines. Thus, the students' understanding expands from perceiving the creative intelligence in their immediate surroundings and how it develops within themselves, to appreciating the creative intelligence of the entire universe. They see that the same laws of nature guide their own growth and the evolution of everything in nature.

Maharishi has explained that the SCI curriculum introduces the children to basic laws of nature presented in a form that is appropriate to their age, so that "the children are thinking natural law from their very earliest days." In the lower grades, the children learn about the SCI principles through stories, songs, and plays. For example, they first learn the principle "Order is present everywhere" in simple terms such as the orderliness of a snowflake.

Roxie Teague, introduced earlier, comments on how the practice of Transcendental Meditation complements the students' intellectual understanding of the SCI principles: "The students look at the formation of leaves, seeds, and pods, and see orderly growth and patterns. But because TM expands their awareness, they are able to look beyond the surface level and see the universality in nature. Then the principle is lively — order is present *everywhere.*"

Kathleen Tachet told us, "The children enjoy their SCI classes very much. They experience a great deal of happiness and bliss as a result of their practice of TM and their growing knowledge of the principles that contribute to their personal growth."

"You learn about life," says Mary, a 5th-grader, about why she likes SCI. "You're more balanced because you know more about yourself. When you know the fundamentals, it makes it easier to learn things."

On the secondary level, the students go more deeply into the SCI principles, relating them to their growing experience of the unified field through the TM technique. For example, the Upper School students locate the SCI principle of orderliness in the Third Law of Thermodynamics in physics, which describes the mechanics by which reduced excitation brings increased order to physical systems.

Kathy, an 11th-grade student, comments on her experience of studying SCI in high school: "It helps to know SCI, because SCI relates to everything; it relates to yourself and what you are doing in school. Principles of SCI are just common principles that are known to everyone, but because we study them in a systematic way, relating them to our own lives, they become an important source for being successful in everything we do."

How SCI is Taught at the Elementary Level

Grades 1 to 3: "What's Inside? What's Outside?"

The youngest students, in grades 1 to 3, study the theme, "What's Inside? What's Outside?" The goal of this first part of the curriculum is to open the children's awareness to the inner, more precious values of life and how these values enhance the outer expressions of life. Here the children first learn the 16 principles of SCI, including "The nature of life is to grow," "Order is present everywhere," and "Life is found in layers." They study each principle for two weeks in their SCI class at the beginning of the school day, after practicing the Children's TM technique.

Through the learning activities designed by their teacher, the children come to thoroughly understand each SCI principle. They hear stories which inspire them to appreciate more pleasing, subtle inner values and to become great. They are often encouraged to draw pictures to make their understanding of each principle more concrete.

Maharishi has explained that it is the skill of a teacher to relate to the underlying reality of life without losing the concrete perceptual levels of the child's experience.[5] Dr. Dillbeck points out that

"You learn about life. You're more balanced because you know more about yourself. When you know the fundamentals, it makes it easier to learn things." — 5th-grade student

in grades 1 to 3 the children gain knowledge principally through their senses. "This is how they discover the universe," she says. "To awaken their minds to the inner realities of life we bring their attention to processes in nature that they can see, touch, and feel."

Dori Jackson, a teacher in the Maharishi Lower School, says, "SCI is unquestionably the children's favorite subject. I think it's because the principles and qualities of SCI are connected so closely to the child's life."

A Sample 1st-Grade SCI Lesson: "Order Is Present Everywhere"

In Werner Pfleger's 1st-grade class, the children are studying the principle, "Order is present everywhere." Two weeks ago they learned the first SCI principle, "The nature of life is to grow," and this lesson integrates that principle, keeping it lively in the children's awareness. The children gather around Mr. Pfleger on one side of the classroom, sitting in an area with a thick carpet and pillows that is often used for story-telling. He

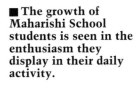

■ The growth of Maharishi School students is seen in the enthusiasm they display in their daily activity.

arranges seven cards along the ledge of an easel. Each card shows one word, and they are all mixed up and upside down: IS LIFE THE ꟽOЯƆ OF TO NATURE. "Not very orderly, is it?" he says to the children. "Who can help put them right?" One boy stands up and rearranges them, getting them almost right. Another boy moves the last card into the right spot. "Now the order of the words is correct, so everyone can read and understand them," says Mr. Pfleger. The children read all together, as their teacher points to each word: "THE NATURE OF LIFE IS TO GROW."

Then they sing a song that demonstrates different kinds of orderly growth:

> The nature of life is to grow, grow, grow
> High and low, fast and slow.
> The nature of life is to grow, grow, grow
> Growing all around us.

As they sing, the children illustrate each kind of orderliness with motions of their hands and arms. Next, Mr. Pfleger picks up a clock with large red numbers on its face. "How does this clock show orderliness? That's right, the numbers are all in order. Not 1, 4, 7. How do they go? 1, 2, . . ." They all join in, saying each number as he points to it. He goes on: "Did you ever see a clock that went 12, 9, . . .?" The children giggle. "No," he continues, "they are always the same, because otherwise no one could tell time. What else is orderly? How many minutes are there between 12 and 1, 1 and 2, . . .? That's right, five. Who can count by fives?" They all call out, "5, 10, . . ." They finish counting. "So how many minutes in an hour?" The children crow triumphantly: "Sixty!" "Right!" he answers, "so this is another example of how order is present everywhere." Thus a simple lesson in counting and telling time is transformed into knowledge about a fundamental principle of life.

Mr. Pfleger explains that often the children carry their understanding of the SCI principles into their activities at home. One parent told him recently that she left her shoes in disarray on the floor, and her daughter, a student in his class, stopped her and urged her to arrange them neatly, saying, "You know, order is present everywhere."

The principles act as "advance organizers" for the children, putting their experience into a larger context. "The children really

"SCI is unquestionably the children's favorite subject. I think it's because the principles and qualities of SCI are connected so closely to the child's life."
— Lower School teacher

incorporate these principles in their own minds and use them to process what they learn about the world," Mr. Pfleger says. "One day we were discussing the principle, 'Water the root to enjoy the fruit,' and got onto the idea of 'enjoying the fruit of all knowledge.' Maharishi has said this will mean you can know anything, do anything, achieve anything. I told them this and one boy took it literally, and had a completely blissful expression on his face. He said, 'Gosh, that's just *incredible* — there's nothing greater than that!' It was a powerful experience, to see how he absorbed that idea and took it into his heart. For me it was very clear how our children really are growing up enlightened."

Even children in preschool understand the SCI principles and find them to be familiar and intimate to themselves. Roxie Teague describes a conversation with a 3-year-old boy about a blade of grass he had picked. He wanted to know what the seeds were, why the grass had seeds, and how they made the grass grow. "Everything has seeds," she told him. "Why?" he asked. The conversation continued in this vein. Several "Why's" later, she finally said, "It's *nature*. It's the nature of life to grow." When he heard this simple SCI principle, the boy just said, "Ohhh . . . ," and a look of deep satisfaction came over his face. "There is some intuitive knowingness in the children," she says. "They are searching for truth, for knowledge. When you give them pure knowledge, they recognize its profundity, because it's nothing outside of themselves. You can see the integration taking place. It's like nothing I've ever seen at any other school."

A Sample 3rd-Grade SCI Lesson: "Every Action Has a Reaction"

In Anne Love's 3rd-grade SCI class, the students are discussing their favorite SCI principles. Sally likes "Opposites are found together." As an example, she points out that "a tree has soft and bendable leaves, and a hard, sturdy trunk." Mrs. Love joins in: "My favorite principle is 'Enjoy and accomplish more,' because I find that when I'm having the best time at something, I accomplish the most." Alison likes "'The world is as we are' — because if you're really nice to everybody, everyone wants to play with you." The SCI principles help the children to organize the information they gain about their environment in a way that helps them to progress in their thinking and activity.

In Rosemary Collins's 3rd-grade class, the children are studying another of the 16 SCI principles, "Every action has a reaction." Pointing to a chart posted at the front of the classroom, Ms. Collins copies "Every action has a reaction" onto the blackboard. She asks the children to define "every," "action," and "reaction"; with the use of a dictionary, she helps them to understand each of these key words. Then, they discuss the proverb "As you sow, so shall you reap" in relation to the SCI principle.

Next, she shows the children a set of pictures. In the first picture, a child invites another to join a game; the other child responds: "Thank you, I'd like to play." After each set of pictures, the teacher asks the class what the pictures mean to them. After presenting several sets, she asks the students to draw their own pictures illustrating how every action has a reaction.

When they finish, Ms. Collins invites them to show their work. One by one, they stand and explain their pictures. In a variety of ways, ranging from playing on the playground to helping a fellow classmate in school, the children's pictures convey the idea that when you are kind to someone, the other person will in turn be kind to you. Then the teacher summarizes the lesson, reminding the children that their own practice of Transcendental Meditation is the most effective way to generate positivity for oneself and others. She explains, "We become more kind and considerate of others, and in return, others become happy and express their kindness back to us."

According to Roxie Teague, "Because the children are so receptive to patterns, you'll find that they say, 'Guess what! That's a good example of the nature of life is to grow.' It just happens spontaneously throughout the day. Or 'Every action has a reaction' — it just pops up all the time. There are no boundaries on SCI."

Perhaps most striking are examples of how SCI helps children to think and act in an evolutionary way outside the classroom. This, according to Maharishi, is the purpose of the study of SCI. Dori Jackson explains the value of SCI in the primary grade levels:

The children not only enjoy learning the principles of SCI in class but also spontaneously make use of them in their daily activity. For example, a situation on the playground may arise

In a natural way, which uplifts the children's hearts and minds, the study of SCI helps even the youngest ones to grow in the ability to spontaneously think and act in an evolutionary way.

that involves a disagreement of opinions between two children. The children have a way of handling these situations themselves. Quite often we observe the children saying to each other, "Every action has a reaction" in discussing the ramifications of their actions with each other. In this way they appear to be sorting out for themselves what would be the appropriate action in a specific situation based on a broader principle. The younger children appear to be most concerned with the feelings of other children. If they find that some child becomes sad or unhappy, most children will immediately begin to reflect on their action to see whether they did something which was not right, or what could be done to help.

In a natural way, which uplifts the children's hearts and minds, their study of SCI helps even the youngest ones to grow in the ability to think and act spontaneously rightly; this is based on the development of creative intelligence they experience through their practice of the Children's TM technique.

Grades 4 to 6: "The Nature of Life Is to Grow and Progress"

In grades 4 to 6, the main SCI theme is "The nature of life is to grow and progress." In these three years the students study 16 fundamentals of growth, including Creativity, Intelligence, Orderliness, and Knowledge. By this time, their understanding has matured to the point that they can understand in more detail the mechanics of growth.

Here is a story by Annie, a 4th grader, which illustrates how important the children feel it is to understand these principles and how studying the SCI principles uplifts them:

THE 16 RAINDROPS OF KNOWLEDGE

Once upon a time there was a little girl named Alice. Her problem was she wasn't very self-confident. She was very shy and if she heard giggling around her she always thought they were laughing at her. She was a very pretty girl with long black hair that looked golden in the sun. After school she walked home feeling sad. Every day when she got home she would look out the window to see the other children pass by. Suddenly it started to rain. She counted 1, 2, 3, 4, 5 raindrops, and she counted 16 and it stopped. That's very odd, she thought. I'm going outside to see what's going on, she said. When she got there she could

still see full raindrops, not just water. Each one had a number,
and said, "Fundamental." This is what they said: Creativity,
Energy, Intelligence, Purposefulness, Rest and Activity, Orderliness, Purification, Knowledge, Integration, Stability, Adaptability, Resourcefulness, Vigilance, Insight, Foresight, Happiness. After she read them she realized she had all that. At
school the next day she sat with the girls in her class, got an A+
on a science test, and she won a spelling bee. She has been like
that ever since the raindrops of knowledge fell.

Annie has clearly integrated the value of knowing the 16
fundamentals of growth into her own understanding. Once the
little girl in her story learns these fundamentals, she immediately realizes that "she had all that" — that they are her own inner nature. As we pointed out earlier in this chapter, the students' deep understanding of these principles is based on their
growth of consciousness through Transcendental Meditation,
through which these fundamentals of natural law are enlivened
in their awareness. Annie's story echoes the feelings of many of
the other children we talked to at the school, that SCI with its
practical aspect, TM, makes them happy and makes it easy for
them to learn and understand things.

When asked why they like SCI, many of the children simply
answer, "It's fun!" Chris, a fifth grader, expands on this: "It's
fun and work both together. You learn a lot and you have a lot
of fun. . . . It makes math more creative and fun, and you have
more energy, because math is right after SCI — you think about
SCI and get it done faster. SCI makes you feel happy, because
everyone likes SCI — everyone's always happy when doing SCI.
Everyone likes to be creative."

Kathleen Tachet gives an insight into why the study of the
SCI principles brings happiness and fulfillment to the children,
and how this is connected to their practice of Transcendental
Meditation: " These principles are the same principles at the basis of their own lives.They give the children a deep, positive
way to see how life is organized. Their appreciation of nature is
always on the basis of these uplifting, progressive SCI principles. The technique of TM is absolutely necessary—the basis of
it all—because that gives them the experience of their own inner nature, the basis of themselves and everything else."

When asked why they like SCI, many of the children simply answer, "It's fun!"

A Sample 5th-Grade SCI Lesson: The Fundamental of Adaptability

In the 5th grade, the students continue to study the 16 fundamentals of growth in the context of the SCI theme, "Developing the Outer by Enlivening the Inner." By this time, they are all practicing the TM technique practiced by adults, and enlivening these fundamentals of growth in their own lives.

One 5th-grade SCI class is discussing the fundamental of adaptability, relating it to their own lives and to the lives of great people. "As we study this fundamental," says the teacher, "we have to study number ten, stability, because adaptability and stability go hand in hand, right?"

First the class establishes the meaning of each term. "Adaptability means to fit into the environment easily without any trouble," says Edward. Another boy adds, "Stability means the ability not to get disoriented when you have to make a very big change, sort of like being in a boat on the waves of change. Your stability is that anchor that keeps you calm." Michael contributes an analogy to explain stability: "You can't have a strong building without a strong foundation."

"Why are stability and adaptability both necessary for developing greatness?" asks the teacher. "When you are adapting," answers David, "you are changing, and you have to be stable to do that. Your system has to be able to adjust and to be strong. You have to be adaptable so you can roll with the punches."

What is the basis for being adaptable in one's own life? "When we contact the unified field during TM," says Richard. "We've all done our [TM] program," adds Donald, "and that helps us adapt to different situations that might disturb us otherwise. And we are all going to a wonderful school, and that'll help us to adapt to problems we might have on our own."

They think of examples of how they have been adaptable. Ron thinks of his experience of moving to Iowa to go to Maharishi School: "We travelled across the United States to come to Iowa, and we have to adapt to new things here. We're not used to the things here, because we used to live in a different place and have to make different friends here. This is adaptability."

Then they identify other types of people who are both adaptable and stable. "Astronauts are very adaptable," says Richard, "because they have to go into space. But first, they have to have their body withstand an immense amount of pressure. Going up there, they have to be alert. They have to be very stable to be able to operate in zero gravity, because you can't really walk or anything. If they weren't very adaptable, they wouldn't be able to work in space."

The students have been learning about Abraham Lincoln in their social studies class. They draw on this study to give examples of how Lincoln was adaptable.

"Abraham Lincoln was adaptable because he guided us through the Civil War," says Edward. "I think he had to be very adaptable to lead this country," says Tom. "This is one of the biggest, most complex countries of the entire world. I'm not saying that he alone controlled it, but that he was placed in a very high position of power. In fact he was a very adaptable and stable person not to crack under the pressure."

The students' homework assignment is to write a short essay relating the fundamental of adaptability to another great man or woman. The lives of great people are used as examples in all the courses at Maharishi School, to inspire students to develop greatness in their own lives. By studying the achievements of great people from their own country, they also grow in appreciation for their country's tradition of greatness. The great men and women selected represent various fields of knowledge—scientists, artists, businessmen, statesmen. "In this way the student grows in appreciation of the rich and varied expressions of each quality [of creative intelligence]," states a curriculum description, "while simultaneously growing in appreciation of all fields of knowledge and their applied value in enriching the quality of life in his culture."[6]

How SCI is Taught at the Secondary Level

Grades 7 to 9: "Discovering the Full Creative Potential of Natural Law"

In Grades 7 to 9, the students return to the 16 principles of SCI, the same principles they studied in grades 1 to 3. In the first grade, as they learned the principle, "The nature of life is to grow," the children studied growth and change on a concrete, sensory level as it related to their own physical growth and that of their immediate environment.

In the 7th grade, with a more mature awareness, they bring a deeper understanding to the same principles. They start to explore the Self — the field of consciousness. As they grow in understanding and experience of creative intelligence through their practice of Transcendental Meditation, they can appreciate how creative intelligence guides their own personal development. "As their consciousness develops, the students can more easily relate these SCI principles to the deepest level of their lives, the Self — the fountainhead of every aspect of their existence," explains Dr. Dillbeck. "A whole new reality unfolds for the students."

The SCI Principle: "Knowledge Is Structured in Consciousness"

One important SCI principle the students encounter in grades 7 to 9 is "Knowledge is structured in consciousness." They have already studied this principle in grades 1 to 3, in the terms "The

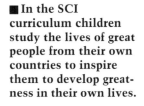

■ In the SCI curriculum children study the lives of great people from their own countries to inspire them to develop greatness in their own lives.

world is as we are." One meaning of "Knowledge is structured in consciousness" is that the ability to gain knowledge depends on the clarity, depth, and comprehensiveness of one's consciousness. Teachers at Maharishi School often refer to Maharishi's explanations and analogies when presenting this and other SCI principles. The passage on the next two pages contains excerpts from a lecture by Maharishi which explain "Knowledge is structured in consciousness."

The 7th-grade SCI curriculum also includes the scientific research on the TM technique, which shows the psychophysiological correlates of the experience of pure consciousness. The research brings home to the students in concrete, objective terms how their experience of pure consciousness improves the functioning of their minds and bodies.

In the 8th grade, while continuing to study the 16 principles, students also relate the principle "Knowledge is structured in consciousness" to world peace. They see how a permanent state of world peace will be achieved when enough people permanently establish within themselves the state of unbounded awareness (see Chapter Eight). And in the 9th grade, students apply this principle to different fields of study such as art, music, literature, psychology, the physical sciences, and government. By the end of these three years, the students have understood and experienced creative intelligence and its expressions in every aspect of life. On this basis, the curriculum in grades 10 to 12 focuses on full development of the student for the full expression of creative intelligence in practical life.

Grades 10 to 12: Perceiving, Developing, and Living the Fullness of Life

The main theme of grades 10 to 12 is "Fullness of Life" — the goal is to enliven the students' ability to perceive, develop, and live the fullness of life. This is the fulfillment of the SCI curriculum for elementary and secondary education. Maharishi explains that the 10th-grade SCI curriculum "is designed to culture every student's vision to appreciate the full potential of life. To perceive the fullness of life everywhere is to enliven wholeness in one's life."[7]

In the 10th grade, students study 50 qualities of creative intelligence, which are actually 25 pairs of opposite or complementary

Studying the scientific research on the TM technique brings home to the students in concrete, objective terms how their experience of pure consciousness improves the functioning of their minds and bodies.

qualities — for example, *stable/adaptable*, *gentle/strong*, *harmonizing/diversifying*, and *thoughtful/spontaneous*. Through the practice of TM, the students enliven all the qualities of creative intelligence in their awareness. On this basis, their study of these qualities helps enliven students' perception of the fullness of life all around them, as well as within themselves. According to Maharishi, the fulfillment of the 10th-grade curriculum is "in developing the ability of every student to spontaneously use the qualities of creative intelligence in thought and action."[8]

Following are some examples of one pair of opposite qualities, "gentle/strong," used in the SCI curriculum:

• The root is the stable basis that gives strength to the towering tree and to its more delicate expressions in tender petals and gentle fragrance around the flowers.

• Water, so gentle and soothing to the touch, yet has the strength and power to sustain life and uphold the progress of civilization.

Excerpts from a Lecture by Maharishi on the Principle "Knowledge Is Structured in Consciousness"

DIFFERENT STATES OF CONSCIOUSNESS, ON THE basis of different levels of creative intelligence, produce different knowledge. It is our experience that knowledge varies with our state of consciousness. The knowledge of a room, viewed in the waking state, shows us walls, people, colors, etc. If we remain exactly where we are and fall asleep, we experience nothing, or we may dream and find ourselves, instead of in the room, in a forest or a cave, in the Himalayas or the Atlantic, in the air or on the moon!

The room, experienced in the waking state, has a particular structure. Where is that structure structured? In consciousness. Only in the waking state is the room as it is. When we have a different state of consciousness, the structure of the room may be completely different.

A child sees the inside of a watch and it is a mystery to him. From his level of consiousness it is a mystery. He grows and becomes a watchmaker and on that level of consciousness the watch is no longer a mystery. He is the creator, the maker of watches. The watch is the same but the knowledge of the watch depended on his level of consciousness, on whether he was a child or a grown-up manufacturer of watches.

"When we study a pair of opposites such as gentle and strong," says Dr. Dillbeck, "first we look at an obvious example such as a willow tree, which gently bends with the wind, but is sturdy, too. Then the students see what gentle and strong means in themselves, physically and psychologically."

Then the students are asked, "What demonstrates this principle in our practice of TM? And in higher states of consciousness?" They see that seeming opposites are found together in the fifth state of consciousness, cosmic consciousness, in which unbounded awareness coexists permanently with the boundaries of waking, dreaming, and sleep states of consciousness [see Chapter Two]. In this way they come to appreciate a fuller range of life. As the students become more in tune with natural law through their practice of TM, they experience more integration between the gentle and strong aspects of their lives, between silence and dynamism.

So the state of consciousness decides the nature of knowledge, and knowledge is different in different states of consciousness. . . .

"Knowledge is structured in consciousness" . . . means that if we want knowledge to be invariably true we should have a level of consciousness which is most comprehensive. The expanded, unbounded state of consciousness should be permanently established. On that basis, whatever knowledge is gained will be true and complete. When one sees that knowledge truly is structured in consciousness, one is inspired to gain that comprehensive and complete state of awareness on the level of which the truth of life will always be cognized. When unbounded awareness is established it will not change with other states of consciousness. Waking, dreaming, and sleeping will continue to change, but when that unbounded awareness which develops through Transcendental Meditation becomes permanently established it does not change. That non-changing field of pure consciousness, because it does not change and because it is unbounded, will always give the same knowledge. Then knowledge will be complete. Only incomplete knowledge changes. Complete, decisive, full knowledge gained on the level of pure consciousness never changes. This is what we aim at when we say, "Knowledge is structured in consciousness."[9]

Through SCI, students learn and begin to experience that all seemingly opposite values are found in their own pure consciousness, which is at once completely silent and infinitely dynamic.

"They learn and begin to experience", Dr. Dillbeck says, "that the most extreme opposite values are found in their own pure consciousness, which is at once completely silent and infinitely dynamic." When the students become fully awake to this reality through their practice of TM, then they experience all seeming opposites as coexisting harmoniously in their daily lives — they are stable and adaptable, traditional and innovative, orderly and spontaneous.

A Sample 11th-Grade SCI Lesson: The Value of "Purposefulness"

The theme of the 11th-grade curriculum is "Developing the Fullness of Life." The core of the curriculum is the study of 16 values of creative intelligence and their application to the personal life of the student. The following sentence expresses the dynamics of these 16 values, illustrating how, from the fullness of the field of pure creative intelligence, life can be developed to the state of fulfillment: "Fullness, being Purposeful, Spontaneously becomes Active, takes a Direction towards Progress, and Transcending, Accelerates Integration of Stability and Adaptability, and Enjoys Evolution in Self-Purification, Harmony, and Fulfillment."

One SCI class is studying the second value, Purposefulness. "Our natural desire for more and more, and our efforts to achieve more and more demonstrate the purposefulness of activity in life," Lawrence Eyre tells his class. Reading from Maharishi's *Science of Being and Art of Living*, Mr. Eyre says,

> Expansion of happiness is the purpose of life, and evolution is the process through which it is fulfilled. Life begins in a natural way, it evolves, and happiness expands. The expansion of happiness carries with it the expansion of intelligence, power, creativity, and everything that may be said to be of significance in life.

Mr. Eyre continues, reading Maharishi's words:

> If one is not happy, one has lost the very purpose of life. If one is not constantly developing his intelligence, power, creativity, peace, and happiness, then he has lost the very purpose of life. Life is not meant to be lived in dullness, idleness, and suffering; these do not belong to the essential nature of life.

"In our own practice of TM," Mr. Eyre explains to the students, "the purposeful nature of our mind allows us to spontaneously

experience the unified field of natural law in the simplest state of
our own awareness. This unified field is the source of our happiness, creativity, and intelligence. We also find that great men and
women are very purposeful in their activity, never wasting any
time or energy on things that do not contribute to their goals."

As the class continues discussing great men and women,
one student comments that Olympic athletes have to be very
purposeful — every day for four years, they must constantly
work towards the goal of being the best in the world.

Mr. Eyre smiles and says, "I'm very glad that you understand that to be purposeful in your activity, you must have a
goal that you want to achieve and should take steps to plan out
how you can achieve the goal. I have a simple exercise that will
help you become more purposeful in achieving your goals."

He tells his students about the need to manage their time
properly. He explains that the most successful people plan very
carefully how they want to use their time, both day-to-day and
on a yearly basis. In describing the class exercise, which the students will do in small groups, Mr. Eyre shows them how to set
daily and yearly time schedules. The students are then encouraged to think about what goals they want to achieve and what
would constitute an "ideal daily routine" to achieve their goals.

One student, after sharing his daily and yearly schedules with
his small group, volunteers to show the entire class how he
planned his time. His overall goal is to evolve and become enlightened as quickly as possible. His schedule shows him arising
at 6:30 a.m. and preparing to go to the MIU Golden Domes, where
he will practice the Transcendental Meditation and TM-Sidhi
program (see Chapter Eight). Back home after the program, he has
breakfast, finishes his homework, and arrives at Maharishi School
at 9:20 a.m. in time for his morning classes. These end at 12:10
p.m., and then he eats lunch; afternoon classes begin at 1:00 p.m.
The last class of the day is the group practice of the TM and TM-
Sidhi program. Following this, he has varsity soccer practice until
about 7:00 p.m., and then he goes home to eat dinner with his
family, and does homework until 9:30 p.m.

"This exercise, which occurs during the second week of the
school year when we study Purposefulness, sets the tone for the
whole year," Mr. Eyre explains to us later. "Through a simple

time management exercise, the students plan out their day so that they can take maximum advantage of the knowledge presented in school, extra-curricular activities, and Maharishi's Transcendental Meditation program."

Furthermore, the students understand the value of purposefulness in their lives as it relates to the other 15 values of creative intelligence they study throughout the year. The students realize that careful planning eliminates wasted time and wasted mental energy, and thus they become more effective in activity. They see that maximum growth can occur on the basis of having a well-structured routine that includes the regular practice of the Transcendental Meditation technique. By becoming more purposeful, the fullness of life spontaneously blossoms in their lives.

Grade 12: An Overview of 24 Academic Disciplines in Light of the Knowledge of SCI

Fullness can only be lived on the basis of the physiological and psychological ability to naturally maintain and not lose the grip of the totality of life, even when one is within boundaries of thought, speech, perception, and action.

Throughout the SCI curriculum, students probe deeply into the principles and qualities of creative intelligence — the natural laws that guide their own personal development. They learn about the highest reaches of human potential and how to most rapidly develop their own inner genius to its fullest extent. Throughout all grade levels, the students' understanding deepens and matures through both the theoretical knowledge and direct experience of the field of pure intelligence provided by Maharishi's Science of Creative Intelligence. This cultures a greater depth of personality, a sharper intellect, more developed feelings of compassion, and more happiness and bliss throughout the school day.

The theme of grade 12 is "Living the Fullness of Life."

It is obvious that fullness can only be lived on the basis of the physiological and psychological ability to naturally maintain and not lose the grip of the totality of life, even when one is caught up within boundaries of thought, speech, perception, and action. This implies a normal physiology and psychology, which display maximum stability and flexibility at the same time.[10]

The purpose of the 12th-grade SCI curriculum is thus "to enable the students to live the fullness of life, by developing in their physiology and psychology the necessary flexibility and stability."

This year presents an interdisciplinary overview of all fields of knowledge through a study of 24 academic disciplines.

> Psychological flexibility and stability are developed through this examination of all fields of knowledge in the light of one common basis, creative intelligence. This development in psychology is supported and made permanent by a corresponding development on the physiological level, which comes through . . . the practice of Transcendental Meditation.[11]

Rather than bringing out the knowledge of the disciplines in great detail, the lessons aim at giving the student insight into the relation between the knowledge of the discipline and the field of pure intelligence as brought out by SCI. This not only makes all fields of knowledge relevant to the life of the student, but, by presenting all disciplines on the common ground of intelligence,

> gives such an interesting and inspiring synthesis of all knowledge that it warms up the emotions of the students for higher knowledge and inspires them to develop higher consciousness to derive maximum from higher education.[12]

Locating the principles of SCI in 24 academic disciplines cultures in the students a deep familiarity with the basis of knowledge in each field. Their growing understanding and experience through SCI and its practical aspect, TM, enables students to connect all the expressions of knowledge to their own lives. Nothing is foreign to them. This is how the 12th-grade SCI curriculum profoundly prepares students for studying the academic disciplines at the university level.

In Chapter Four we'll see how, on the basis of their study of SCI, the students at Maharishi School come to understand the different subjects of study as different expressions of the field of pure intelligence, the unified field of natural law, which is their own Self.

SCI and the Study of the Seven States of Consciousness

SCI on the secondary level includes a detailed analysis of the full range of human development in terms of Maharishi's description of the seven states of consciousness.

In Chapter Two we saw how higher states of consciousness develop naturally and spontaneously through regular practice of

Presenting all disciplines on the common ground of intelligence, gives such an interesting and inspiring synthesis of all knowledge that it warms up the emotions of the students for higher knowledge and inspires them to develop higher consciousness to derive maximum from higher education.

Maharishi's Transcendental Meditation technique. As part of their curriculum and their daily life, Maharishi School students regularly experience transcendental consciousness, the fourth state of consciousness — the basis for rapidly developing higher states.

Maharishi emphasizes that, for complete development, students need intellectual understanding of higher states of consciousness as well as personal experience. In the passage at the beginning of this chapter, Maharishi explains that by intellectually understanding higher states of consciousness, the students at Maharishi School become inspired to gain enlightenment as soon as possible.

A comment by Jeffrey, a 12th-grade student, bears this out: "By studying SCI, we have a better understanding of enlightenment. Because of this understanding, we want to do everything possible to grow towards enlightenment as quickly as possible." Based on their personal experiences and their knowledge of SCI, students understand which kinds of activities will promote their development and which ones are detrimental. Chapter Six describes more fully the moral development of Maharishi School students.

The knowledge of higher states of consciousness also clarifies experiences the students are having through their practice of Transcendental Meditation. Kathy, the junior we introduced earlier, emphasizes this point:

> In the beginning of the year when we were discussing the seven states of consciousness, the new students would ask lots of questions to clarify what is meant by each state. When we went over the higher states of consciousness more slowly for the benefit of the new students, they would then remark, "Oh yes, I've had that experience." Everyone would remark that they do go to a deeper state while meditating and discuss their experiences of being able to do things more efficiently in activity. I would be surprised if everyone was not having regular, clear experiences of higher states of consciousness. The experience of unbounded awareness is just a part of our lives now.

John, another senior describes the practical value of SCI in helping students to understand their growth: "Instead of just being caught up on the level of problems, we learn through SCI that more fundamental levels of creation are levels of greater

"I would be surprised if everyone was not having regular, clear experiences of higher states of consciousness. The experience of unbounded awareness is just a part of our lives now."
— 11th-grade student

harmony." The students directly experience these fundamental levels during their practice of the TM technique, and thus experience greater harmony in their activity. Their understanding of this principle is therefore a result of the growth of consciousness based on their experience during meditation. "Problems may arise in life," says John, "but by experiencing a more unified level of life, students can learn to see the harmony that exists within the diversity." By developing higher states of consciousness, students acquire the ability to live the fullness of life.

CHAPTER   FOUR

Connecting All Knowledge to the Self: Teaching the Academic Disciplines in Light of Maharishi's Science of Creative Intelligence

Unless knowledge is learned with reference to the universe and oneself, it will leave the mind in doubt. "What is the connection of this to everything else? And to me?" Unless this is made clear the thirst for knowledge will never be satisfied.[1]   — *Maharishi*

IN GUY HATCHARD'S 9TH-GRADE GEOMETRY CLASS AT Maharishi School, the students learn about axioms and angles, vectors and vertices, definitions and deductions. The students learn about all the parts of geometrical knowledge — spheres, parabolas, polyhedrons, and so on. But this class is different from other 9th-grade geometry classes. In every lesson, the students learn the *parts* of knowledge in relation to the discipline *as a whole.* And they connect the whole discipline to its source in the unified field of natural law, the same unified field they experience every day during their practice of TM. Every class in every secondary-level course at Maharishi School is taught this way.

This integrated approach is one of the secrets behind the success of Maharishi School. It also sets Maharishi School apart from other schools. Schools nationwide have been criticized for not producing well-rounded, educated people. The 1983 report of the National Commission on Excellence in Education brought national attention to this problem and urged schools to adopt higher academic standards. The report recommended a more comprehensive study of English, social studies, mathematics, natural science, and computer science.[2]

Since the school's founding, well before the National Commission's report, the Maharishi School curriculum has upheld rigorous academic standards. After their first-period SCI class, the Middle and Upper School students take courses in all the standard academic areas — for example, biology, chemistry, physics, algebra, geometry, precalculus, computer science, foreign languages, American history and government, world cultures, and English, American, and world literature.

But the Maharishi School curriculum goes far beyond the Commission's recommendations. In addition to teaching traditional academic knowledge, the purpose of every academic course at Maharishi School is to develop the full potential of the knower. On its own, each course offers the student the *content* of knowledge — for example, the formulas and equations they need to master the field of mathematics. But if students study the content of mathematics alone, they understand only the particular laws of nature of that discipline, without knowing how it is connected to the total range of knowledge.

The value of Unified Field Based Education for the students is immense: they automatically connect whatever they study to themselves.

At Maharishi School, the content of knowledge is always connected to the unified field, the basic level of existence and the source of every discipline of knowledge. Because the unified field is also the source of intelligence in the student, this approach to learning directly connects the known — the content of knowledge — to the knower, the student. The value of this approach for the students is immense: they automatically connect whatever they study to themselves. We'll come back to Mr. Hatchard's geometry class later in this chapter and see that this process is often delightful and exhilarating.

How is the unified field the source of every academic discipline? We discussed in Chapter One how everything in creation is an expression of the laws of nature — a result of the unified field, the field of pure intelligence, reverberating within itself and creating the universe. An academic discipline takes a specific angle on this vast, interconnecting web of intelligence — it studies the laws of nature operating in one particular area of life.

Chemistry, for example, studies the interactions among the

chemical elements, which arise from the fundamental interactions of the force and matter fields. Since the basis of all the force and matter fields is the unified field, the source of the discipline of chemistry is also the unified field — the same field of pure intelligence that is the basis of human awareness. If every discipline has its source in the unified field, then all the branches of learning are connected at their source.

Throughout the centuries, education has reinforced the notion that the knower and known, the student and the content of the disciplines, are fundamentally separate. The laws of nature studied in physics and astronomy, for example, are held to be distinctly different from those guiding human development. Current-day education perceives nature and human nature as distinctly different phenomena.

In the Science of Creative Intelligence, Maharishi explains that nature and human nature are unified at their source: "Human life as a whole has the total potential of natural law to guide it. All the laws of nature which can be seen governing the multitude of galaxies in the universe govern the billions of neurons in the human brain, and give man the ability to be a whole universe in himself."[3]

We saw in the previous chapter that through the study of Maharishi's Science of Creative Intelligence, students learn that the laws of nature guiding evolutionary development in the physical universe are the same laws of nature guiding human growth. They also learn that the field of pure consciousness, one's own Self, is the home of all the laws of nature. Maharishi's system of education thus identifies consciousness as the total potential of natural law, which opens to the student's awareness through the practice of the Transcendental Meditation technique.

In describing the value of integrating the traditional academic disciplines with the knowedge of the unified field of natural law, Maharishi states:

> In Unified Field Based Education the students connect all streams of knowledge with the source of all knowledge, the unified field, which they experience in their own transcendental consciousness. The student grows in the awareness that all streams of knowledge are expressions of his own intelligence.

"Human life as a whole has the total potential of natural law to guide it. All the laws of nature which can be seen governing the multitude of galaxies in the universe govern the billions of neurons in the human brain, and give man the ability to be a whole universe in himself."
— Maharishi

Maharishi explains that in his Unified Field Based Education, the knowledge of the lesson becomes a living reality in the student's daily life. "It is not merely information on the level of memory, but it goes deeper into his own pure intelligence, which guides all his thoughts and actions."

The knowledge of the lesson becomes a living reality in his daily life. It is not merely information on the level of memory, but it goes deeper into his own pure intelligence, which guides all his thoughts and actions.[4]

SCI-Based Teaching Methods that Connect the Knowledge of the Academic Disciplines to the Student's Self

The entire curriculum at Maharishi School is structured to present all streams of academic knowledge in the light of Maharishi's Science of Creative Intelligence, and thus to connect all knowledge to the student's own life. The faculty at Maharishi International University and Maharishi School have developed effective SCI-based teaching methods to accomplish this. These include the use of large graphic charts in every course on the secondary level to connect the knowledge of the academic disciplines to the unified field of natural law — the student's Self. Among these are Unified Field Charts, Main Point Charts, and Unity Charts. Because they present knowledge in a form that is more abstract than the younger students are used to, these charts are mainly used in the Middle and Upper Schools.

Unified Field Charts

The most comprehensive of all the charts is the Unified Field Chart. Unified Field Charts show the entire discipline at a glance. They show how the structure of a discipline emerges from the unified field of natural law, and unfolds sequentially from its most abstract, basic levels to its most applied areas that serve society. At Maharishi School, teachers use Unified Field Charts for a few minutes during each lesson to locate all the important principles of the lesson in the context of the entire discipline, and to connect them to the source of the discipline — the unified field, the field of pure consciousness.

For example, the Unified Field Chart developed by the MIU physics faculty is used in the Upper School physics course at Maharishi School. This chart, which appears on the following pages, shows how the unified field of natural law gives rise to all the various force and matter fields in nature, and how these fields in turn are the basis for all areas of theoretical and applied physics and technology. It also shows how the unified field, the field of pure intelligence, is experienced in transcendental consciousness during Maharishi's TM technique.

A 12th-grade student, Dan, explains that "The Unified Field Chart is like a 'map' that shows there are two ways of gaining knowledge — the objective way, through the study of the academic disciplines, and the subjective way, through the Transcendental Meditation technique. You can gain the experience of the unified field through Transcendental Meditation and then gain an objective understanding of knowledge through the study of each discipline," he says. "In the Unified Field Chart for physics, you can see how everything is related and how all the more expressed levels of physics are connected through processes of unification — like a family tree. The fundamental level of unification is the unified field of natural law, which we experience twice a day during our Transcendental Meditation program."

"Students at other schools do not know how the disciplines they are studying are relevant to their own lives," he continues. "Unified Field Charts allow the student to see not only how each discipline is related to the others but also how each discipline relates to one's own life. When you transcend the surface parts of the discipline and go to the unified field, you can see the connectedness of all knowledge. All disciplines are unified at that level where the knower, process of knowing, and known are fully united." (Maharishi has also used the terminology observer, process of observation, and observed to refer to these three aspects of the unified field.)

Julie Hane, a 12th-grade physics teacher at Maharishi School, explains how the job of making new knowledge relevant to the lives of the students is easy when a teacher integrates SCI into an academic course:

> I wanted them to have a clear foundation in the knowledge of the physical world, a foundation they could relate to current theories of cosmogenesis, to other areas of physics, and most importantly to their own lives. This foundation is provided by the Science of Creative Intelligence, and presented graphically through the use of the Unified Field Chart for physics.

She explains that through the repeated use of the Unified Field Chart, "students could see how all the various facts and theories we were discussing related to each other." Also, she says,

"Unified Field Charts allow the student to see not only how each discipline is related to the others but also how each discipline relates to one's own life."
— 12th-grade student

THE MAHARISHI TECHNOLOGY

CREATING HEAVEN ON EARTH THROUGH THE APPLICATION OF
EVERY PROFESSION TO RISE TO PERFECTION AND PROVE TO

PHYSICS

HEAD OF STATE

MINISTRIES OF GOVERNMENT

PHYSICS SERVING ALL AREAS OF NATIONAL LIFE ADMINISTERED BY GOVERNMENT

LEVEL 4

NAVIGATION AND TELEMETRY · TELECOMMUNICATIONS · LASER TECHNOLOGY · COMPUTER SCIENCE · MECHANICAL AND STRUCTURAL ENGINEERING · CHEMICAL ENGINEERING · BIOMEDICAL ENGINEERING · HYDRO-DYNAMICS AND HYDRO-ELECTRICITY · AERO-DYNAMICS AND AEROSPACE TECHNOLOGY · METEOROLOGY · GEOLOGICAL ENGINEERING

RADIOWAVES AND MICROWAVES · OPTICS · ELECTRONICS · MATERIALS SCIENCE · PHYSICAL CHEMISTRY · BIOPHYSICS · FLUID MECHANICS · ATMOSPHERIC PHYSICS · GEOPHYSICS

INFRARED AND VISIBLE LIGHT · SOLID STATE PHYSICS · CLASSICAL MECHANICS · QUANTUM CHEMISTRY · THERMO-DYNAMICS · PLASMA PHYSICS · PLANETARY SCIENCE

ULTRAVIOLET LIGHT · QUANTUM MECHANICS NON-RELATIVISTIC · ATOMIC PHYSICS · STATISTICAL MECHANICS · ASTRO-PHYSICS

LEVEL 3

X-RADIATION · NUCLEAR ENERGY AND NUCLEAR MEDICINE · ASTRONOMY · GALACTIC SYSTEMS

β-RADIATION · NUCLEAR PHYSICS · COSMOLOGY

From GRAVITY

MESONS · BARYONS

To ASTROPHYSICS · To COSMOLOGY

10^{-14}cm →

ELECTRO-MAGNETISM QUANTUM ELECTRODYNAMICS · WEAK FORCE FERMI THEORY · STRONG FORCE QUANTUM CHROMODYNAMICS · GRAVITY GENERAL RELATIVITY · N = 1 SUPERSYMMETRY · UP-TYPE QUARKS · DOWN-TYPE QUARKS · NEUTRINOS · CHARGED LEPTONS

10^{-16}cm →

ELECTRO-WEAK UNIFICATION · STRONG FORCE QUANTUM CHROMODYNAMICS · GRAVITY GENERAL RELATIVITY · N = 1 SUPERSYMMETRY · QUARKS · LEPTONS

10^{-29}cm →

LEVEL 2

GRAND UNIFICATION · GRAVITY GENERAL RELATIVITY · N = 1 SUPERSYMMETRY · LEPTOQUARKS

FORCE FIELDS · MATTER FIELDS

BOSE FIELDS · SUPERSYMMETRY · FERMI FIELDS

10^{-33}cm Planck Scale

SUPER ● UNIFICATION

LEVEL 1 · MAHARISHI TECHNOLOGY OF THE UNIFIED FIELD

UNIFIED FIELD
TOTAL POTENTIAL OF NATURAL LAW

UNIFIED FIELD

UNIFIED FIELD
TOTAL POTENTIAL OF NATURAL L

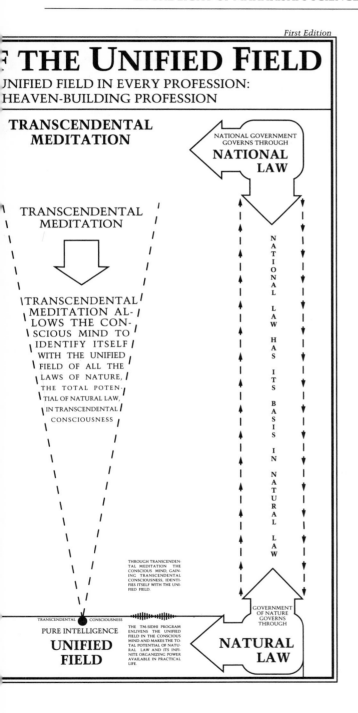

First Edition

THE UNIFIED FIELD

UNIFIED FIELD IN EVERY PROFESSION:
HEAVEN-BUILDING PROFESSION

TRANSCENDENTAL MEDITATION

NATIONAL GOVERNMENT
GOVERNS THROUGH
NATIONAL LAW

TRANSCENDENTAL
MEDITATION

TRANSCENDENTAL
MEDITATION AL-
LOWS THE CON-
SCIOUS MIND TO
IDENTIFY ITSELF
WITH THE UNIFIED
FIELD OF ALL THE
LAWS OF NATURE,
THE TOTAL POTEN-
TIAL OF NATURAL LAW,
IN TRANSCENDENTAL
CONSCIOUSNESS

NATIONAL LAW HAS ITS BASIS IN NATURAL LAW

THROUGH TRANSCENDEN-
TAL MEDITATION THE
CONSCIOUS MIND, GAIN-
ING TRANSCENDENTAL
CONSCIOUSNESS, IDENTI-
FIES ITSELF WITH THE UNI-
FIED FIELD.

TRANSCENDENTAL   CONSCIOUSNESS
PURE INTELLIGENCE
UNIFIED FIELD

THE TM-SIDHI PROGRAM
ENLIVENS THE UNIFIED
FIELD IN THE CONSCIOUS
MIND AND MAKES THE TO-
TAL POTENTIAL OF NATU-
RAL LAW AND ITS INFI-
NITE ORGANIZING POWER
AVAILABLE IN PRACTICAL
LIFE.

GOVERNMENT
OF NATURE
GOVERNS
THROUGH
NATURAL LAW

■ **Figure 8.** This chart illustrates how the unified field of natual law is the source of all the fundamental force and matter fields in nature, and how these fields in turn provide the basis for all areas of physics and technology and their applications throughout society. The Maharishi Technology of the Unfied Field — which includes Transcendental Meditation, its advanced techniques, and the TM-Sidhi program — unites the knowledge of the unified field discovered by the objective approach of modern physics with the direct experience of the unified field provided by the subjective approach of ancient Vedic Science. It enlivens the unified field in the awareness of the individual, bringing thought and action spontaneously in accordance with natural law so the individual enjoys the full support of nature in very aspect of life.

"**The knowledge of the unified field is important because you begin to see where everything springs from; the nature of life becomes clear and more orderly.**" **— 12th-grade student**

the students could see from the perspective of physics how everything in the manifest world emerges from this most fundamental field of existence, which we know from Maharishi's Vedic Science is the student's own consciousness. "It would not have been possible to accomplish all that I wanted to in this course and make the knowledge relevant to the students' own lives without the use of this chart. The chart organizes the discipline of physics so well and really makes the course easy to teach."

Ms. Hane presented a paper on her physics class at the 1987 meeting of the American Association of Physics Teachers in San Francisco.[5] As part of her presentation, she described the results of an evaluation she conducted on her course. Students gave the course high ratings. At the end of the year students responded to the item, "Overall this course was a valuable learning experience for me," with an average rating of 4.8 out of 5. They responded to "My interest in the discipline has increased as a result of this course," with an average rating of 4.9.

One student said, "The knowledge of the unified field is important because you begin to see where everything springs from; the nature of life becomes clear and more orderly." Another said that the course gave an introduction to physics and provided "many of the concepts which are important to life. It was one of the most valuable experiences in my high school career."

The Unified Field Chart developed by the MIU faculty for physiology illustrates how the entire range of human physiology emerges from the self-referral, three-in-one structure of pure knowledge — the unified state of knower, process of knowing, and known at the level of the unified field. The chart also shows how the practice of TM strengthens all aspects of the body. Scientific research on TM indicates that it enlivens the self-referral nature of the unified field within the physiology, giving rise to improved health and longevity. For example, one study found that TM meditators had significantly younger biological age than controls and norms for the general population, and that the strength of this effect is related to the length of practice of Maharishi's TM technique.[6]

Nina Meade, the Upper School physiology teacher, explains that throughout the course students study the different topics displayed on the chart. They learn, for example, all about the cells, tissues, organs, and systems that make up the human body.

But the most important knowledge the chart displays is how consciousness transforms itself into matter. "Through its own self-interacting dynamics, consciousness — the unified field of all the laws of nature — transforms itself into DNA. DNA is the most concentrated expression of intelligence in the body, and as such reflects most completely on a physiological level the pure intelligence contained within the unified field. It is this intelligence which is transferred to RNA, and then becomes manifest in proteins, which give rise to the rest of the physical body," she says.

"It's fun to teach physiology using this chart," she adds, "because everything on the chart relates to the students' experiences. They see clearly how their practice of Maharishi's TM technique produces a coherently functioning physiology that supports the full range of consciousness."

Teachers use Unified Field Charts in every Middle and Upper School course to help students see knowledge in a holistic context. Learning every subject in this light, the Maharishi School students grow in the awareness that all the knowledge in the various academic disciplines is an expression of their own intelligence — that they contain within their own consciousness the totality of knowledge, the totality of natural law.

Dr. Susan Dillbeck, whom we introduced in Chapter Three, comments that the Unified Field Chart "puts the day's discussion in the larger context of the whole discipline. It connects the students to the holistic basis of the subject they are studying and reminds them of their personal, directly-experienced connection with the knowledge." When their use is combined with the practice of Maharishi's TM technique, she explains, Unified Field Charts develop in the student "a more intimate relationship with the disciplines and a greater interest in understanding them more deeply. This approach helps solve two persistent problems in education — students feeling dissociated from what they are studying, and students perceiving knowledge as fragmented."[7]

Main Point Charts

When lecturing to the class, teachers also use Main Point Charts to organize the knowledge in the lesson so students can most easily assimilate it.

The left side of the chart presents the three or four main ideas

THE MAHARISHI TECHNOLOGY

CREATING HEAVEN ON EARTH THROUGH THE APPLICATION OF
EVERY PROFESSION TO RISE TO PERFECTION AND PROVE T[...]

PHYSIOLOGY

HEAD OF STATE

MINISTRIES OF GOVERNMENT

PHYSIOLOGY SERVING ALL AREAS OF NATIONAL LIFE ADMINISTERED BY GOVERNMENT

COLLECTIVE CONSCIOUSNESS

PHYSIOLOGY OF SOCIETY

INDIVIDUAL CONSCIOUSNESS

INDIVIDUAL PHYSIOLOGY

| NERVOUS | ENDOCRINE | IMMUNE | CARDIOVASCULAR RESPIRATORY DIGESTIVE REPRODUCTIVE HEMATOPATIC | MUSCULO-SKELETAL | INTEGUMENTORY |

SYSTEMS

| BRAIN PITUITARY GLAND THYMUS GLAND | HEART LUNGS STOMACH LIVER KIDNEY MARROW | SKELETON SKIN |

ORGANS

| CEREBRAL CORTEX | PERIPHERAL NERVES | LYMPH NODE | HEART MUSCLE ALVEOLUS INTESTINAL EPITHELIUM NEPHRON BLOOD | MUSCLE BONE EPIDERMIS |

TISSUES

| NEURON LYMPHOCYTE | CARDIAC MUSCLE CELL ALVEOLAR CELL HEPATO-CYTE RENAL TUBULAR CELL RED BLOOD CELL | MYOCYTE OSTEOCYTE KERATINOCYTE |

CELLS

| NUCLEUS RIBOSOME | ENDOSPLASMIC RETICULUM GOLGI APPARATUS MITO-CHONDRIA LYSOSOME | CYTOSKELETON PLASMA MEMBRANE |

CELL COMPONENTS

| GENE EXPRESSION MACHINERY CHROMATIN RIBONUCLEOPROTEIN PARTICLES | BIOSYNTHETIC PATHWAYS CARBOHYDRATES AMINO ACIDS LIPIDS NUCLEIC ACIDS | STRUCTURAL MACROMOLECULES MICROFILAMENTS EXTRACELLULAR MATRIX |

MACROMOLECULAR SYSTEMS

| INFORMATIONAL PROTEINS NEUROPEPTIDE RECEPTOR | ENZYMES BIOSYNTHETIC DIGESTIVE | STRUCTURAL PROTEINS LIPOPROTEIN COLLAGEN |

PROTEINS

| MESSENGER RNA TRANSFER RNA | RIBOZYME | RIBOSOMAL RNA |

RNA

INFORMATION FOR GENE EXPRESSION

INFORMATION FOR REPLICATION & DNA REPAIR

DNA

GENE STRUCTURE

ELECTROMAGNETISM QUANTUM ELECTRODYNAMICS	WEAK FORCE FERMI THEORY	STRONG FORCE QUANTUM CHROMODYNAMICS	GRAVITY GENERAL RELATIVITY	UP-TYPE QUARKS	DOWN-TYPE QUARKS	NEUTRINOS	CHARGED LEPTONS
	ELECTRO WEAK UNIFICATION	STRONG FORCE QUANTUM CHROMODYNAMICS	GRAVITY GENERAL RELATIVITY		QUARKS	LEPTONS	
		GRAND UNIFICATION	GRAVITY GENERAL RELATIVITY		LEPTOQUARKS		

FORCE FIELDS   MATTER FIELDS

SUPERSYMMETRY

PLANCK SCALE

LEVEL 6		
LEVEL 5	BIOMEDICAL TECHNOLOGY	
LEVEL 4	HISTOLOGICAL TECHNOLOGY / CYTOLOGICAL TECHNOLOGY	
LEVEL 3	BIOCHEMICAL TECHNOLOGY / GENETIC TECHNOLOGY	
LEVEL 2	QUANTUM MECHANICAL BODIES	

| LEVEL 1 | MAHARISHI TECHNOLOGY OF THE UNIFIED FIELD | UNIFIED FIELD TOTAL POTENTIAL OF NATURAL LAW | **UNIFIED FIELD** | UNIFIED FIELD TOTAL POTENTIAL OF NATURAL [...] |

CONNECTING ALL KNOWLEDGE TO THE SELF: TEACHING THE ACADEMIC DISCIPLINES
IN THE LIGHT OF MAHARISHI'S SCIENCE OF CREATIVE INTELLIGENCE

69

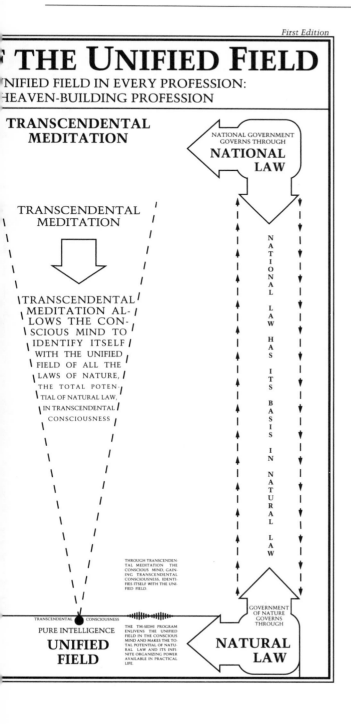

First Edition

THE UNIFIED FIELD

NIFIED FIELD IN EVERY PROFESSION:
HEAVEN-BUILDING PROFESSION

TRANSCENDENTAL MEDITATION

NATIONAL GOVERNMENT
GOVERNS THROUGH

NATIONAL LAW

TRANSCENDENTAL
MEDITATION

TRANSCENDENTAL
MEDITATION AL-
LOWS THE CON-
SCIOUS MIND TO
IDENTIFY ITSELF
WITH THE UNIFIED
FIELD OF ALL THE
LAWS OF NATURE,
THE TOTAL POTEN-
TIAL OF NATURAL LAW,
IN TRANSCENDENTAL
CONSCIOUSNESS

NATIONAL LAW HAS ITS BASIS IN NATURAL LAW

THROUGH TRANSCENDEN-
TAL MEDITATION THE
CONSCIOUS MIND, GAIN-
ING TRANSCENDENTAL
CONSCIOUSNESS, IDENTI-
FIES ITSELF WITH THE UNI-
FIED FIELD

TRANSCENDENTAL CONSCIOUSNESS

PURE INTELLIGENCE

UNIFIED FIELD

THE TM-SIDHI PROGRAM
ENLIVENS THE UNIFIED
FIELD IN THE CONSCIOUS
MIND AND MAKES THE TO-
TAL POTENTIAL OF NATU-
RAL LAW AND ITS INFI-
NITE ORGANIZING POWER
AVAILABLE IN PRACTICAL
LIFE

GOVERNMENT
OF NATURE
GOVERNS THROUGH

NATURAL LAW

■ **Figure 9.** This chart illustrates how the Maharishi Technology of the Unified Field contributes to modern physiology by providing a new integrated approach in which the whole range of physiology can be appreciated from its source in the self-interaction of the self-referral unified field of all the laws of nature. Practice of the TM and TM-Sidhi program ensures that the homeostatic self-regulatory processes functioning at every level of physiology fully reflect the self-referral value of the unified field, establishing all aspects of life in accordance with the total potential of natural law — perfect health for the individual and society.

of the lecture, from the perspective of the discipline. To the right of each main point is a corresponding point from SCI. The main points of the disciplines state the main principles that connect the specific bits of information to the major ideas within the field of study. The SCI points present a more comprehensive perspective on the discipline points and relate the content of the lecture to the students' growth of consciousness. The title for each Main Point Chart gives the main theme of the lesson; the subtitle gives an expanded context for the lesson from the perspective of SCI.

In a week-long 11th-grade American government unit on Constitutional amendments XI to XXVI, the teacher used the following Main Point Chart to show the relationship of the amendments to the qualities growing in the students' lives through the TM program.

Expanding Freedoms Through a Growing Constitution: Enlivening the Unified Field in One's Own Awareness to Gain Greater Freedom in Life

MAIN POINTS

American Government	Maharishi's SCI
1. The Constitution is a living document. While the basic principles underlying the Constitution have remained the same for over 200 years, amendments have been added to meet the needs of the changing times.	**1.** Stability and adaptability are two qualities necessary for maximum progress on any level of life. The stable, nonchanging field of pure creative intelligence, the unified field, is infinitely adaptable and gives rise to the ever-changing expressions to life.
2. The purpose behind most amendments to the Constitution is to provide people with greater freedoms, which are not specifically granted in the main body of the Constitution.	**2.** Through the practice of Maharishi's Transcendental Meditation everyone in society can experience growing freedom. To feel real freedom in life, one must permanently maintain unbounded awareness along with waking, dreaming, and deep sleep states of consciousness.

3. Although amendments were added to the Constitution that granted greater freedom to certain groups who were not previously treated with equal respect, many individuals and even state governments have failed to provide equal treatment to all persons under the law.

3. The existence of law does not guarantee compliance with the law; what is needed is the development of consciousness to ensure right thinking and right action. By establishing one's awareness at the level of the unified field, all thoughts and actions will be fully life-supporting for oneself and society.

As a review exercise at the end of the unit, the teacher invited the students to present their own ideas on the main points covered in the unit. The following comments, from a recording of the class, show that through this approach to learning the students easily connect the knowledge of the discipline with their personal experiences:

Tina: When you contact the unified field, which is in every single individual, in their consciousness, you can then open up your awareness to what's inherent in the person, and some of these qualities are freedom, bliss, and unboundedness. When you have done that, when you have opened your awareness to these qualities, then you can begin living them in your life. And that's essentially what the amendments are — the springing up of these qualities of the unified field into . . . written documents, and [they are] evidence of growing collective consciousness.

John: With SCI, with the practice of TM, it lets people grow in freedom, bliss, and unboundedness. These are also structured into the Constitution. Freedom has been guaranteed in the Constitution, that man was created equal and free and it's intended to always be that way. There's bliss, because freedom naturally brings about bliss, but also if there's any disharmony within the Constitution then people can change it, amend the Constitution, to make it better for the people and to make the people more happy. And there is unboundedness also, because amendments can make the Constitution change in any direction; there's no limit to which the Constitution can be changed.

Kathy: I see an SCI principle that relates to this, and that's "Purification leads to progress," because the Constitution in the beginning was imperfect; it was a document that was meant to bring about perfection. As the consciousness of the people became higher, new things needed to be added and other things needed to be purified out for progress to take place. For instance, slavery needed to be taken out, needed to be purified out of our national consciousness. And once it became purified out, then other things could be added, like blacks could vote and women could vote.

Pam: Amendments XIII to XV, and XIX . . . mainly granted freedom for blacks and extended the rights of women, so they could vote and have their equal share of influence in the government. As we see, Transcendental Meditation has a much grander, more basic influence in life. Everyone who contacts the unified field through TM and the TM-Sidhi program has a profound influence on all [levels] of consciousness. And not only that, they can change the trends to bring about new amendments to further the evolution of all of society.

Unity Charts

The Unity Chart accompanies the Main Point Chart, and is used at the end of each lecture to "connect the parts of knowledge to the wholeness of knowledge." This chart presents the topic of the lesson from four different perspectives, of increasing subtlety and organizing power.

The first point shows the common textbook understanding of the lesson's main theme. The second point states a more profound and abstract way of perceiving this theme, still from the perspective of the discipline. The third point relates the topic to the experience of transcendental consciousness. And the fourth examines the topic from the perspective of the highest state of human consciousness, unity consciousness, in which all activity is perceived as the dynamics of one's own consciousness — "wholeness moving within itself." (See Chapter Two for a description of higher states of consciousness.)

Following is the Unity Chart used in the same 11th-grade lesson on Constitutional amendments. This chart gives four perspectives on the concept of freedom. It starts with an obvious point from the discipline and proceeds to a second point which presents a deeper perspective. Further explanation appears following the chart.

Connecting the Parts of Knowledge to the Wholeness of Knowledge: Freedom

1. Individual freedoms are guaranteed by written laws and amendments contained within the United States Constitution.

2. Individual freedoms are upheld when society as a whole acts in ways that support the written laws and amendments to the Constitution.

....

3. Transcendental consciousness, the unified field of natural law, is the state of perfect freedom — the total potential of natural law, full of all possibilities.

4. Wholeness Moving Within Itself: Complete freedom is gained in the state of unity consciousness. At this level of human development, all the laws of nature are perceived as expressions of one's own Self — the unified field. Life is a field of all possibilities — one can know anything, do anything, and accomplish anything.

The dotted line separating the first two points from the second two signifies the shift from the surface level of life, represented by the discipline, to the underlying wholeness of life, the unified field, pure consciousness. The arrow at the side indicates that from the perspective of unity consciousness, all surface values of life are perceived in terms of the Self. By concluding every lesson with the perspective of unity consciousness, the student leaves each class with the impact of wholeness rather than the impact of parts, and the awareness that every facet of life is an expression of his own intelligence, his own Self.[8]

The Value of SCI-Based Teaching Methodologies

Upper School students appreciate how the SCI principles help them integrate their knowledge of the academic disciplines. Tim, a 12th-grade student, says, "SCI gives you a bigger picture of life. In my opinion, SCI principles give you a basis, a foundation, to work with everything. You can take SCI principles and see how they apply and link the different disciplines." He gives examples of the SCI principle "Order is present everywhere" in numerical

Maharishi explains that knowledge results from the integration of the knower, the known and the process of knowing within the consciousness of the student.

systems and physiology. "The main principle is that numbers are orderly — they follow each other sequentially. When you go to physiology, you also find the principle of order. . . . The physiology embodies this orderliness principle throughout its structure."

Mark, a junior, says that SCI makes whatever he's learning easier to understand. "It's like when you are reading a book in a dark room, and you turn a light on; it makes it easier to learn." Betty, a sophomore, says that SCI helps her to relate all her academic studies to each other in terms of natural principles. "This in turn helps you see more clearly what you are studying so you do better in school."

Research shows that using a broad conceptual framework, in which the specific details of knowledge are organized into greater wholes, is important in promoting students' cognitive learning. According to current cognitive learning theorists, learning occurs when new information is connected to students' "prior knowledge base" — the knowledge and skills they already have. Learning is not a passive process — it does not occur simply because the teacher presents some new material. For learning to take place, students must actively reorganize and reconstruct incoming information. This leads to greater meaning in their classroom experience.[9]

This view of learning is consistent with Maharishi's theory of how knowledge is gained. Maharishi explains that knowledge results from the integration of the knower (the student), the known (the content), and the process of knowing (that which links the two). These three fundamental elements of the educational process are not integrated outside the knower, but rather within his own consciousness. For this reason, Unified Field Based Education emphasizes expanding students' conscious capacity by opening their awareness to the unbounded field of pure intelligence during TM, the practical aspect of Maharishi's Science of Creative Intelligence. It also prescribes the theoretical study of SCI, to give students a comprehensive intellectual framework that connects all knowledge.

Further Examples of How Maharishi's SCI Integrates and Illuminates Knowledge in the Classroom

In our classroom observations, we found that students were able to integrate easily and profoundly the specific details of knowledge from their academic subjects into the holistic frame-work provided by SCI. The following excerpts from an 11th-grade student's presentation and a 9th-grade geometry play are further examples of how SCI integrates and illuminates the knowledge of the academic disciplines.

A Student's Presentation on William Blake

As part of our research, we observed an 11th-grade English literature class in which one of the students, Jan, gave a presentation on two works by William Blake in the light of SCI principles. Jan discussed slides of Blake's *Songs of Innocence and Experience* in terms of the growth of higher states of consciousness. She then presented slides from Blake's *Four Zoas* in light of the different levels of the mind arising from the unified field of natural law.

The unifying theme of Jan's presentation was the necessity of regaining innocence through contact with the unified field. In the growth to enlightenment, she explained, the "innocence" of the unified field becomes stabilized when it is never lost, even during all the experiences of the waking state of consciousness.

Jan located the concepts of the Science of Creative Intelligence in the writings of Blake with an ease that was particularly striking. Her classmates' attentiveness to her 30-minute presentation was also impressive. When she asked them to elaborate on how SCI could be applied to Blake's works, they were quick to respond and readily integrated Blake's concepts with their own understanding and experience.

> **Jan**: To really understand William Blake is to not look at instances in his life but to understand his works. He had a way to tap into what we call the unified field.... The main thesis is that all his writings centered around the human soul.
>
> During the practice of Transcendental Meditation, we experience what Blake calls "silence." This is the innocence part. The experience is the coming out into activity. Then there is the self-referral process of coming back to the state of innocence again. Can anyone relate this to enlightenment?
>
> **Student**: First, one transcends the environment and experiences transcendental consciousness, innocence. Then there is the experience of our daily activity. By alternating meditation with

our daily activity, we begin to infuse pure consciousness, the unified field, into our daily activity so that pure consciousness becomes stabilized in our awareness all the time. Then we have gained the state of enlightenment. This is innocence and experience together.

Jan: When one is enlightened, one has a balance between innocence and experience.

Jan then described how Blake consistently showed innocence and experience side by side. For example, the tiger, representing experience, is shown next to the lamb, representing innocence. In Jan's view, Blake was emphasizing the importance of regaining a state of innocence, which she equated with the unified field of natural law.

In the second part of the talk, Jan discussed her interpretation of Blake's *Four Zoas*. She explained the relationship between the main characters and the levels of the mind described in SCI (see Chapter Two). She equated Tharmas (body) with the senses, Urizen (reason) with the intellect, Luvah (emotion) with feeling, and Urithona (soul) with the unified field. "These four in their pure state represent man in his most unified state of awareness. Together they can be seen to represent the state of enlightenment," she said.

Jan then described Blake's conception of the "fall of man," illustrated by the disconnection of the four Zoas, and the regeneration of man, illustrated by the return to the unified field: "The senses, intellect, and feelings, disconnected from the unified field, represents the 'fall of man.' The 'fall of man' is when experience is not connected with innocence, in Blake's words. Man is regenerated through innocence — regeneration into enlightenment through innocence. The unified field is strategic to bringing about innocence. Due to innocence, one rises to perfect harmony."

The last slide depicted experience and innocence in perfect harmony. "This is mankind in innocence and experience together, because it shows perfect symmetry," she said. She concluded by saying, "Blake wants the audience to learn from his writings and have his fellow men share the ecstasy of bliss."

Afterwards, Jan said, "Without SCI, I would have only been able to pick up the surface understanding of innocence and experience, without realizing the real significance of Blake's writings."

"His whole emphasis on the higher dimension of human experience would have gone right by me. While other students are groping just to understand the significance of Blake's works, students at Maharishi School have a practical means for developing enlightenment, which is what these two works are essentially about."

The Geometrical Musical Play of the Unified Field

Another way students use SCI to connect their academic coursework with the unified field is by enacting on stage the Unified Field Chart for a discipline or area of study. By acting out the dynamic interactions among the parts of knowledge and between the parts and the unified field, the "unified field play" makes the knowledge of a particular discipline and its applications to society come alive.

The original "Play of the Unified Field" was written by MIU physics professor John Hagelin and performed for the whole community by over a hundred undergraduate and graduate MIU students in the fall of 1987. The play was a great success — the students enjoyed themselves immensely and, in the process, learned a great deal about the fundamental transformations at very fine time and distance scales that create the elementary forces and particles of nature.

Using witty Gilbert and Sullivan-type songs, marching bands, and dialogue, the play presented these concepts in the language of both physics and Maharishi's Vedic Science, and made especially clear to both students and audience how the unified field, the source of the "building blocks of nature," is the same field of pure consciousness at the basis of their own lives. With the help of elaborate stage machinery, the climax of the play portrayed the physicist transcending the surface layer of existence and directly experiencing the unified field. He then gains the fruit of all knowledge, and lives a life of complete fulfillment in accord with natural law.

Inspired by the success and fun of Dr. Hagelin's play, Mr. Hatchard and his 9th-grade geometry students, whom we introduced at the beginning of this chapter, wrote "The Geometrical Musical Play of the Unified Field." All 33 of the 9th-grade students performed in this play, with the help of 16 8th-graders. The play

By acting out the dynamic interactions among the parts of knowledge and the unified field, the "unified field play" makes the knowledge of a particular discipline and its applications to society come alive.

was written, Mr. Hatchard says, "in just five 40-minute lessons and a weekend of fun!"

The play was based on the Unified Field Chart he uses in his geometry classes. Complete with costumes and music, the play educated the audience in the essential concepts of geometry and showed how geometry is applied to all areas of society. As Professor Hagelin's play showed for physics, this play clearly illustrated that the source of all geometry is the field of pure consciousness, the unified field of natural law; the "geometer," experiencing the unified field through Maharishi's Transcendental Meditation and TM-Sidhi program, becomes enlightened and gains complete mastery of natural law. At the heart of the play were amusing songs to the tunes of "Old MacDonald Had a Farm," "Michael, Row the Boat Ashore," and "Old Man River."

As the play begins, the audience sees the knower, process of knowing, and known emerging from their unified state in the unified field of all the laws of nature. As the play unfolds, the stage gradually fills with characters as the students enact the sequential emergence of the more concrete, applied levels of each of these three.

First, they portray the known — the subject matter of geometry. Its first expressions are the abstract geometrical concepts of the particle, direction, and space-time. Wearing imaginative costumes that depict each "character," they show how these three concepts take form as the Point, the Angle, and the Line:

> **Point**: I'm smaller than the smallest.
> **Line**: I'm taller than the tallest.
> **Point**: But when I form a vertex,
> **Line**: And I the rays,
> **Together**: Our gap becomes an angle to amaze.
> [The angle jumps out onstage]

These interact onstage to become the concepts of congruence, transformations, vectors, and scalars, which are always connected to the three-in-one structure of the unified field — the unified state of knower, process of knowing, and known.

These concepts become the Forms, the Platonic solids. They come onstage dressed and named in the shapes Tetrahedron, Cube, Octohedron, Dodecahedron, and Icosohedron and sing "Old MacDonald Had a Form." The song begins,

Old MacDonald had a form, E-I-E-I-O
And on that form he had a line, E-I-E-I-O
With a line here, and a line there,
Here a line, there a line, everywhere a line, line
[Students join lines to make a triangle.]
Then we have a triangle, E-I-E-I-O

As the song progresses, the students show how the triangle gives rise to every form. They:

- unfold a triangle into a square
- stretch a square into a rectangle, showing how the polygons are generated
- tie a knot in a rectangle to create a pentagon, then a geodesic dome
- with conic sections, convince a skeptical sphere that even its perfect curves are generated from the triangle.

Meanwhile, the audience has been seeing how the different levels of the knower, the mathematician, evolve — how the advanced knowledge arrived at through the mathematical processes of knowing (inference, classification, measurement, and application) transforms the Theoretician into a Geometer, and then into an Applied Scientist.

The students show how geometrical concepts are practically applied in engineering, architecture, and graphic design. In the process, they connect the SCI principles they have been studying in class with the concepts of geometry.

"The nature of life is to grow."
Building and construction show
The triangle's a rigid shape
That every builder has to make.
"The whole is contained in every part."
The DNA in every cell and in the heart
Makes and guides the hands and eyes
To find the helix where its secret lies.

Finally, through Maharishi's Transcendental Meditation and TM-Sidhi program, the Applied Scientist is transformed into an Enlightened Scientist. Just before a rousing finale with the entire cast of geometrical characters, the Enlightened Scientist says:

Plato said that "Geometry will draw the soul towards truth
   and create love for knowledge."

And so it is now taught in every college,
But somehow through the ages
Geometry failed to provide the wisdom of the sages.
Now with the TM-Sidhi program of Maharishi,
Inspired by the ancient sage Patanjali *
Geometry is fulfilled when the student experiences
The self-interacting dynamics of consciousness.
He gains mastery over space-time
And creates world peace just in time.

[*see Chapter 8]

"Writing and acting out the play was a big motivator that helped the students understand concretely how the geometry of the universe emerges from the unified field, which is nothing other than their own consciousness," Mr. Hatchard says. "Also, the play increased their interest in studying mathematics. In performing the play, they could concretely see how the fundamental principles of geometry give rise to its more applied aspects."

Since performing in it, his students frequently refer to the play in class. "For example," he says, "whenever we discuss the concept of symmetry, the students mention that the twins in the class acted out this concept in the play. And when we come to some particular topic on the Unified Field Chart, they often exclaim, 'Oh, I remember that!' and start to sing the song from the play about that topic. The play was an ideal method for teaching — it gave them knowledge and enjoyment together. It definitely uplifted their hearts and minds, and made the whole year a success."

We have consistently found that the Upper School students enjoy connecting the details of their academic subjects with the universal principles of Maharishi's Science of Creative Intelligence. SCI adds richness and vitality to the study of the traditional academic disciplines, by giving a framework of knowledge that integrates the content of each discipline with the life of the student.

The first four chapters have illustrated the holistic approach of Maharishi's Unified Field Based Education. This integrated approach effectively connects all knowledge to the consciousness of the student. This contrasts with the present system of education, which emphasizes the content of knowledge but excludes the domain of consciousness.

There is clearly a need today for a new and holistic approach to education. Our schools must give every student the total range of knowledge. Maharishi's Unified Field Based Education presents the knowledge of the objective world, the subjective field of consciousness, and the relationship of the two. In Maharishi's words, the holistic knowledge gained through his system of education allows the student "to imbibe total knowledge and live it in daily life."

In the next two chapters, we'll see the effects of Unified Field Based Education on student academic achievement and social development at Maharishi School. Then we'll discuss how Unified Field Based Education promotes a more positive school climate, helps to create world peace, and is laying the foundation for Heaven on Earth.

Maharishi explains that his system of education allows the student "to imbibe total knowledge and live it in daily life."

C H A P T E R　　F I V E

Excellence in Education:
Gaining the Fruit of All Knowledge

N IRMAL SMILES PROUDLY AS HIS NAME IS CALLED AS THE first place winner in the junior biological division of the 1986 Eastern Iowa Science Fair. Many months of work at the MIU chemistry lab — learning how to use equipment, analyzing assays, and writing his report — have finally borne fruit.

As a Maharishi School 8th-grader, Nirmal decided to conduct his own original research project. He started going to the MIU chemistry lab on Saturdays, to watch the scientists conduct research on neurotransmitters associated with feelings of happiness and well-being. Nirmal was fascinated by what he saw, and asked the scientists many questions. They explained how their research was determining if the increase of these biochemicals in TM meditators was associated with the experience of bliss and unbounded awareness during meditation. Nirmal asked if more people were needed to do research. The answer was yes.

Nirmal went to the lab director and asked if he could do his own research project. The director hesitated, not at all sure this was a good idea either for the boy or for the lab. Not wanting to discourage him, the director decided to let Nirmal clean test tubes for a few weeks. When Nirmal's interest in doing research showed no signs of waning, the director finally agreed to teach him the necessary steps. Normally, only graduate students were permitted to train and conduct research in the lab, so it was quite extraordinary for the director to devote his time and attention to training an 8th-grader.

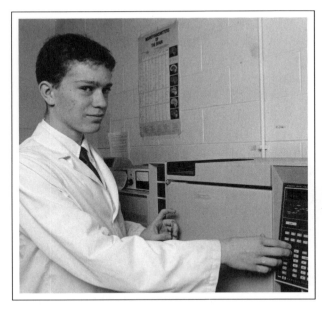

■ Previous research on Maharishi's Transcendental Meditation and TM-Sidhi program gave Nirmal the idea for his award-winning research project.

The MIU scientists had hypothesized that serotonin, a neurotransmitter associated with feelings of well-being, was increased by the practice of Maharishi's TM and TM-Sidhi program. Nirmal's visits to the chemistry lab had given him the idea of investigating if serotonin increased still further when Maharishi's TM and TM-Sidhi program was practiced together in a group with other individuals. In Nirmal's study, serotonin levels were monitored by measuring the urine concentrations of 5-HIAA, one of its principal metabolites.

Over the next several months, Nirmal spent every spare moment at the lab learning how to conduct his study. The scientists were delighted and impressed by his extraordinary dedication and acute attention to every detail of his project. Nirmal never seemed to tire of sitting at the computer and analyzing his data. In the end, his hypothesis was confirmed — 5-HIAA was found in greater concentration in meditators as a result of their group practice of Maharishi's TM and TM-Sidhi program.

Nirmal acknowledged that his project was not typical for an 8th-grader, even at a state science fair. "The judges thought I knew the material pretty well. At first they kind of wondered if I had done the work myself, but after I answered all their questions, they were convinced," he said. Three pairs of judges quizzed him for half an hour each. Then four other judges came by just to hear about the project for their own interest. Later, Nirmal was also invited to present his research at several scientific conferences. Now in his senior year at Maharishi Upper School, Nirmal continues to win awards for his research projects.

Success in Academic Competitions

Nirmal is obviously a boy of extraordinary talent and ability in the sciences. But he is just one of many students at Maharishi School of the Age of Enlightenment who have won awards at regional and state fairs.

For example, during the past two years, Maharishi School students won over 70 awards at the Eastern Iowa Science and Engineering Fair. This included first place in both the senior biological science and physical science divisions, and first place in the papers competition for each division. During the 1987–1988 Hawkeye Science Fair, Maharishi School students won 10 awards, including second place in the research paper competition and fourth place in the biological science division. During the past two years, three Maharishi School students have been invited to present their research at the annual meeting of the Iowa Junior Academy of Sciences. During the 1988–89 school year, a Maharishi School student won a first place award and was

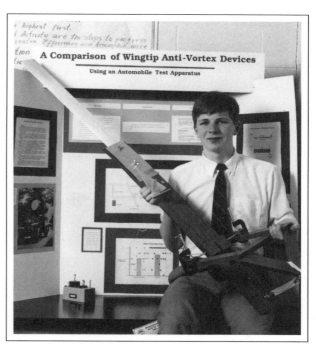

■ (Above) Another student displays an award-winning science project.

■ (Left) Students shown here at the MIU Spayde Theater were preparing to compete in the 1989 speech competition, for which they won the highest rating at the District level.

■ This Maharishi
School student won
first place in the Iowa
High School Music
Association
competition.

selected to be one of only two students representing Iowa at the prestigious American Association for the Advancement of Science annual convention. Also, for the fourth consecutive year, Maharishi School students have been selected to present their research at the International Science and Engineering Fair.

During the 1988–89 school year, a Maharishi School student won a second place award at the State History Fair in individual media for her presentation on Louis Armstrong, which qualified her to represent the State of Iowa at the National History Day competition in Washington, D.C. Another student won third place in the senior paper category for her essay on "The Italian Immigrant." Maharishi School students also won awards in regional art and music competitions, including Gold Medals for flute, violin, and voice performances.

During the 1987–1988 school year, a Maharishi School entry won the state championship and was declared the "Critics' Choice" in the Iowa High School Speech Association competition, which had over 200 entries. In 1988–1989, all three Maharishi Upper School entries in the Speech Association's District competition earned the highest rating; two of three entries went to the All State competition, where one group was invited to perform and the other received special recognition.

The 1988 Maharishi School senior class distinguished itself by having two National Merit Scholars, one National Merit finalist, two State of Iowa Scholars, and two Iowa Math and Science Scholars.

These awards and honors reflect the academic excellence of students at Maharishi School, which is also seen in their annual performance on standardized academic achievement tests.

Research on Improved Academic Achievement at Maharishi School

In August, 1985, the Associated Press circulated a story describing the academic performance of Maharishi School students on the nationally administered Iowa Tests of Basic Skills (ITBS) and Iowa Tests of Educational Development (ITED). The ITBS is given to students up through grade 8, the ITED to secondary students. The article cited statistics showing consistently high performance in all grade levels at Maharishi School.[1]

Over the past several years, the test scores of the average class at Maharishi School ranked at or above the 95th percentile nationally. Grades 10–12 all scored in the 99th percentile nationally on overall academic achievement. A percentile rank is a comparison of one student or class of students to a larger group, in this case to all classes that were tested nationwide. To say that a class is in the 99th percentile means that as a whole the class performed as well as or better than 99 percent of all other classes taking the test.

Table One shows the class percentile ranks for grades 10–12 on all scales of the ITED.[2]

TABLE ONE

Percentile Ranks on the Iowa Tests of Educational Development (ITED) for Grades 10-12 at Maharishi School

Grade	CE	QT	SS	NS	LM	GV	SI	RT	COMP
Grade 10[a]	99	99	99	99	99	99	99	99	99
Grade 11[b]	80	99	97	99	99	99	99	99	99
Grade 12[c]	78	98	99	98	99	99	99	99	99

CE = Correctness of Expression   GV = General Vocabulary
QT = Quantitative Thinking (Math)   SI = Sources of Information
SS = Social Studies   RT = Reading Total
NS = Natural Science   COMP = Composite
LM = Literary Materials   [a]n=20   [b]n=15   [c]n=19

Considering the school's liberal admissions policy, these high percentile ranks are impressive. However, further research reveals something even more striking — the academic achievement of individual students significantly increases over a year's time. Of particular interest are the findings that students who transfer to Maharishi School from other schools show significant increases in academic development. New students entering Maharishi School typically show about average academic ability. Thus the high level of academic achievement at the school can't be said to arise simply because the school attracts the best students. Rather, the findings show that attending Maharishi School makes the difference.

The following case study of Mark, an 11th-grade student, demonstrates this point. Before coming to Maharishi School, Mark went to a public school in an affluent Long Island suburban neighborhood. There, he got B's and C's and felt he was not gaining much from school. Within one year of coming to Maharishi School, which he considers to be more academic than his old school, Mark has achieved nearly an A average. He has improved on the ITED by 16 percentile points in overall academic achievement —from the 56th percentile, about average, to the 72nd percentile, which is very good. He also improved substantially in mathematics (22

■ Students throughout Maharishi School typically exhibit significant improvements in academic achievement, as measured by standardized tests over a one-year period.

percentile points), the natural sciences (41 percentile points), and reading ability (26 percentile points). Now, Mark looks forward to going to school and to being challenged in his coursework.

Mark is one of many students who have made considerable academic progress at Maharishi School. Other students have increased in overall academic achievement by as much as 21, 24, 27, and even 40 percentile ranks in one year. These changes are striking. To show an increase in percentile rank a student must exhibit a greater increase in the knowledge of a specific area than other students would normally attain. The typical student does not show a marked change over time in percentile rank on standardized tests of academic achievement; for example, if a student starts out in the 3rd grade with a percentile rank of 50, we would expect him to still be about at the 50th percentile upon entering senior high school.

Research shows that these gains in academic achievement made by new students in their first year at Maharishi School are statistically significant. In one study, we assessed changes in academic achievement for new students in the Lower and Middle Schools by comparing their ITBS scores from the fall and spring of one school year. We found that students improved significantly on the composite (overall) academic achievement, mathematics,

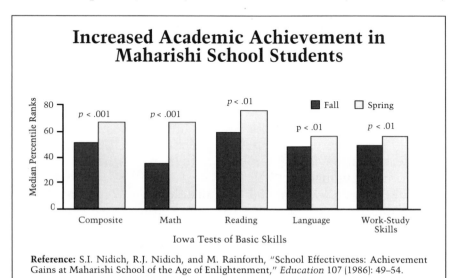

■ Figure 10. New students at Maharishi School of the Age of Enlightenment, grades 3 to 8, exhibited significant increases in academic achievement as measured by the nationally standardized Iowa Tests of Basic Skills (ITBS). Substantial gains in achievement were found within one academic year of attending Maharishi School of the Age of Enlightenment.

Reference: S.I. Nidich, R.J. Nidich, and M. Rainforth, "School Effectiveness: Achievement Gains at Maharishi School of the Age of Enlightenment," *Education* 107 (1986): 49–54.

"I've learned more in one semester here than I learned in an entire year at my previous school."

— 10th-grade student

reading, language, and work-study skills scales of the ITBS.[3] Figure 10 illustrates these improvements in academic achievement.

Additional analysis showed that whereas "grade level" ITBS scores (50th percentile or higher) were achieved by 58 percent of new students at the start of their first year at Maharishi School, 82 percent were at or above grade level by the end of the year. A second study on new students entering grades 3 through 7 also showed significant improvements in overall academic achievement, reading, vocabulary, language, and work-study skills over approximately a 12-month period.[4]

Other findings indicate that continuing students at Maharishi School exhibit marked improvement on the ITBS in overall academic achievement, language, and work-study skills within a single school year.[5] And on the ITED, new Upper School students have shown significant gains on the scales for reading, quantitative thinking, social studies, and knowledge of literary materials.[6] ITED scores for continuing Upper School students as a group remain at a high level over time, without showing significant changes.

Principal Richard Beall says of the academic performance of new Upper School students:

> Students who come to our school are typical of students everywhere. Many of them have a fear of not doing well in school. As a result of Unified Field Based Education, the students grow in their appreciation for studying the various academic disciplines. They become more receptive to learning, and their ability to learn is enhanced tremendously.

Sue, a 9th-grade student who recently transferred to Maharishi School, says: "I've noticed that here one understands absolutely everything about a subject. Attending Maharishi School increases the capacity to learn and understand. One's grades go up; students are very happy here." John, a new student in the 10th grade, adds: "I've learned more in one semester here than I learned in an entire year at my previous school."

One parent, who moved to Fairfield from Trinidad, notes: "My daughter loves school so much. Before coming here, she never really showed much joy in going to school. Now it is different. Every day she wants to tell the whole family what she has learned; she looks forward to going to school so much. She's blossoming so quickly due to Unified Field Based Education."

The mother of Mark, the 11th-grade student mentioned earlier in this chapter, comments on the change in her son: "Since coming to Fairfield, a complete change has occurred. My son became very happy in school, and is now an honors student. I mainly attribute this positive development to his regular practice of Transcendental Meditation and the fact that all the students and teachers practice Transcendental Meditation together."

Together with Patrick Moulin, Fred Travis, and Maxwell Rainforth, we conducted research on the relationship between the number of years that students at Maharishi School had been practicing Maharishi's Transcendental Meditation technique and their overall academic achievement scores on the ITBS and ITED. As predicted, we found that the number of years Maharishi School students had been practicing TM was significantly correlated with their overall scores of academic achievement. Those students who had been practicing TM the longest tended to have the highest percentile ranks for academic achievement. In addition to this finding, we found that the relationship between length of time practicing TM and academic achievement was independent of the students' IQ.[7] A second study also showed a significant, positive correlation between length of time practicing TM and academic achievement independent of students' age and sex.[8] All of the above findings taken together suggest that the longer students practice Transcendental Meditation, the better they do in school.

Subjective reports by the students confirm that TM makes a noticeable difference in their academic performance. They attribute this to their increased ability to work efficiently and to concentrate. Richard, a 9th-grade student, states: "Maharishi School has helped me to grow a lot, because I have the advantage of Transcendental Meditation to help me cope with problems. It clears my mind so I can work efficiently." James, an 11th-grader, remarks: "I have better concentration and energy throughout the day because of Transcendental Meditation."

Research on students practicing TM in other high schools and colleges has also found a strong relationship between the practice of Transcendental Meditation and academic performance. Two studies showed significant increases in grade point average (GPA) within one semester after students began the TM technique. Another study found that students with a C+ GPA improved to a B+

Those students who had been practicing TM the longest tended to have the highest percentile ranks on standardized tests of academic achievement.

GPA within three semesters of learning the TM program, with a further increase to nearly an A– GPA after six semesters. Also, research has found positive changes in the academic performance of graduate students practicing Transcendental Meditation.[9]

Levels of the Knower and Academic Development

In addition to studies showing a significant relationship between the practice of Transcendental Meditation and improved academic performance, there have been studies showing the positive effects of TM on factors influencing academic performance.

Educational researchers have found that academic performance is related to such factors as time-on-task, organization of memory, intelligence, creative thinking, and student self-concept.[10] These factors can be understood to correspond to the different levels of the knower — senses, mind, intellect, feelings, and ego — described in Chapter Two.

Time-on-task, the percentage of time students are alert and engaged in lesson-related behavior, is related to the level of the senses. Organization of memory evaluates how effectively new information is stored in the student's mind. Intelligence refers to the students' ability to think logically, act purposefully, and deal effectively with the environment, and equates with the intellect. Creativity adds the dimension of intuitive and original thinking, that is, being able to discover new ideas and relationships. Creativity can therefore be related to the feeling or intuitive level of the mind. Self-concept refers to how students feel about themselves; it affects their academic motivation, and relates to the ego.

Figure 11 illustrates the relationship of these factors to the levels of the knower and their source, the unified field of natural law. Each factor may include other levels of the knower, but here they are associated with the most predominant level.

All of the above factors have been found to be positively influenced by the practice of TM. For example, research studies have indicated that the practice of TM increases alertness, organization of memory, recall ability, intelligence, learning ability, creativity, and self-concept.[11] Research conducted on high school students in Canada found that within two and a half months of beginning the practice of TM, students showed increased creativity, intellectual performance, energy level, innovation, tolerance, self-esteem,

Research studies have indicated that the practice of TM increases alertness, organization of memory, recall ability, intelligence, learning ability, creativity, and self-concept.

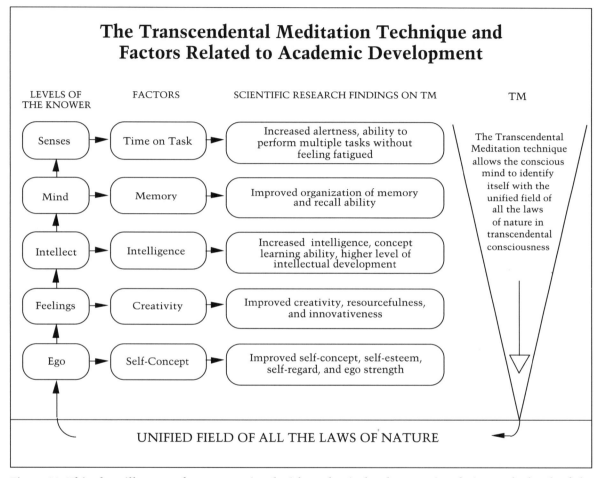

The Transcendental Meditation Technique and Factors Related to Academic Development

LEVELS OF THE KNOWER	FACTORS	SCIENTIFIC RESEARCH FINDINGS ON TM	TM
Senses	Time on Task	Increased alertness, ability to perform multiple tasks without feeling fatigued	The Transcendental Meditation technique allows the conscious mind to identify itself with the unified field of all the laws of nature in transcendental consciousness
Mind	Memory	Improved organization of memory and recall ability	
Intellect	Intelligence	Increased intelligence, concept learning ability, higher level of intellectual development	
Feelings	Creativity	Improved creativity, resourcefulness, and innovativeness	
Ego	Self-Concept	Improved self-concept, self-esteem, self-regard, and ego strength	

UNIFIED FIELD OF ALL THE LAWS OF NATURE

Figure 11. This chart illustrates factors associated with academic development in relation to the levels of the knower, as described by Maharishi. Research indicates that all levels of the knower and corresponding factors associated with academic development are enriched by the direct experience of the unified field during TM.

greater ability to deal with abstraction and complexity and decreased anxiety, compared to students not practicing TM.[12]

Taken together, these studies demonstrate that Maharishi's unified field based approach to improving student academic development is holistic — it spontaneously enhances the full range of mental functioning.

Most of the above factors associated with academic development have also been studied at Maharishi School. Research has been conducted on student time-on-task, intelligence, creativity, and self-esteem. A preliminary study of time-on-task was conducted several years ago by Charles Matthews, then Professor of Science Education at Florida State University. Of his findings on the percentage of lesson-related student behavior, i.e., time-on-task, he said:

> The students at Maharishi School of the Age of Enlightenment have the longest attention span of any students I have observed during my 18 years of research in public and private schools. I found that the students were "on-task" more than 95 percent of the time. This is quite extraordinary. Usually, I find that students attend to their lessons less than half the time they are in class. The rest of the time they are doing other things that are not related to learning such as looking out the window or passing notes to each other. Throughout all grade levels at Maharishi School, I have observed a high degree of attention to learning.[13]

Regarding intelligence, we recently found in a study we conducted with Fred Travis that new students in grades 4 to 11 at Maharishi School showed a significant increase in IQ over a one-year period, as measured by the Cattell Culture Fair Intelligence Test. Students showed an average improvement of 5 IQ points, increasing from an average IQ score of 114 to an average IQ score of 119 (see Figure 12).[14] Tifra Warner, as part of her doctoral dissertation at York University, found that Maharishi School elementary school students exhibited a higher level of intellectual development than students from similar backgrounds at a school in Toronto, Canada. She also found that the length of time students practiced the Transcendental Meditation technique was significantly correlated with their intellectual performance scores. Students who had been meditating for a greater number of months tended to exhibit higher scores on tests of intellectual development than students meditating for fewer months.[15]

Research we conducted with John Zanath, Selwyn Bhajan, and Laura Rose, using the Torrance Test of Creative Thinking Demonstrator Form A, showed that overall creativity scores of Maharishi School students in grades 5 through 8 were significantly higher than the scores of control students. For grades 5 and 6, Maharishi School students scored approximately 80 percent higher than non-meditating students in creative thinking.

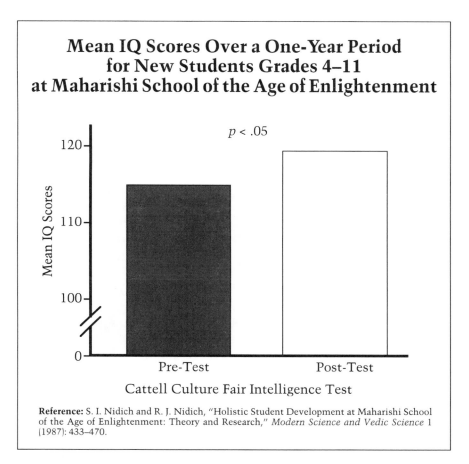

Mean IQ Scores Over a One-Year Period for New Students Grades 4–11 at Maharishi School of the Age of Enlightenment

$p < .05$

Mean IQ Scores

120 —
110 —
100 —
0 —

Pre-Test   Post-Test

Cattell Culture Fair Intelligence Test

Reference: S. I. Nidich and R. J. Nidich, "Holistic Student Development at Maharishi School of the Age of Enlightenment: Theory and Research," *Modern Science and Vedic Science* 1 (1987): 433–470.

■ **Figure 12. IQ scores for new students at Maharishi School of the Age of Enlightenment, grades 4 through 11, significantly increased over a one-year period. During this period an average increase of 5 IQ points was found. The norm for IQ is 100.**

Figure 13 illustrates the mean scores for the four grade levels tested in this study.[16]

Data collected in a survey of self-concept showed that secondary school students at Maharishi School have a very positive perception of themselves. One hundred percent of the students reported that they feel good most of the time, are happy, can make up their own mind about things, and are able to do school work at least as well as most other students. Ninety-six percent reported that they are easy to like and are popular with students their own age, and 93 percent said that students usually follow their ideas. Eighty-one percent reported that they are good readers, 77 percent that they are doing the best work they can, 73 percent that they are good

■ Figure 13.
Differences between
the mean creativity
scores of students at
Maharishi School of
the Age of
Enlightenment and
controls selected from
Torrance's data bank
are illustrated.
Maharishi School of
the Age of
Enlightenment
students at each grade
level exhibited a
significantly higher
degree of creative
thinking than controls.

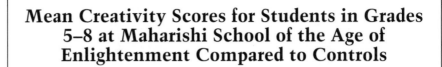

Mean Creativity Scores for Students in Grades 5–8 at Maharishi School of the Age of Enlightenment Compared to Controls

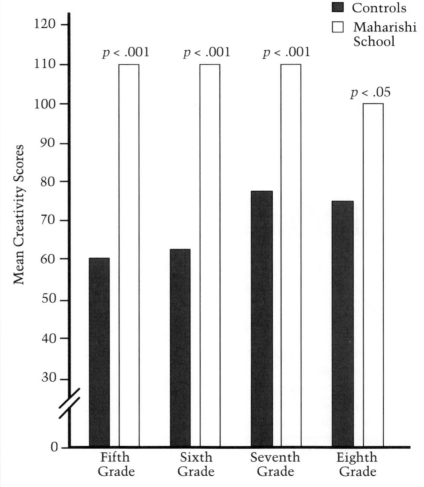

Torrance Test of Creative Thinking

Reference: S.I. Nidich and R.J. Nidich, "Holistic Student Development at Maharishi School of the Age of Enlightenment: Theory and Research," *Modern Science and Vedic Science* 1 (1987): 433–470.

at mathematics, and 96 percent that they are proud of their school work.[17]

We have also observed that students at Maharishi School possess a strong sense of self-confidence, both during and outside their classes. We have found students to be very willing, even eager, to stand up in class and present their ideas. They appear not to have any of the inhibitions about speaking in front of a group that other elementary and secondary school students typically have.

Maharishi School students have repeatedly exhibited great self-confidence when performing in front of large audiences. In the winter of 1988, we attended the Children's SCI Theater, in which 120 students in grades 1 to 5 displayed principles of SCI through song and dance to packed audiences in MIU's Spayde Theater. All the children radiated an impressive degree of self-confidence, self-sufficiency, and happiness. Even when a younger child missed a line, he would simply continue without hesitating.

■ Maharishi Upper School science fair winner exhibits his research on the effects of Maharishi Amrit Kalash on the immune system. Maharishi Amrit Kalash is an herbal preparation derived from the knowledge of natural law contained in Maharishi Ayur-Ved — the complete science of health.

In the 1988 All-State Festival sponsored by the Iowa High School Speech Association, performances from both Maharishi School groups received praise from the judges. As mentioned in the section on "Academic Competitions," the school won the state championship when its one-act play, "A Young Lady of Property," was judged "The Critic's Choice." Following the performance, one of the judges told the students: "I've been judging high school pieces for the last four years and this is without doubt one of the two or three strongest pieces I've seen." Then the judge asked, "Are you sure you're in high school? You have tremendous maturity. I don't mean your age, but something inside you. . . . I was completely captivated."[18]

Gaining the Fruit of All Knowledge

The above results on academic achievement and its related factors — e.g., intelligence, creativity, and self-concept — provide

Maharishi points out that our most precious educational resource is the human brain physiology, because it is capable of sustaining the experience of the unified field of all the laws of nature.

concrete evidence of the practical value of Maharishi's Unified Field Based Education. Ultimately, though, Unified Field Based Education aims at unfolding full knowledge of the knower, full knowledge of the total potential of natural law residing in the consciousness of every student.

The common goal of all educational systems is to provide students with the knowledge they need to lead successful, fulfilling lives. Today, educational institutions attempt to provide all knowledge on one campus. But, as Maharishi points out, all the knowledge in every school and college library, is still incomplete — it is insufficient to provide students with fulfillment. It is a common experience, especially in higher education, that the more students learn the more they realize how much remains unknown. The further students pursue their education, Maharishi states, the more isolated the details of knowledge become. "He discovers a particle but sees a greater field of knowledge lying ahead."[19]

Maharishi points out that our most precious educational resource is the human brain physiology, because it is capable of sustaining the experience of the unified field of all the laws of nature. When this experience is lively in human awareness one gains the "fruit of all knowledge" — the ability to know anything, do anything, and achieve anything. By culturing the brain physiology to maintain higher states of consciousness, Unified Field Based Education bestows the fruit of all knowledge on students.

Through this system of education, Maharishi says, "every student can live in higher states of consciousness — enjoying increasing levels of achievement and fulfillment in daily life."[20] Thus, Maharishi's system of education has transformed the concept of a university from "all knowledge on one campus" to "all knowledge in one brain."[21] According to Maharishi, this can be accomplished through proper education:

> Proper education means giving the fruit of all knowledge to everyone — the ability to think and act spontaneously in accord with natural law. Now that the self-interacting dynamics of unity have been discovered in the self-referral transcendental consciousness of everyone, it has become easy to develop this ability of spontaneous thought and action according to natural law. This has provided a system of education whereby everyone could be offered the fruit of all knowledge without

having to go through the endless path of gaining knowledge and never reaching the goal of knowledge.[22]

Maharishi emphasizes that educated people should possess more than an abundance of facts and information and some professional skills. They should be fulfilled, possessing the practical ability to spontaneously fulfill their desires without causing suffering to others. In summarizing the attributes of an educated person, Maharishi states:

> An educated man is one who habitually thinks and acts rightly. Education, so far, has succeeded in producing skilled and professional people, but something is certainly lacking because these people are unable to live their own lives with enough skill to avoid suffering. . . . They are not taught anything about the deep level of intelligence which is the origin of everything. . . .

> Through the Transcendental Meditation program, the individual grows in his ability to fulfill desires, because they arise from the field of all possibilities [the unified field of natural law] which is maintained consciously in his awareness. No wrong can spring from these desires because they come from the home of all the laws of nature; nature works only one way — in the direction of evolution. Because of this experience the individual will be an enlightened and orderly person. He will not make mistakes against the laws of nature.[23]

The academic success of the Maharishi School students described in this chapter is simply the by-product of developing higher states of consciousness — the primary goal of Unified Field Based Education. Maharishi School of the Age of Enlightenment is setting a new standard of excellence in education by applying the theoretical and practical aspects of Maharishi's Science of Creative Intelligence to ensure the complete development of every student.

In the next chapter, we will describe findings on student social development at Maharishi School and bring out the importance of experiencing the unified field of natural law to promote right thinking and action.

The academic success of the Maharishi School students described in this chapter is simply the by-product of developing higher states of consciousness — the primary goal of Unified Field Based Education.

C H A P T E R   S I X

Social Development: Action in Accord With All the Laws of Nature

Besides academic excellence, we emphasize the quality of life of the student at Maharishi School. We feel that it is our responsibility to educate the whole person. In addition to promoting academic excellence, we want students to become integrated in every way. A successful student is one who thinks and acts according to natural law. This results in students being happier and more fulfilled while at the same time promoting the happiness and well-being of everyone around them. As they grow this extends to include all of society.
—Robin Rowe, Ph.D., Academic Director
Maharishi School of the Age of Enlightenment

UNIFIED FIELD BASED EDUCATION DEVELOPS THE STUDENT both academically and socially. In most schools, these two goals are addressed separately. At Maharishi School, student academic and social development are the natural result of the development of consciousness through Maharishi's SCI, and its practical aspect, the TM program.

Guy Hatchard, the Middle School mathematics teacher whose geometrical play of the unified field we presented in Chapter Four, has taught in private schools in England, Australia, and New Zealand. He observes: "There are many good academic schools around the world, but at Maharishi School students not only develop academically but grow in the higher human values of kindness, respect, honesty, responsibility, forthrightness, and caring. Because our students are experiencing the unified field of natural law every day in their Transcendental Meditation program, the teachers do not have to do much to facilitate the students' social growth. It happens automatically and spontaneously due to their experience of this fundamental field of life which nourishes every aspect of their personality."

During the last two decades, educators have become increasingly concerned that we are not doing enough to promote student social development. Gerald Grant observed in his study of American schools that the major emphasis is on preparing students to do well on standardized tests, with virtually no attention to social values.[1] In *A Place Called School*, John Goodlad cites John Raven's studies on the attainment of educational goals in British and Irish schools. Raven found that although student character development was considered very important, "nevertheless, all the evidence, both circumstantial and direct, suggests that these goals are not being well attained and that schools may be having . . . harmful effects in this area."[2] In a broader context, the report by the National Commission on Excellence in Education emphasized that:

> Our society and its educational institutions seem to have lost sight of the basic purpose of schooling, and of the high expectations and disciplined effort needed to attain them. . . . Our concern, however goes well beyond matters such as industry and commerce. It also includes the intellectual, moral and spiritual strengths of our people which knit together the very fabric of our society.[3]

All educators, regardless of their philosophical tenets, attach importance to students developing thinking and behavior that produces harmony and coherence in the school and society. Educators especially want students to develop feelings of responsibility and care for others, and to feel committed to upholding society's conventions and laws. Following are the results of a study we conducted on the moral development of students in the Maharishi Upper School. This study examined students' prosocial thinking and behavior with respect to caring, keeping agreements, not stealing, and restitution. Behavior and thinking is considered prosocial when it contributes to the cohesion and harmony of the group, and not merely to one's own self-interest.

A Study of Moral Development

As part of our study, we individually interviewed 24 students in grades 10 through 12. Each interview lasted for almost an hour, with students responding to four practical school dilemmas adapted from the Moral Atmosphere Interview (MAI), developed by Higgins, Power, and Kohlberg of the Center for Moral Education at Harvard University. The students were asked how they would think and act in several practical school dilemmas and how they felt most students in their school would think and act. For the purpose of comparison, they were also asked how they felt students from the school they attended prior to Maharishi School would respond. Maharishi School responses were then compared to responses by students at special alternative schools in Massachusetts and New York designed to promote moral development.[4] The four practical school dilemmas used in this study were:

Dilemma One: Helping Out an Unpopular Student

The college Billy applied to had scheduled an interview with him for the coming Saturday morning at 9:00 a.m. The college was 40 miles away from Billy's town and Billy had no way of getting there. The guidance counselor wanted to drive him but had already made an appointment at that time. The guidance counselor decides to go to Billy's homeroom and ask the students if there is anyone who could drive Billy to the college. No one volunteers to drive him. Most students say they do not like Billy, because he shows off a lot. One student, Harry, knows he can use his family car, but he wonders whether he should do something for Billy when the few students who know him best say they are busy or just can't do it. Besides, he would have to get up really early on a Saturday morning which is the only morning during the week he can sleep late. Should Harry drive Billy to his college interview?

Dilemma Two: Keeping An Agreement

Before the junior class trip the faculty told the students the whole class had to make an agreement not to bring or use alcohol. If the students were found using alcohol they would be sent home. The students knew that without faculty approval they would not be able to have their trip. The students said in a class meeting they all agreed to these conditions. While on the trip, several students ask Jim, a fellow student, to go on a hike with them to the lake. When they get to the lake, they pull out a bottle of alcohol and pass it around. Should Jim refuse to drink?

Dilemma Three: The Issue of Stealing

When Mary arrived at her history class, she noticed that although the students were all there the teacher had not arrived. She sat down for a few seconds but decided to chat with a few of her friends in the hall until her teacher came. She opened her pocketbook, pulled out a letter she wanted to show her friends and ran out of the classroom, leaving her pocketbook unsnapped and lying on her desk. Tom, a student in the class looks into Mary's pocketbook and sees a twenty dollar bill. He thinks about taking the twenty dollar bill from her pocketbook. Should Tom take the money?

Dilemma Four: Restitution or "Chipping In"

When Mary comes back into the class, she notices that a twenty dollar bill is missing from her pocketbook. She tries to find out who stole the money. None of the students admit to stealing the money, including Tom, who stole the money. When the teacher arrives, Mary tells the teacher what has happened. The teacher suggests to the class that since none of the students have come forward to give Mary back the money, all the students in the class could chip in about 50 cents to repay Mary. Should the students chip in money to repay Mary?

The first dilemma is whether or not to help an unpopular student. Typically, students at other schools fear that by doing so they may be ostracized by their friends. Students commonly say that "it's not cool to help out someone who is unpopular" or "why should I be expected to help out someone if no one else will?" This kind of attitude creates student "cliques" and cultures exclusion. "Students don't really care about each other anyway at my school," is another frequent comment.

The second dilemma is whether or not to keep an agreement not to use alcohol on a class trip. Today, students typically feel that it's all right as long as they don't get caught. Many students don't fully appreciate how breaking an agreement affects responsibility and trust. Also, the use of alcohol and nonprescribed drugs is so pervasive among high school students that this situation is felt to be commonplace. Recent Gallup Polls found the use of alcohol and drugs to be one of the major problems in schools nationwide.

The third dilemma is whether or not to steal money from a classmate's purse. Even though most students would agree that stealing is both illegal and wrong, many give reasons for taking the money. Some say it is really Mary's fault for leaving her purse unattended. Others respond that if Tom needs the money he should take it. Students typically say that money left lying around a classroom will most certainly be taken. These responses indicate that theft of personal property on school premises is a real problem.

The last dilemma results from the previous one. Tom steals the money but doesn't admit it. The teacher suggests that each student help repay Mary's stolen money. This dilemma is similar to the first one, in that the student's good will is necessary to perform the prosocial action. Because there are no rules stipulating the right course of action, students have to rely on their own personal sense of responsibility and community. This dilemma typically receives the lowest percentage of prosocial responses; students blame Mary for being careless and decline to contribute.

Student Responses Indicating a
High Level of Social Development

The following table shows the high percentage of prosocial responses to the four dilemmas by Maharishi School students. The total prosocial responses ranged from 94 percent to 97 percent. *Choice* refers to how one feels one *should* act in a given situation, and *behavior* refers to how one thinks one actually *would* act. *Self* refers to *one's own* behavior while *others* refers to the behavior of *other* students.

TABLE TWO

Total Percentage of Prosocial Choice and Behavior
Responses for Self and Others by Maharishi School Students

DILEMMA	CHOICE FOR SELF	BEHAVIOR FOR SELF	CHOICE FOR OTHERS	BEHAVIOR FOR OTHERS
Caring	100%	100%	100%	100%
Keeping agreements	100%	100%	100%	100%
Not stealing	100%	100%	100%	100%
Restitution	79%	88%	88%	88%
Average	**94%**	**97%**	**97%**	**97%**

"It's the natural thing to do to help others. By helping others, you help them evolve faster and easier. Students at Maharishi School realize the value of helping others."
— 10th-grade student

Considering each dilemma separately, 100 percent of the Maharishi School students said they and others in their school should and would help out an unpopular student, keep an agreement not to drink alcohol, and not steal. A slightly lower percentage said they and others should and would chip in money to repay a fellow student.

In the following responses Maharishi School students explain why they would help an unpopular student:

It's the natural thing to do to help others. By helping others, you help them evolve faster and easier. Students at Maharishi School realize the value of helping others. . . . Like in team volleyball, you always win when you play together. In school, we help each other and everyone improves. (Teri, 10th grade)

By helping him out, you may improve the quality of life of all those around. A leader should bring out the positive qualities of a person. By being positive yourself, you automatically get positivity in return. [The students at Maharishi School] like to help others. They see that everyone is worth being helped. By helping others, they see that they can also improve the quality of the environment. (Karla, 12th grade)

When asked whether they would keep an agreement not to drink alcohol on a class trip, Maharishi School students stated:

It's important to keep a promise. A relationship is based on trust. If you can't trust a person, it lessens the ability to communicate. It's important to be responsible. People can always trust you, you can be counted on. I think that people expect other people to trust each other, because it would ruin the coherence of the group if one person didn't trust another, or if everybody didn't trust one person. They wouldn't be united as a whole; they wouldn't act as one.

That's what this school is all about, just being as one, being as a whole, acting together and being invincible. That's what makes this school different. Because acting together, you are invincible; you are more boundless. There's more you can do together. A whole group can do more than one person can do if you are focused. (Mary, 12th grade)

He made a commitment to the school, saying he will not drink. He made the decision himself that he wouldn't drink on the trip.

I'd refuse to drink, to maintain the stability. In a community, you need to reinforce the things you say by your actions.... Students [at Maharishi School] would do everything they could to be positive and have a good quality of life. (Karen, 12th grade)

Below are representative responses to the stealing dilemma:

I would feel that if they did that to someone else, they would be doing it to me; it would show lack of respect. (Sara, 11th grade)

They should know better; it shows a lack of self-control. Community is based on truthfulness, not stealing. Stealing would do something to the community on the fine feeling level. (Jim, 11th grade)

It's Mary's money. If you take something that someone else owns, it hurts them and your own development of enlightenment. It's not mine. If I want twenty dollars, I should go out and earn it. It's not right action. It's not good for them, for me, for the school, for the community, or for the world. Every thought and action influences the environment either positively or negatively. (Teri, 10th grade)

Following are responses to the last dilemma on whether to help repay a fellow student:

Something lost by someone is pretty much lost by everyone. The person should not suffer. It's closer here. Most people would feel obligated to do it. Being in the school atmosphere grows on you; it gives you the feeling of helping rather than acting negatively. (Ken, 11th grade)

I would feel obligated out of kindness to help someone in need. It's like a big family here. There is a lot of love and compassion. (Jim, 11th grade)

Most students here would chip in. It would be for someone they liked, and people here help each other. Students here would want to make everyone happy and make it come out as smooth as possible. (Teri, 10th grade)

One student felt at first that she *should* not have to help repay a fellow student: "It's not my responsibility. The person who stole the money is responsible for the situation." But after pausing for a moment, she continued: "If everyone decided to do it (chip in), I *would* also." While the majority felt responsible for the situation, this student's response points out the strong positive influence that the students at Maharishi School have on each other. This student also acknowledged that her classmates would try to make others happy and resolve the situation as harmoniously as possible.

Overall, Maharishi School students responded to the dilemmas in a prosocial manner and felt that most students in their school would do the same. Many students considered the ramifications of their decisions for the coherence and unity of the school. Also it was common for students to base their decisions on what they felt would further (or restrict) their own personal growth and the development of others. The following excerpt from an interview with Robert, a 12th-grade student, sheds more light on how Maharishi School students reason about moral dilemmas.

Excerpts from an Interview
with a Maharishi School Student

Robert began attending Maharishi School three years ago when his family moved to Fairfield from a small town in southern California. At the time of our interview, Robert was a 12th-grade student and president of the student government. Robert's responses to the dilemmas on the Moral Atmosphere Interview are representative of the attitudes of Maharishi School students.

The interviewer began by asking Robert about his background. After a few minutes, the interviewer read Robert the first dilemma, on helping an unpopular student.

Interviewer: Should Harry help out Billy?

Robert: I would say yes. It is a big decision in his life to go to college, and he needs a lot of help with that. Harry shouldn't think what others think; he should do what he thinks is right and that is helping him out, and he would make a friend for a later date when he needed help.

Interviewer: Should you help out an unpopular student in a situation like this?

Robert: Sure. Because they are the ones that need the friends the most. Unpopular students are unpopular because they don't have a chance to do things other students do. A lot of unpopular students are not that outgoing, and one way to be more outgoing would be to have friends who could help you become more outgoing.

Interviewer: Assuming you could help out, would you try to help out an unpopular student in a situation like this?

Robert: Yes, for sure I would, just for the same reasons that I said before. It's not that the person isn't a good person, or is a bad person; it is just that they don't have a chance to become popular.

Interviewer: Would most students at Maharishi School feel they should help out an unpopular student?

Robert: Yes, . . . Actually at [Maharishi School] I don't know any really unpopular students. We don't really look at students as being popular. There are some students who are more active in certain areas of the school than others . . . but I wouldn't really say that anyone is unpopular. When a new student comes to the school, I guess you could say that they wouldn't be as popular because they wouldn't know as many people. But it seems to me — and I see it every day and know I do it — my friends and I go out of our way to make the new students feel at home, make them feel comfortable, and help them, especially in a situation like this.

Interviewer: Would most students at Maharishi School actually help out an unpopular student in a situation like this?

Robert: Yes, for sure.

Interviewer: Any particular reasons?

Robert: Because . . . an unpopular student at our school would probably be somebody new, because they wouldn't know as many students. They would feel obligated to help this person feel more comfortable at the school and have the same chances that everyone else has.

Interviewer: Why would they feel obligated?

Robert: Because they know that in the school there is a group coherence created and if one person doesn't feel at home then it . . . subtracts from the group coherence. . . . But also for the other person's benefit, the students who go to the school are very loving and very caring and I'm sure that they wouldn't want to see someone who didn't have the same chance to do something.

In the next segment, Robert is asked whether he thinks most students at his previous school would help out an unpopular student. He is also asked whether helping out would be a generally expected behavior at Maharishi School and his previous school.

> "My friends and I go out of our way to make the new students feel at home, make them feel comfortable, and help them."
> — 12th grade student

"There are a lot of different interest groups, but the school has a wholeness, a unity that works together.... A lot of people describe our class as being one unity working together."
— 12th-grade student

Interviewer: Would students at your previous school feel they should help out in a situation like this?

Robert: No. Most students wouldn't.... There are a lot of different cliques ... and not much unity at the school.

Interviewer: How about at Maharishi School, are there different cliques?

Robert: There are a lot of different interest groups, but the school has a wholeness, a unity that works together.... A lot of people describe our class as being one unity working together.... For studying purposes out of school, we have study groups. And for fun things outside of school, for different kinds of activities — dances and things like that — we see each other. Everyone is included who wants to be included....

The classes have their own different personalities.... But they all work together. When you walk into the school, you feel the wholeness in the school, you feel the common connection. We do group program [collective practice of the TM program] and everyone has a common reason to come to the school. It's because of the program and because of SCI ... that pulls people together....

Interviewer: Would there be a general feeling of expectation at Maharishi School that students should help out each other?

Robert: Very much so. It seems that if a person needs help in a certain area ... he is bombarded by people who want to help. People enjoy helping you out, and they are always wanting to.... You will often find students studying in pairs, because some students are stronger in certain areas than others. ... One learns a lot by teaching others.

Interviewer: Would there be a general feeling of expectation at your previous school that students should help each other out?

Robert: Most students would be having a hard enough time themselves; they wouldn't want to help someone else out.... The ones that want to learn get pulled down by the ones who don't want to learn. [In terms of the situation presented], it would be real hard to get somebody to give you that kind of help.... You kind of fend for yourself.

Interviewer: Would you be disappointed if another student at Maharishi School did not help out in a situation like this?

Robert: Yes, I would be disappointed. I would not only feel bad for the person who wasn't helped out, but I would feel bad for them too because there must be some kind of roughness or problem [to cause them not to feel] the friendship to want to help the fellow student. That would probably mean that they were not feeling at home themselves if they didn't feel obligated to help this other person out. . . . I would want to see what the reason was. . . .

As in the responses from other Maharishi School students, Robert bases many of his decisions on whether the action would help or hinder the unity of the group. At the school, we have repeatedly seen that the feeling of "group coherence" deeply permeates the way in which students interact with one another.

The interviewer then read the second dilemma, on keeping an agreement. The following excerpt shows Robert's reason for why he and other students would refuse to drink.

Interviewer: Do you think you would refuse to drink?

Robert: Yes. In that situation, having the understanding [of] the damage that alcohol does to the nervous system . . . I would refuse. It is just a needless thing to do. . . .

For what I am trying to accomplish right now . . . enlightenment, bringing out my full potential . . . this would just set me back. . . . I know that in one's life it is natural to want to grow and accomplish as much as one can, and these things would be subtracting from that. And if I want to gain my full potential, I have to take the steps in my life that are responsible and do the things that will actually bring me more fulfillment than drinking alcohol.

Interviewer: Would most students at Maharishi School not drink?

Robert: Most students at the school, from what I can see, have the same feelings towards this as I do. . . . It is not something that is evolutionary and worthwhile. In the long run it is just not worth it. . . . It is not like it is a big decision you have to make. The students just don't do it. . . .

This is unsupported by natural law, it violates the integrity of the individual, and in turn violates the integrity of the whole group. And it subtracts from the ideals of the group, what the group is trying to achieve. So naturally the group would want everyone to have the same high ideals, the same high focus. . . .

Unlike typical instances of peer pressure, the kind exerted by students at Maharishi School promotes students' personal and social development.

During this segment of the interview, Robert also referred to the influence students have on each other. "Peer pressure" has been researched by educators and found to be one of the main motivating factors in adolescent behavior. Usually we hear of "peer pressure" in a negative context. A typical instance of peer pressure would be the alcohol dilemma, in which a student is coaxed by others to do something wrong.

Robert indicated that students at Maharishi School are also under peer pressure to do what the group deems desirable. But unlike typical negative instances of peer pressure, the kind exerted by students at Maharishi School promotes students' personal and social development. Also, in responding to the dilemma, Robert places a striking emphasis on his own personal development. This appears to be the main motivating factor guiding the behavior of students at Maharishi School.

In responding to the third dilemma, Robert states that stealing someone else's money shows a lack of integrity and respect. He also says that he feels his possessions are safe at Maharishi School.

Interviewer: Would you take the money?

Robert: No, not at all. It is also that kind of activity that is not supportive to the other person and not supportive to yourself. It shows a lack of respect; it shows a lack of dignity and weakness in your own personality. . . . It violates the integrity of the individual and therefore violates the integrity of the group. If one person is doing something like this then it is subtracting from the group. . . .

Interviewer: Would you be as trusting as Mary with your possessions?

Robert: Yes, for sure. I know that the students at the school have all the same high ideals that I do. They have respect for me, the same respect that I have for them. There is no way that something like that would occur.

Interviewer: Would you be as trusting as Mary with your possessions at your old school?

Robert: No. I wouldn't even keep money in my locker because lockers get broken into. People at my old school don't have the same knowledge and integrity and the same knowledge of respect and the same knowledge of coherence. Through ignorance, they would steal. I just couldn't trust [the students], because it would be gone.

Interviewer: What would most students at Maharishi School do in a situation like this, steal or not steal?

Robert: I know all the students and none of them would. It's because they have the same knowledge I have about self-integrity and the respect for other people . . . and how that not only affects the other person but affects themselves. . . . The level of coherence [at Maharishi School] is much higher. Even if a stranger came into the school, the atmosphere within the school would let a person know that this is not a place where this kind of activity happens.

Here are Robert's responses to the final dilemma on whether to help repay another student whose money was stolen.

Interviewer: Do you think that you should chip in money to repay Mary?

Robert: Yes, I do. The reason why is that the class is a group of people. . . . So you are partly responsible for that, and you're responsible for that person's actions. If something like that were to happen then it would show a weakness in the group and a weakness in yourself, because you are a reflection of the consciousness of the group and vice versa. And besides that, it would be a nice thing to do.

Interviewer: Would you actually chip in money?

Robert: Yes. For the same reason.

Interviewer: Would most students feel they should chip in money?

Robert: Yes. . . .

Interviewer: Would most students actually chip in money?

Robert: They would chip in. They would feel badly something like this would actually happen and the person was subjected to that. They would feel partly responsible for that happening. If you are not maintaining a high level of integrity there must be something wrong and you have to blame everyone. . . .

[Rules] are introduced in a more loving way, a more nurturing way. We are always looking to the positive side of things.

Robert believes that students at Maharishi School would assume responsibility for this kind of behavior at their school. He emphasized that it is the students' responsibility to ensure that all the other students know the difference between right and wrong actions. This response exemplifies the social maturity of Maharishi School students. Students feel responsible not only for their own actions, but also for how others act in their school.

Comparison With Other Schools

As you can see from the interview with Robert, students were also asked to describe how most students at their previous school would act in similar situations. On the whole, Maharishi School students felt that other students at Maharishi School would be more likely to respond prosocially to the dilemmas than students from their previous schools. Table Three shows these responses:

TABLE THREE

Comparison of Students' Perceptions of Maharishi School and Their Previous Schools

SCHOOL	N	PROSOCIAL CHOICE FOR OTHERS	PROSOCIAL BEHAVIOR FOR OTHERS
Maharishi School	24	97%	97%
Combined previous schools	24	36%	26%
Private schools	6	63%	53%
Public senior high	11	29%	22%
Public junior high	7	20%	4%

Students' responses from Lawrence Kohlberg's "Just Community Schools" provided a means for further comparison of Maharishi School student responses. Dr. Ann Higgins and Dr. Lawrence Kohlberg of the Center for Moral Education at Harvard University provided us with their data on Just Community Schools (JCS) — special alternative high schools established specifically to promote student moral development. These schools were established as a special alternative program within selected regular public high schools. They are based upon the concept of a participatory democracy and use the forum of community meetings and small group discussions to facilitate higher levels of moral reasoning and prosocial behavior[5] JCS students have been found to have a much higher level of moral development than students from their counterpart regular public high schools.

Responses by Maharishi School students were compared with two of the most academically and socio-economically advanced JCS schools, one just outside Boston (JCS #1) and the other near New York City (JCS #2). We found that a larger percentage of Maharishi School students responded prosocially to *all* of the dilemmas than JCS students. The difference between the percentage of Maharishi School and JCS prosocial *behavior* responses was statistically significant, both for *self* and for *others*.[6]

Figure 14 shows the *total* percentage of responses for Maharishi School, the two JCS schools, and the schools previously attended by Maharishi School students. The figure also indicates some incongruence between the prosocial *choice*

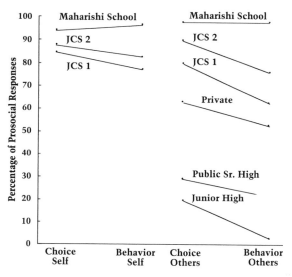

Percentage of Prosocial Responses for Students at Maharishi School, Just Community Schools (JCS 1 and JCS 2), and Other Private and Public Schools.

Percentage of Prosocial Responses

Maharishi School
JCS 2
JCS 1

Maharishi School
JCS 2
JCS 1
Private
Public Sr. High
Junior High

Choice Self   Behavior Self   Choice Others   Behavior Others

Reference: R.J. Nidich and S.I. Nidich, "An Empirical Study of the Moral Atmosphere of Maharishi International University High School [Maharishi School of the Age of Enlightenment]," presented to the American Educational Research Association (Chicago, Ill.), April 1985.

and *behavior* responses by JCS students. This incongruence was not found in the Maharishi School responses. In other words, Maharishi School students felt that they would act on their prosocial beliefs more often than did the JCS students.

Levels of the Knower and Social Development

Social psychologists have identified several factors associated with student moral development. These include degree of distractibility when performing a task, cognitive style, moral reasoning ability, empathy, ego-strength, self-esteem, and ego development. Grimm, Kohlberg, and White found that students who showed higher distractibility and lower ego strength are generally considered more disobedient and untrustworthy by

■ Figure 14. This graph illustrates the total percentage of prosocial responses for Maharishi School, two Just Community Schools, and Maharishi School students' perceptions of the schools they previously attended. Prosocial responses were found to be highest for Maharishi School.

their teachers. These researchers also suggested that a field-independent cognitive style (indicative of a more inner-directed, self-sufficient style of thinking) is also associated with positive social behavior. Other studies have found that individuals who exhibited higher levels of moral reasoning ability tended to exhibit prosocial behavior under experimental conditions. Research shows that empathy — the ability to understand and appreciate how another person feels — is an important factor related to social development. There is also evidence that both self-esteem and ego-development are associated with moral development.[7] Figure 15 illustrates how these various factors associated with social development can be related to Maharishi's model of the levels of the knower.

All of the above factors associated with social development have been found to be enhanced through the practice of Maharishi's Transcendental Meditation. For example, individuals practicing TM exhibit more focused attention compared to non-meditators, as indicated by measures of vigilance and reaction time. In terms of cognitive style, practice of the TM technique significantly increases field independence.[8] Dr. Paul Gelderloos and co-workers found that elementary school students at Maharishi School exhibited a higher level of field independence than students from other schools.[9]

College students practicing TM have also exhibited significantly higher levels of moral reasoning than nonmeditating students.[10] Studies indicate that the practice of TM increases empathy, affiliation, nurturance, tolerance, capacity for intimate contact, and feeling reactivity. Other research has indicated improvement in ego development, self-esteem, self-concept, and ego strength.[11]

In addition, educational research has shown that there are psychophysiological correlates to social development. In one study, EEG brain wave coherence, a measure of the functional organization of the brain, was found to be related to students' moral reasoning ability. A second study found that brain wave coherence was positively related to instructors' ratings of student prosocial behavior in the classroom. As mentioned earlier, research has found that the practice of TM increases brain wave coherence.[12]

A study by Farrow found that subjective reports of the experience of the unified field during TM were closely correlated with

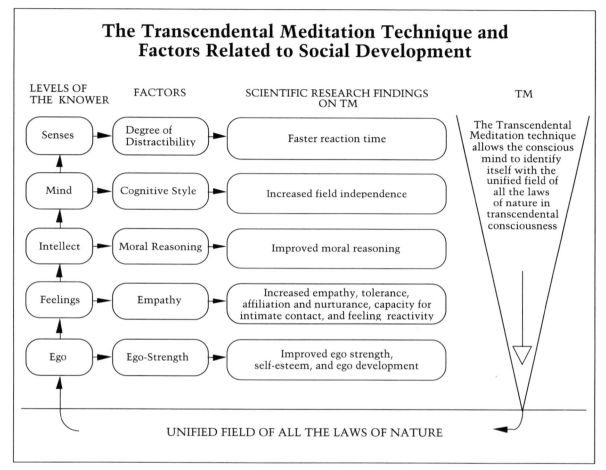

The Transcendental Meditation Technique and Factors Related to Social Development

LEVELS OF THE KNOWER	FACTORS	SCIENTIFIC RESEARCH FINDINGS ON TM	TM
Senses	Degree of Distractibility	Faster reaction time	The Transcendental Meditation technique allows the conscious mind to identify itself with the unified field of all the laws of nature in transcendental consciousness
Mind	Cognitive Style	Increased field independence	
Intellect	Moral Reasoning	Improved moral reasoning	
Feelings	Empathy	Increased empathy, tolerance, affiliation and nurturance, capacity for intimate contact, and feeling reactivity	
Ego	Ego-Strength	Improved ego strength, self-esteem, and ego development	

UNIFIED FIELD OF ALL THE LAWS OF NATURE

■ Figure 15. This chart illustrates factors associated with social development in relation to the levels of the knower, according to Maharishi's theory. Research has indicated that all the levels of the knower and the corresponding factors associated with social development are enriched through the direct experience of the unified field of natural law provided by the practice of Maharishi's Transcendental Meditation technique.

increases in EEG brain wave coherence. Orme-Johnson and others found that clarity of experience of transcendental consciousness was positively related to degree of EEG brain wave coherence during the practice of Maharishi's TM and TM-Sidhi program. Also, Dillbeck and Bronson found that over time individuals practicing the TM technique exhibited marked increases in EEG coherence.[13]

These findings further support the claim that Maharishi's

Transcendental Meditation and TM-Sidhi program enhances student social development.

Knowledge of the Self as the Basis for Right Action

As the studies described previously show, Unified Field Based Education promotes students' social development by giving them the experience of the unified field of natural law — the Self. By establishing their awareness at the level of the unified field, they gain the ability to think and act spontaneously in accord with all the laws of nature. Being in accord with natural law ensures that their thoughts and actions will be fully life-supporting, both for themselves and their environment.

Since the time of Socrates, self-knowledge has been valued as the most important knowledge we can gain. The axiom "Know thyself" has been passed down through the ages to the youth of every culture. Yet at no time has education had a proper and complete understanding of the essential nature of human life. The most complete understanding, provided by Maharishi, is that the Self is the unified field of natural law, the totality of the laws of nature responsible for structuring the entire universe.

Maharishi cites a verse from *Rig-Ved*, the central text of the Vedic literature, as expressing this principle:

> *Richo akshare parame vyoman*
> *Yasmin deva adhivishve nisheduh*
> *Yastanna veda kimricha karishyati*
> *Ya ittadvidus ta ime samasate*
> (Rig-Ved I.164.39)

The verses of the Ved exist in the collapse of fullness
in the transcendental field,
in which reside all the devas, impulses of creative intelligence,
the laws of nature responsible for the whole manifest universe.
He whose awareness is not open to this field,
what can the verses accomplish for him?
Those who know this level of reality
are established in evenness, wholeness of life.

This verse shows that the self-referral state of consciousness, transcendental consciousness, is the home of all the laws of nature that structure the entire manifest universe. It further emphasizes the importance of human awareness being open to this level of reality so that fulfillment can be lived.

In commenting on this verse, Maharishi explains:

> That knowledge of the Self is the basis of all the laws. It is the first law. That is natural law. That is the reason why self-realization has been emphasized throughout the ages. In every generation there has been an emphasis on realizing the Self. In terms of law, it is realizing the home of all the laws of nature, and that is within yourself....
>
> ...for he who does not know that first law, he who does not know himself, he who does not know that eternal seed of wisdom of life in the transcendental area of consciousness... what can the expression of law do for him? This [is the] eternal expression of law — 'know the home of all the laws of nature which is in your own Self; if you do not know that, what can the expressions of law do for you?[14]

According to Maharishi, the ability to act in accord with natural law comes from being established in the Self, and not from merely knowing the rules and laws of society. "Those who know the law are found violating the law...just because it is not possible through knowing something that one can act according to it.... Often people know that what they are doing is probably not right, but then they still do it anyway." Maharishi summarizes this principle by stating: "Action is always on the level of consciousness, not on the basis of knowing what one should or should not do."[15]

Experience of the unified field transcends the duality of subject and object — it is the unified state of knower, known, and process of knowing. Maharishi explains that this three-in-one structure within one's own consciousness contains the total potential of natural law — it is the basis of all the diverse values of natural law guiding the progress and evolution of everything in nature, including one's own individual life. Thus, repeated experience of the unified field promotes action in spontaneous accord with all the laws of nature that benefits both the individual and the whole of society. One's own interests and the progressive interests of society no longer conflict — what is good for oneself is also found to be good for society.

The experiences of higher states of consciousness reported

According to Maharishi, the ability to act in accord with natural law comes from being established in the Self, and not from merely knowing the rules and laws of society.

by people practicing Maharishi's Transcendental Meditation technique for several years further indicate how TM promotes spontaneous right action by giving experience of the unified field — the Self. Following are two examples of such experiences recorded in Maharishi's *Creating an Ideal Society*:

> There are many examples of growing intuition, but basically what is experienced is foreknowledge of an event or sequence of events, giving rise to the increased ability to fulfill the needs of the environment in a spontaneous manner. I seem to say and do the right thing at the right time. The intellect does not seem to be relied upon as much, just the intuitive feelings. I am just doing right action spontaneously. This, I think, may be the most refined level of intuition. (D.S., California)

> I now find my individual interests have broadened to include universal interests — my awareness has expanded to such a degree that I can undertake world-wide desires and responsibilities. Naturally, I still have concern for my individual affairs, but the ideas and projects that really interest and inspire me these days are ones that extend to all mankind. (C.P., Colorado)[16]

Along with the direct experience of the unified field of all the laws of nature, Maharishi has emphasized the importance of gaining intellectual knowledge of the unified field. According to Maharishi, this is because the knowledge gained through Unified Field Based Education "enlivens that most fundamental value of consciousness from where all thoughts and actions come out."[17]

Through the knowledge and technology of the unified field a sense of wholeness and the "totality of life" develops in the student's personality rather than a sense of division and conflict.

Together, the knowledge and technology of the unified field refine the intellect so that it identifies more and more with the unified field of natural law, the unified state of knower, known, and process of knowing. A sense of wholeness and the "totality of life" develops in the student's personality rather than a sense of division and conflict. Through Unified Field Based Education, students spontaneously begin to make more life-supporting decisions that promote their own growth and the well-being of those around them.

Students at Maharishi School emphasize the importance of being in tune with natural law so that they can live in complete fulfillment without causing suffering to others. Patrick, a 12th-grade student, stated:

Action in accord with natural law would be the action that brings the most good to the doer and the environment — everyone and everything. Good means that which brings happiness and greater fulfillment in life. It's not just some immediate effect, it's the overall effect. It brings about evolution to myself and all that exists around me. Violation of natural law would be detrimental to my growth and everything around me — it brings about bad feelings and uncomfortable situations.

[When somebody does something wrong,] he knows he is wrong but he thinks he'll gain happiness from it. He'll feel guilty about it for a long time and this will create stress in his nervous system and because he is stressful his future actions will also not be in accord with natural law — they won't be right. Overall, the action doesn't bring happiness because he feels guilty and others around him will feel uncomfortable.

The following comments by 10th-grade students at Maharishi School further show the beneficial effects of Unified Field Based Education on their social development:

I have found myself growing up in incredible spurts. All of my actions now are based not only on how they will affect me but also how they affect the people involved in my life. I have learned not to think only for myself but also for others. I am always happy to share myself and happiness with others. (Gail)

Since attending Maharishi School, my attitude toward myself and my peers has changed greatly. Before coming here, I didn't get along with anybody and really was never at ease with myself. Now, I have a great respect for everybody. (Jim)

I've noticed a great difference in my attitude.... Now I think more clearly about right action. I am much more thoughtful about the people around me and my environment. (Arlene)

These examples show the effectiveness of Maharishi's Unified Field Based Education for developing higher values of thinking and behavior in students. Enlivening the total potential of natural law in the consciousness of the individual students is the basis for ideal social behavior. In the next chapter, we will see how the experience of the unified field, the home of all the laws of nature, by students, teachers, and administrators creates a positive, harmonious social climate in the whole school.

C H A P T E R   S E V E N

School Climate: Producing a Coherent Collective Consciousness Within the School

Maharishi School of the Age of Enlightenment left an indelible impression on me when I saw the amount of affection and respect the students have for their teachers and peers, as well as the appreciation and support the teachers give to the students. Such a wholesome, cheerful atmosphere among the students exists wherever you go on campus. This is so noticeably different from any other school I have ever attended or visited.
—Oberdon J. Raimondi, retired principal
Union City, New Jersey

Anyone who comes to Maharishi School is struck by the brightness and happiness of the children, the orderliness of the environment, and the love and good feeling that the children and teachers express. There is something about the atmosphere of the school. A very good feeling of collective consciousness has developed at Maharishi School due to the group practice of Maharishi's Transcendental Meditation program.
—George Balf, former Lower School Principal
Maharishi School

TO A VISITOR STANDING IN THE SECOND-FLOOR HALLWAY of Maharishi School between classes, the hustle and bustle, the unmistakable thunder of 57 pairs of 5th-grade feet coming down the stairs on their way to PE class, don't seem much different from any other elementary school. The children call to one another: "Hi, Sarah!" "It's going to be *boiling hot* tomorrow!" "*My* birthday is December 4th!" Smothered giggles and high spirits. But you notice immediately that it's an *orderly* bustle. The children are eager and excited to get to PE, but they are courteous to each other — there is no shoving or pushing. They respond immediately to their teacher's directions. And their faces glow with happiness.

Every school has its own atmosphere, which reflects the collective consciousness of all the students and teachers. This "personality" of the school is often referred to as school climate. Professor Edgar Kelly, an expert on school climate, notes: "Some schools are cheerful and hum with excitement and purpose. Others seem to lack enthusiasm.... Feelings of satisfaction and productivity constitute school climate."[1]

Over the years, educational researchers have devoted increasing attention to assessing school climate. Researchers now recognize that a student's performance, both academically and socially, depends not only on IQ and socio-economic status but on the school environment. A positive school climate tends to enhance student development while a negative one restricts it. Michael Rutter, who conducted a landmark study on school climate in Great Britain, states: "To an appreciable extent children's behavior and attitudes are shaped and influenced by their experiences at school and, in particular, by the qualities of the school as a social institution."[2] According to Kurt Lewin, a noted social psychologist, understanding the effects of climate on individuals' behavior in social institutions is as important as understanding gravity for explaining physics.[3]

Emile Durkheim, the eminent French sociologist, explained that the collective consciousness of an institution, such as a school or even a class within a school, forms a wholeness that is more than the sum of its constituent parts. Durkheim wrote: "When one says of a class that it has good or bad spirit, that it has warmth of life or that on the contrary it is dull and dead, it is the collective individual that is being judged and qualified."

Durkheim believed that the collective consciousness of a school, or even a single class, could not be changed at will. "A teacher can no more make the temper of a class than a king can fashion that of a nation," he wrote.[4] Until recently, there was no systematic way to substantially improve school climate. With the advent of Unified Field Based Education, however, our research indicates that it is now possible to systematically promote a more positive school climate.

According to Maharishi, the individual is the basic unit of collective consciousness. The progress and well-being of any social entity — from a family to an entire nation — depend on the quality of consciousness of each of its members. Similarly, the productivity, positivity, and harmony of a school depend on the quality of consciousness of each student, teacher, and administrator. The nourishing climate of Maharishi School of the Age of Enlightenment is a by-product of its unified field based educational system: the collective practice of Maharishi's Transcendental Meditation program by students, teachers, and administrators enriches the school's climate by enlivening the field of pure consciousness — the unified field of natural law.

Since school climate cannot be directly measured, reseachers look at the interactions among students, teachers, and administrators as a reflection of the school's overall atmosphere. They often solicit the opinions of parents as well. In this chapter, we will discuss the climate of Maharishi School from the following angles:

- quality of interactions among students
- quality of interactions between teachers and students
- teacher morale and quality of interactions among teachers
- quality of interactions between administrators and teachers
- parents' opinions.

Interactions Among Students

One important indicator of school climate is students' interactions with each other — whether they are harmonious and coherent or full of conflict and division.

We saw in the previous chapter that consideration for the effects of their actions on others and for the overall harmony of the school dominates the thinking and behavior of Maharishi School students. Research indicates that they hold strong values for caring, keeping agreements, honesty, and harmonious resolution of negative situations. The students' responses to the four dilemmas on the Moral Atmosphere Interview showed that they value their own personal development as well as the development of others.

According to Maharishi, the individual is the basic unit of collective consciousness. The progress and well-being of any social entity — from a family to an entire nation — depend on the quality of consciousness of each of its members.

"It is common for young children to be egocentric and not immediately extend themselves to others. In our school, children seem to be different. They have a very healthy respect for other children."
— Former Lower
    School principal

Making New Students "Feel at Home"

Perhaps the most conclusive indicator of the quality of students' interactions is how the "old" students treat the "new" students. In many schools, new students are initially rejected. According to George Balf, students at Maharishi School go out of their way to make new students feel at home. "I have been impressed with the relationship that students develop with new students," he says. "One of the common complaints about moving to a new school is that it takes a long time to make friends. Children say that at other schools there is usually a clique of students that they have to try to get into. Here, they find that within a day or two they feel they have been here their whole lives. The children go out of their way to welcome new students into their circle of friends. Right away they go up to them and invite them to join them in their games."

"It is common for young children to be egocentric and not immediately extend themselves to others," Mr. Balf added. "In our school, children seem to be different. They have a very healthy respect for other children."

These observations are consistent with those by the Maharishi School secondary students we reported in Chapter Six. Students say that cliques are not dominant at Maharishi School and that the school is like "one big family." In several instances, students said that new students are made to feel welcome at Maharishi School on their very first day. For example, a 10th-grade student says: "When new kids come here, they don't get rejected or made to feel embarrassed. We try to make them feel at home." Joyce, a 9th-grader, says:

> I used to have a problem making friends. When I came here I made lots of friends. Maharishi School is a good school, and everyone here is like a family. We all get along and are close friends. People have a good attitude about school and towards their friends and family.

Teachers also report that Maharishi School students reflect positive qualities in their interactions with other students. In a questionnaire given to teachers, 100 percent described the students as being friendly, trustworthy, supportive, helpful, knowledgeable, flexible, confident, motivated, cooperative, and responsible in their interactions with other students. The teachers did not feel that such negative attributes as being aloof, alienated, rigid, scared, or uncaring were applicable to Maharishi School students.[5]

Cooperation and Competition

Another indicator of school climate is the degree of cooperation versus competition among students. Educators generally believe that there should be a balance between cooperation and competition in classroom and extracurricular activities. Experience has shown that when competition is emphasized at the expense of cooperation, negativity and conflict often arise.

In our observations and interviews with teachers and students at Maharishi School, we have found a healthy, positive blend of cooperation and competition. Students are encouraged to always strive to do their best, but at the same time they are encouraged to help their fellow students.

At Maharishi School, one finds 5th-graders going into 1st-grade classes to help the younger children learn to read. Another example of their helpful attitude is the way the Upper School students work together when studying for the National Merit Scholarship test. Nancy Messinger, who has taught high school English at Maharishi School, comments:

> It is very rare to see so many students wanting to be Merit Scholars. At other schools there's usually an aggressive competition and a feeling of not wanting to help somebody else do well on the test out of fear that that person will do better than you and reduce your chances of placing in the competition. Here at Maharishi School, students are very open to helping other students. In fact, as a teacher, that's something I'll often use. I'll take the students who are better academically and have them help the students who are having a problem with their work. They often explain the material to the other students better than I can. They are very open to that, and it is really great.

A 4th-grade teacher at Maharishi School says, "There is less of the aggressive kind of behavior that results from competition at Maharishi School, because in class we are always upholding the values of positivity and harmony." She explained that the children feel "each person's work is worthwhile and [they] never denounce another's work or make fun of another person. The children are careful about feelings because the fine feeling level is important to them. They realize that feelings are a delicate source of much of their motivation. They understand this very well and do not want to hurt others." A 6th-grade teacher says: "Competition is a feeling for gaining excellence. The students cooperate with one another in order to raise the level of excellence of their peers."

Says Charles, an 11th-grader:

> In my class there isn't competition against other students. Everyone is helping everyone else all the time. If you're having a hard time in one of the subjects, you can always ask another student to explain the material to you. If another student explains it to you, you can generally understand the material better. There is always someone there to help you.

"Competition is a feeling for gaining excellence. The students cooperate with one another in order to raise the level of excellence of their peers."
— Lower School teacher

Emphasis on Academic Excellence

Much of the school climate research evaluates the "academic climate" of a school — how well the school's atmosphere supports student academic achievement.[6] For example, prep schools are known for their academic climate.

We found a very positive academic climate at Maharishi School, as indicated by the strong motivation among students to excel academically. Melanie, an 11th-grade student who recently came from Los Angeles, describes with amazement the difference in attitudes towards schoolwork between students at Maharishi School and her previous school:

> In L.A. when school is out, it is out. Even during lunch break, for that matter, no one mentions school. Here, our school work is integrated into everything we do, because the knowledge is so well integrated. After school and even over lunch time, students at Maharishi School are always discussing what they learned in class. At first . . . I wondered why they were doing this when they could talk about anything they wanted to during this time. I thought it must be a joke they were playing. But I soon found that it wasn't a joke at all; the students were really enjoying discussing the knowledge they were learning in class. They got me doing it too. It's fun to talk about knowledge at this school.

■ Maharishi School students are strongly motivated to excel academically, indicating a very positive academic climate at the school.

Melanie also comments on how students behave in class at Maharishi School compared to her previous school:

> In L.A. my classmates were reasonably quiet and well behaved, although they didn't really pay attention; they just tuned out. The talking that went on among students was not related to the information being presented by the teacher. Here, at Maharishi School, students really are paying attention and are tuned in to what the teacher is saying. Sometimes, out of enthusiasm, the students may talk out of turn, but it is always related to what the teacher is saying. Even conversations among students in class are almost always about the knowledge we are learning.

Melanie attributes the enthusiasm for knowledge among Maharishi School students to their practice of the Transcendental Meditation program. "Knowledge is growing within me due to my TM practice," Melanie says. "What I learn in my classes, whether it's literature or math, relates to my experiences during meditation. Now, when I study lines from poems, I really understand where they are coming from. Poems have more meaning to me now. In math, I can see that the math formulas reflect mathematicians' insights into the way nature functions. Since coming to Maharishi School I can really appreciate the value of gaining knowledge much more."

According to Upper School teacher Rod Magoon, the new students at Maharishi School quickly adopt the norms that have

■ The bliss experienced during the practice of the Transcendental Meditation technique spontaneously extends into teacher-student relationships.

already been established by the other students. "The norm is to always do the best one can," he explains. "The students have a self-image of wanting to excel in everything they do. Because of this self-image, they see themselves as capable of learning anything. Unlike students at other schools, these students are not anxious about learning; there is a sense of ease, comfort, and confidence in class. They don't have a fear of failure or being laughed at by other students in class, and the students aren't afraid to participate and show how smart they are."

Interactions Between Teachers and Students

"The children in my class are so sweet and innocent and so open to learning," says 3rd-grade teacher Anne Love. "It seems that when I put my attention on their sweetness and innocence, some of that rubs off onto me. Their openness to learning is my inspiration; it draws from me the desire to give them whatever they need. Teaching at Maharishi School is where I want to be for many years to come."

One of the most obvious effects of Unified Field Based Education is the productive, harmonious quality of interactions between teachers and students. All the students and teachers are practicing Maharishi's Transcendental Meditation technique and experiencing bliss and happiness in their own lives, and this blissful quality naturally extends into their relationships.

Kathy, a 12th-grade student, describes her class environment as "really open and friendly." Asked what she means by "open and friendly," she said:

The teachers are great. They obviously really care about the students and try to inspire all the students to do the best they can. The teachers speak to each student as a person, as someone who is intelligent and wants to learn. They seem to bring up knowledge that you want to know. When students discuss things in class it seems that they really begin to "own" the

■ Happiness and coherence are the dominant feelings in Maharishi School classrooms.

knowledge.... The teachers are really interested in the students as individuals and want to help them. They make it known that students can speak with them and get their help.

Some students who have attended other schools have said that they rarely used to volunteer to answer a question in class because they were afraid that others would make fun of them. Here, the teachers encourage the students to raise their hands. Even if it is a wrong answer, it can lead to something worthwhile.

Alice, another 12th-grade student, says: "The teachers are always there to help us and support us. They're open, giving, loving, and kind. They're always eager to teach us more. If one of the students wants to move faster, the teachers accommodate with special assignments. They are very sincere in their desire to help us grow."

A poem by a 3rd grader shows how the younger children feel about their teachers:

My teacher is sweet.   *She is always caring.*
My teacher is neat.   *She is always sharing.*
She is giving.   *She is very pretty.*
And she makes a perfect living.   *And she's always witty.*

She is kind.   *She is very nice.*
She always has something on   *And she's not a block of ice.*
*   her mind.*
She is full of knowledge.   *She is fun.*
And I know she went to college.   *And occasionally makes a pun.*[7]

In terms of student-teacher relations, teachers also reported that students were cooperative, friendly, communicative, responsible, flexible, and supportive. Says elementary teacher Dori Jackson:

> People who come to visit the school are impressed . . . it's the feeling in the school, the feeling in the classroom that they immediately observe. The . . . interactions with the children seem to convince the visitors that there is something very special going on at this school that is not found at other schools. I think that this plays a major role in the quality of education at Maharishi School. It is easy to cultivate a close bond and level of intimacy with the students. I feel a deep and strong connection with them.

An educator from Japan comments that the difference she observed between Maharishi School and schools she has visited in other countries is the "stability in relationships between teachers and students." She says she experienced a strong feeling of "love, integration, coherence, and silence" in the Maharishi School classes.

Dr. Max Raines, Professor of Higher Education at Michigan State University, observes:

> When I visited Maharishi School, I noticed how naturally learning was taking place. At other schools, learning appears unnatural. Students and teachers are constantly struggling — there is a noticeable stress and strain that comes with learning. At Maharishi School, from kindergarten through 12th grades, I saw a naturalness and joy in learning that is truly remarkable.

"At Maharishi School, from kindergarten through 12th grades, I saw a naturalness and joy in learning that is truly remarkable."
— Visiting educator

What is responsible for the nourishing effect of interactions at Maharishi School? According to Maharishi School teachers and students, it is their twice-daily practice of Transcendental Meditation, which enlivens the qualities of the unified field of natural law in their thinking and behavior. We described some of these qualities in Chapter Two — harmony, infinite correlation, perfect orderliness, simplicity, and bliss. As these evolutionary qualities develop, students at Maharishi School spontaneously reflect them in their interactions with others. And because the teachers also practice Maharishi's TM and TM-Sidhi program, they reflect these qualities in their teaching.

The net result is that learning becomes more ideal. Dr. Susan Dillbeck comments on the quality of interactions she has observed between the teachers and students at Maharishi School: "The students are receptive and focus intently when they work. They ask penetrating questions and clearly enjoy being in school. They are respectful and kind to each other and to their teachers, and the teachers in turn always give their best. Knowledge seems to flow easily in such an atmosphere."

■ Maharishi School teachers experience less teacher stress than norms, as indicated by lower levels of emotional exhaustion and depersonalization, and a greater sense of personal accomplishment.

Teacher Morale and Interactions Among Teachers

Educators have found that the level of teacher morale and the quality of interaction among teachers directly affects student academic and social development. High teacher morale is associated with good academic performance and positive student behavior. Low teacher morale is strongly related to inferior academic performance and negative social behavior.

In *A Place Called School*, Dr. John Goodlad explains: "The emerging hypothesis is that schools staffed by teachers who are less than satisfied are likely to be schools perceived by teachers, parents, and students as having a greater array of problems. Conversely, schools in which teachers are more satisfied with their careers and teaching circumstances are relatively unlikely to be perceived by teachers, parents, and students as having serious problems. Happily, these are likely also to be the schools most frequently perceived by students as giving them a good education."[8]

We have found that teachers at Maharishi School are happy people who are satisfied with their jobs. Teachers report that they maintain high standards of performance for themselves, are continually learning and seeking new ideas, support and encourage each other, and have a high degree of commitment to their jobs. Overall, teachers indicate that a friendly atmosphere prevails among the staff members, and that they are proud to be working at Maharishi School. Responses by the teachers to the Maslach Burnout Inventory (MBI) also showed that they experience less teacher stress than norms, as indicated by lower levels of emotional exhaustion and depersonalization and a greater sense of personal accomplishment.[9]

On teacher morale at Maharishi School, Dori Jackson says:

> When I came here I had been teaching for about seven years and had just finished a master's degree in reading. I was looking for something more in the field of teaching. This was just the right place to move to, because there are a lot of opportunities to do things and for growth. All of the teachers are growing so much — personally and professionally — at Maharishi School; this I feel is the main reason why the morale of teachers is so high and we all work so well together.

Candace Greenley, who taught in the Connecticut public school system for 13 years before coming to Maharishi School, says, "This is the only place I've ever been where it's 'one for all and all for one,' a community in the true sense of the word. We're all here to grow, to help each other."

Although it is challenging to teach children who are developing so rapidly, we have found that Maharishi School teachers look forward to and enjoy this challenge. For example, when Kathy Siemsen first came to Maharishi School, she was concerned that she wouldn't have enough energy to keep up with the children. But she soon found that her practice of TM was the key to meeting this challenge. "I marvel over and over again at how Maharishi's Transcendental Meditation program provides me with what I need," she says. "Ideas pop into my head spontaneously at just the right moment. I feel I'm growing every day. Every day I look forward to teaching these bright, energetic students."

On teacher morale and interaction, George Balf observes:

> There is no jealousy; there is no envy or professional conflict among the teachers or between the teachers and the principal. We have a good group of teachers and I can't think of any of them who would want to do anything else. It's the best faculty I have ever seen. They are helpful and competent, and they really do love the children.

The teachers are open and sharing with each other and help each other. For example, one 1st-grade teacher, Susan Chipman, did an exceptionally creative unit on trucks with her children. As soon as she finished her unit and reported its success, two other teachers immediately did a similar unit on trucks.

Teachers agree that the practice of Maharishi's Transcendental Meditation technique and the knowledge of SCI contribute significantly to the high level of teacher morale at Maharishi School. Dori Jackson notes that "there is a tremendous camaraderie between teachers. What brings out the qualities of the heart in everyone is the common focus on enlightenment through the TM program and the knowledge of SCI." Joanne Orange, an Upper School teacher, says, "There is a constant refreshment in Unified Field Based Education. I don't feel any strain or loss of energy, because teaching SCI is so special. Most importantly we have the benefit of the practice of Maharishi's Transcendental Meditation program."

Interactions Between Administrators and Teachers

According to educational researchers, the principal plays a crucial role in determining the climate of the school. A study by Professor Edward Wynne on Midwest schools found a higher level of coherence where principals regularly visit teachers' classrooms, review student records, and keep abreast of new developments.[10] Dr. Goodlad found that "good principals are associated with more satisfying schools." He states that teachers perceive a good principal as one who is "relatively autonomous as a person and leader, treats staff members as colleagues and professionals, and is consistent in dealing with teachers and students."[11] The attitudes and behavior of the Lower, Middle, and Upper School principals at Maharishi School reflect all these traits.

Teachers report that the principals at Maharishi School are very "strong in leadership" and "enthusiastic in spirit." Teachers also feel that the principals tend to be personally involved in school improvement, are committed to instructional improvement, reward work well done, set realistic standards, believe in accountability, and communicate clearly.

There is a high degree of teamwork among administrators and teachers at Maharishi School. Teachers report that administrators

"There is a tremendous camaraderie between teachers. What brings out the qualities of the heart in everyone is the common focus on enlightenment through the TM program and the knowledge of SCI."
— Lower School teacher

and teachers collaborate in making the school run effectively, trust each other, and support and encourage each other.

An example of this teamwork is the way administrators and teachers worked together to complete the school's curriculum guide for accreditation.

As part of the accreditation process for the Independent Schools Association of the Central States (ISACS), Maharishi School developed a comprehensive description of its entire curriculum, from kindergarten through 12th grade. According to Dr. Robin Rowe, Academic Director of the School, "The creation of the curriculum guide for all 13 grades in just a year's time was a formidable task, requiring input from every teacher in the school. Included in the curriculum guide are the rationale and objectives for each course along with 'scope and sequence charts' that specify exactly when knowledge and skills should be introduced, developed, and mastered by students at each grade level. All of the teachers and the administrators worked together very closely on this project and because of their collective consciousness produced something quite wonderful."

The harmonious, productive interactions among Maharishi School administrators and teachers are further evidence of a positive school climate. From our observations and research it is clear that the basis for such interactions is their practice of Transcendental Meditation, which enlivens in their awareness the qualities of the unified field, e.g., infinite dynamism, infinite correlation, harmony, and bliss. Thus, Transcendental Meditation is not only a significant factor in student academic performance and social development, as described in Chapters Five and Six, but is equally significant for producing a positive school climate as reflected by the interactions of teachers and adminstrators.

Opinions of Parents

The opinions of parents are one of the most important indicators of school climate. In this section we give examples of parents' opinions of the climate of Maharishi School Their comments on the liveliness, intelligence, creativity, coherence, sweetness, and harmony, and the lack of negative influences common at other schools are particularly striking.

Mrs. Eileen Dannemann, mother of three children at Maharishi

School, compared the school's climate to that of the private school her children previously attended in New York City:

> Compared to the previous school that our children attended, I would say that there is more of a liveliness and quality of intelligence that permeates Maharishi School. There is also a high level of creativity. The children are more animated and their intellects are more lively. At the same time the students seem more relaxed. They absorb knowledge much more easily and are more at home with knowledge and other people. They seem to appreciate others more and have more respect for their teachers and other students. While the school in Manhattan that our children previously attended is quite a prestigious school, it definitely lacks the means for developing the student's creative potential. The practice of Transcendental Meditation is the main factor I feel is responsible for the difference I see in the atmosphere of the two schools.

■ Many parents have moved to Fairfield so their children can attend school in an environment that supports holistic growth.

"This school is a dream come true for all parents who have been seeking the best education possible for their children."

— Parent

Mrs. Joan Rothenberg, who moved from San Diego with her husband Stuart, a medical doctor, says:

This school is a dream come true for all parents who have been seeking the best education possible for their children. Our child can hardly wait to get to school each morning. She is attracted to this environment of tremendous sweetness and wisdom that stimulates her intellect and nourishes her heart.

Many parents have moved to Fairfield so that their children could go to school in an environment that supports their holistic growth. "We wanted our daughter to have only positive influences in school — academically, physically, and emotionally," comments Tim Hawthorne, a communications specialist who moved from Los Angeles with his wife Tina. "We feel that at Maharishi School of the Age of Enlightenment, our daughter is getting the kind of education that we would like to have had."

The home environment of each student also contributes to school climate. Home environment includes the parents' support and love and their expectations for their children's success. Maharishi School has an advantage over other schools in that the parents are also practicing Maharishi's Transcendental Meditation technique. This supports the children's practice of TM and helps establish a home environment that supports their education at school. We have found that the home environments of Maharishi School children are typically warm, loving, cheerful, and educationally stimulating.

We have also observed that Maharishi School parents hold high expectations for their children's future. "The changes in my expectations for my children are like night and day," says one parent. "Now I have a view of all possibilities and know that my children can achieve anything they want to." Another parent comments that because of his own experiences during the Transcendental Meditation program, he now believes that "enlightenment is really possible" and wants his children to be able to live blissful lives, free from suffering.

School Climate and the Collective Practice of Maharishi's Transcendental Meditation and TM-Sidhi Program

Maharishi School teachers, administrators, students, and parents all feel that Transcendental Meditation is the main reason for the school's positive climate. There are two aspects to this. First, everyone at the school enlivens the evolutionary qualities of the unified field in their own awareness and exhibits them in interactions with others. Second, the collective practice of this technology creates a "field effect" through which these evolutionary qualities radiate to the whole environment.

Maharishi explains that there are many different levels of collective consciousness — families, communities, nations, and the world as a whole. Collective consciousness is like a field that underlies and interconnects individuals. It cannot be directly seen but its presence can be inferred from the interactions of individuals. We have seen that every school has its own collective consciousness which influences the behavior of all individuals at the school.

The unified field is the most fundamental field in nature, the source and essential constituent of all other force and matter fields. The unified field is also the basis of individual human consciousness, the unit of collective consciousness. Thus the unified field underlies all the different levels of collective consciousness in human society.

According to Maharishi, the unified field governs all levels of society simultaneously. When individuals practice TM, they enliven the qualities of the unified field not only in their own consciousness but in collective consciousness as well.[12] Unified field Based Education thus improves school climate by directly handling the school's collective consciousness and making it harmonious and nourishing.

At Maharishi School, the positive effects of students practicing the Transcendental Meditation technique in their classes are immediately obvious. Teachers say that after a group meditation the whole atmosphere is settled and conducive to learning. Says Middle School teacher Guy Hatchard:

> There is an unusually positive and supportive atmosphere that is felt in the classroom at Maharishi School. There is a complete absence of stress and unhappiness in the classroom that makes the teaching process enjoyable. At other schools, I've found teachers to be very caring, but just a caring attitude isn't enough to produce the quality of school climate felt at Maharishi School.
>
> I feel the main factor responsible for this is the group practice of Transcendental Meditation that we do together at the beginning

and end of the school day. Through our group practice, we produce greater happiness and coherence both in ourselves and in the environment of the school. A tangible feeling is produced that is something very special. It is different from the feeling of any other school in which I've taught or which I have visited.

More than 30 scientific research studies have documented the positive effect that groups of people practicing Maharishi's Transcendental Meditation and TM-Sidhi program have on the environment. These studies, discussed in the next chapter, indicate that this collective practice directly improves the quality of life of a community, a nation, even the world.[13]

C H A P T E R   E I G H T

The Technology for Creating World Peace: Maharishi's Transcendental Meditation and TM-Sidhi Program

With the total knowledge of the unified field of all the laws of nature now available, we have an approach to create world peace that is practical, reliable, effective, and certain.[1]   —*Maharishi*

AT 6:45 A.M. ON A CRISP OCTOBER MORNING, JAN HOPS ON her bicycle, rides down B Street, cuts over to Main Street, passes the Grand Assembly Hall and the MIU dorms, and arrives at the Ladies' Golden Dome of Pure Knowledge in the north part of campus. Outside the Dome, the parking lots are filling with cars, and hundreds of students, faculty, and staff from MIU and Maharishi School, along with other Fairfield residents, stream along the walkways.

Greeting her friends, Jan enters the 15,000 square foot wooden structure and removes her shoes and coat in the foyer. In her light blue warm-up suit, she walks into the vast expanse of the Dome's main area, which is completely carpeted by thick foam mats. The first rays of the sun are filtering through the peach-colored velvet draperies that line the interior walls, casting a soft glow over everything.

Seated comfortably next to Kathy and Jill, fellow 12th-graders at Maharishi School, Jan closes her eyes and begins to practice Maharishi's Transcendental Meditation and TM-Sidhi program. Along with the other ladies, and the men who are in a second

Golden Dome nearby, Jan is practicing a natural, effortless technique for experiencing more refined levels of awareness and enlivening the unified field of natural law. As a natural by-product of this experience, Jan and the other TM-Sidhas in the MIU community are increasing coherence in their own brain physiology and spreading waves of coherence throughout society.

Jan and other Maharishi School students practice Maharishi's Transcendental Meditation and TM-Sidhi program morning and evening in the Golden Domes of Pure Knowledge to hasten the growth of enlightenment in their own lives and to help create world peace. "The students at Maharishi School think in terms of all the people in the world, not just myself or my family, but all of humanity," Jan says. "We all feel we can make an important contribution to world peace by practicing the TM and TM-Sidhi program."

Jan's classmate Kathy comments, "I feel that most students would agree with me that we all want to do everything we possibly can to contribute to world peace. The individual is the basic unit of society, the nation, and the world. By individuals being

■ Maharishi School students practice the Transcendental Meditation and TM-Sidhi program morning and evening in the MIU Golden Domes of Pure Knowledge to hasten the growth of enlightenment in their own lives and to help create world peace.

happy and coherent, the whole world can be happy and peaceful. Governments have not been able to produce peace. It is up to individuals like ourselves to do this." She emphasized that "this is why we practice the TM and TM Sidhi program — to help ourselves and to help the world. We want to create world peace. Twice a day we create a positive influence in our nation and our world."

In an essay on "What High School Students Can Do To Create World Peace," Michael, a 10th-grade Maharishi School student, wrote:

> By learning the TM-Sidhi program and practicing it in large groups you can actually affect not only yourself, but everyone around you too. Scientific studies have shown that having the square root of one percent of the world's population practicing this program together can lower the crime rate, accident rate, and military conflicts around the whole world, and increase the stock market. This is the fastest way to bring world peace.

History does not record any approach that has succeeded in securing lasting peace. This chapter discusses the practice of Maharishi's TM-Sidhi program and describes research showing how this advanced technology of consciousness is promoting world peace. Maharishi explains that "the great significance of the knowledge of the unified field for the human race is that it offers the ability to handle the total functioning of nature at once. With this it is possible to successfully handle the collective consciousness of the whole world." The result of this new knowledge for humanity, Maharishi explains, "will be an integrated world family; every nation will flourish in its full dignity, and together all nations will live in perfect harmony and peace."[2]

Maharishi's TM-Sidhi Program

Maharishi's TM-Sidhi program is an advanced program consisting of techniques derived from the *Yoga Sutras* of Patanjali. Practice of the TM-Sidhi program enlivens the self-interacting dynamics of the unified field in one's awareness. It trains the individual to think and act from the level of the unified field. This greatly enhances coordination between mind and body and the ability to fulfill one's desires.[3]

> "The great significance of the knowledge of the unified field for the human race is that it offers the ability to handle the total functioning of nature at once."
> — Maharishi

"During the
TM-Sidhi program,
I experience a
feeling of being
completely
"washed" of
stresses. I can feel
my body and mind
becoming purified
on all levels. I also
experience great
feelings of
immense bliss."
— Upper School
    student

Maharishi explains that once transcendental consciousness is sufficiently established in one's awareness through the practice of the TM technique, it can coexist with faint impulses of mental activity. Then one is ready to learn the TM-Sidhi techniques, which enliven specific impulses of natural law at the level of the unified field. This creates increased coherence in mind and body; collective practice of the TM-Sidhi program extends this coherence to the whole environment.[4]

Students age 13 or older who have been practicing TM regularly for 6 to12 months are eligible to begin learning Maharishi's TM-Sidhi program. The following experiences of Maharishi School students who practice the TM-Sidhi program express the profound bliss and integration of mind and body they experience during this practice:

> Wonderful! Absolute bliss. My whole body feels so good. Afterwards I feel refreshed and rested, ready for activity. During the practice, I feel free, sort of like a bird; my heart is warm and I feel love rushing through me. It's hard to say exactly how I feel. It's great. (Helen, 11th grade)

> During the TM-Sidhi program, I experience a feeling of being completely "washed" of stresses. I can feel my body and mind becoming purified on all levels. I also experience great feelings of immense bliss. (Robert, 12th grade)

The TM-Sidhi program profoundly enhances the benefits gained from Transcendental Meditation. Maharishi explains that it also accelerates the development of higher states of consciousness, by culturing the ability to maintain transcendental consciousness along with mental and physical activity — a characteristic of the state of enlightenment, as we saw in Chapter Two.

Yogic Flying as the Mechanics for Creating World Peace

The most powerful of the TM-Sidhi procedures is the Yogic Flying technique, which students can learn starting at the age of 16. In the Yogic Flying technique, mind-body coordination is maximum, so that a faint impulse of consciousness from the level of the unified field causes the body to lift off the ground. Research has found that the brain waves become more coherent during Yogic Flying to an even greater extent than during TM. As we noted in Chapter Six, EEG brain wave coherence is a measure of the functional organization of the brain. The greatest coherence in brain functioning is found during Yogic Flying at the moment the body is about to lift up.[5]

According to Maharishi, Yogic Flying is the outward expression of an inner experience in which the conscious mind functions from the total potential of natural law, the unified field: "Yoga means union, the union of the individual awareness with the unified field of all the laws of nature in the state of transcendental consciousness. Yogic Flying demonstrates the ability of the individual to act from the unified field and enliven the total potential of natural law in all its expressions—mind, body, behavior, and environment."[6]

From the perspective of modern physics, MIU physics professor John Hagelin explains that the force of gravity, like every other force in nature, has its basis in the unified field. By functioning from the level of the unified field, it is possible to modify the usual effects of the force of gravity, so that the body can lift off the ground. Dr. Hagelin explains this in terms of space-time geometry, which is associated with gravity:

> Yogic Flying demonstrates the ability of individual consciousness to function coherently from the level of the unified field of all the laws of nature. Only from the level at which all four forces are unified, the level of quantum gravity, do we have natural command over the local curvature of space-time geometry. Yogic Flying would demonstrate such a level of mastery.[7]

Dr. Hagelin further states that:

> It is possible, through the generation of a sustained coherent influence at the level of the unified field, to modify the local curvature of space-time geometry described in general relativity in such a way that the body flies up, or to the left, or forward, or in any direction.[8]

Functioning from this most fundamental level of natural law, all aspects of the mind and body become balanced and integrated. The Vedic literature mentions several stages of mastery of Yogic Flying. In the initial stages of the practice, the body "hops" spontaneously, moving up and forward a short distance; as the practice advances, the hops become higher and longer, and eventually one gains the ability of sustained flight. Presently, the students at Maharishi School are experiencing the first stage of Yogic Flying.

"It is possible, through the generation of a sustained coherent influence at the level of the unified field, to modify the local curvature of space-time geometry described in general relativity in such a way that the body flies up, or to the left, or forward, or in any direction."
— Dr. John Hagelin, MIU Professor of Physics

Maximum brain wave coherence during Yogic Flying coincides with the subjective experience of waves of exhilaration, bliss, and deep inner silence. Jan describes her experience of Yogic Flying:

> Yogic Flying is completely effortless. Energy comes to me no matter how tired or alert I am before I start the practice. I feel awake, aware, in tune with everything, full of bliss.

■ **Figure 16. By maximizing EEG coherence, Yogic Flying accelerates individual growth, and when practiced in groups, it creates an influence of orderliness in the whole environment. Research demonstrates that the means to produce coherent world consciousness is the group practice of Maharishi's TM and TM-Sidhi program, particularly the Yogic Flying technique.**

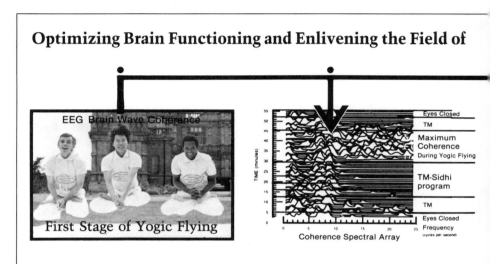

And Kathy says of her experience:

> I enjoy the flying part of the TM-Sidhi program very much. Flying always exhilarates me and gives me a lot of energy.

Yogic Flying not only produces exhilaration, bliss, and more mind-body coordination for the individual, but as Maharishi explains, the coherent functioning of the human brain during Yogic Flying is actually the mechanics for creating something even more significant — world peace:

> The mind-body coordination displayed by Yogic Flying shows that consciousness and its expression — the physiology — are in perfect balance. Scientific research has found maximum coherence in the human brain physiology during Yogic Flying. As the coherently functioning human brain is the unit of world peace, Yogic Flying is the mechanics to make world peace a reality.[9]

The Maharishi Effect — Research on the
Group Practice of Yogic Flying

How does Yogic Flying create world peace? Yogic Flying is such a powerful technology that, when it is practiced in groups, it creates a powerful upsurge of coherence throughout society. Over 30 research studies have shown that the group practice of Yogic Flying

All Possibilities through Maharishi's TM-Sidhi Program

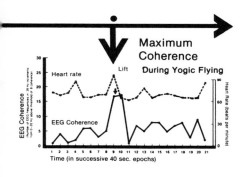

Maximum
Coherence
During Yogic Flying

Maximum coherence in brain waves accomplishes the specific ability. In the case of the Yogic Flying ability, the body lifts up at the point of maximum coherence.

High EEG coherence and heart rate during experience of Yogic Flying

by a small percentage of a population—only the square root of one percent—decreases negative trends, including crime and accident rates, and improves the quality of life in the whole population.

Earlier research showed that when one percent of a population practices Maharishi's Transcendental Meditation technique, the overall quality of life in society improves.[10] Scientists named this phenomenon the Maharishi Effect in honor of Maharishi, who predicted it in 1960.

The effect of increasing positivity through the group practice of Yogic Flying is a further extension of the Maharishi Effect. As we will see in this chapter, when the square root of one percent of the *world's* population practices Yogic Flying in a group, international tension and conflict dramatically decrease, violence is reduced in troubled spots around the world, and indicators of the quality of life rise significantly.[11]

Collective practice of Yogic Flying is referred to as the Super Radiance program, after the superradiance phenomenon of physics. The total intensity of light radiated by a given number of photons is greatly increased when they are in perfect phase correlation — that is, when they function together as one coherent system. In this case, the intensity of light emitted is equal to the number of photons squared. For example, if 100 atoms are perfectly in phase with one another they radiate with an intensity of 100^2, or 10,000 times that of single photon. Superradiance is the principle responsible for the laser and related phenomena in physics.[12]

Similarly, the coherence created by TM-Sidhas is greatly increased when they practice Yogic Flying together in a group. For example, MIU Professor David Orme-Johnson, one of the principal researchers on the Maharishi Effect, describes how people practicing Yogic Flying in Jerusalem, Israel, in August and September, 1983, improved the quality of life in the war-torn Middle East:

> We found that as the size of a group of individuals practicing Yogic Flying together in Jerusalem varied over two months in a virtually random fashion, the number of war deaths in neighboring Lebanon varied in inverse relation. When the group was larger, there were fewer war deaths, and when it was smaller, war deaths increased. We used very sophisticated time series analysis techniques to show that the reduction in war deaths could not have been predicted from any kind of trends or cycles in the data. The effect of Yogic Flying on creating peace was predicted to occur, and it did occur.

Figure 17 shows these results.

In addition, Orme-Johnson and colleagues found that increasing the number of TM-Sidhi participants improved the quality of life in Israel, indicated by decreases in crime rate, traffic accidents, fires in Jerusalem, and the number of war deaths in Lebanon, and by increases in the national stock market and improvement in national mood.[13]

This effect has been repeated in different cultural settings in many parts of the world. The most important study was conducted on the campus of MIU over a three-week period from December 17, 1983, to January 6, 1984. Over 7000 people, approximately the square root of one-percent of the world's population,

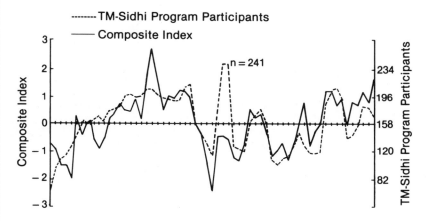

Maharishi Effect: Reduced Conflict and Improved Quality of Life in the Middle East (August-September 1983)

-------- TM-Sidhi Program Participants
——— Composite Index

n = 241

Reference: D.W. Orme-Johnson, C.N. Alexander, J.J. Davies, H.M. Chandler, and W.E. Larimore, "International Peace Project in the Middle East: The Effects of the Maharishi Technology of the Unified Field," *Journal of Conflict Resolution*, 32 (1988): 776–812.

■ **Figure 17.** This study shows that increasing the numbers of participants in the collective practice of the Transcendental Meditation and TM-Sidhi program improved the quality of life in Israel as measured by an index comprised of decreases in crime rate, traffic accidents, fires, and the number of war deaths in Lebanon, and by increases in the national stock market and improvements in national mood.

gathered to practice Maharishi's TM-Sidhi program collectively. Research on world events during the assembly found a dramatic decrease in international conflict, increases in the world's major stock market indices, increased positivity and vitality expressed by heads of state, decreased infectious diseases and traffic fatalities, and increased progress towards peace in Lebanon.[14] (Some of these results are shown on pp. 152 and 153.)

Other studies have been conducted on large groups practicing the TM-Sidhi program in Washington, D.C., Holland, the Philippines, Puerto Rico, India, and Lebanon. All of these studies have shown that when approximately the square root of one percent of a population practices the TM-Sidhi program in one place, negative trends decrease and the quality of life improves.[15]

According to Maharishi, the group practice of the Transcendental Meditation and TM-Sidhi program produces a coherent influence throughout the environment because the coherence is

■ **Over 7000 experts in Maharishi's Transcendental Meditation and TM-Sidhi program gathered for group practice during the historic "Taste of Utopia Assembly" in 1983–84.**

created from the level of the unified field, which is a field of *infinite correlation:*

> The effect produced is from the level of the unified field. Because the unified field is the unmanifest basis of the whole creation, the influence spreads throughout the world. It's just like the effect when you water the root and the nourishment reaches every leaf, branch, flower, and fruit. The unified field is a transcendental reality.... It's a level of infinite correlation which knows no barrier. When we talk by long-distance telephone, it is not that an individual brings the news from here to there. The impulses go on a very quiet level of nature's functioning. Much more quiet than that is the level of the unified field.[16]

The extraordinary effects resulting from the practice of Yogic Flying can only occur from the level of the unified field of all the laws of nature. Maharishi's Transcendental Meditation and TM-Sidhi program enables the individual to enliven the total potential of natural law at the level of the unified field, and from there to create a nourishing effect throughout the environment. The scientific research cited above indicates that for the first time in history there exists a practical technology to put an end to violent and negative tendencies on earth, to remove the basis of terrorism and war, and to create a permanent state of world peace.

Maharishi's Program to Create World Peace

On January 12, 1987, Maharishi inaugurated his Program to Create World Peace, setting three criteria for the attainment of world peace:

- friendship between the superpowers
- a cease-fire in the Iran-Iraq war
- an end to terrorism.

Maharishi predicted that relations among many countries would be found to improve simultaneously as these criteria were achieved.[17]

At the time Maharishi set these goals, world peace seemed far off. But Maharishi was confident that through the continued collective practice of the Transcendental Meditation and TM-Sidhi program at MIU and by meditators and TM-Sidhas worldwide, peace would soon become a reality.

In the summer of 1988, the world press began to document the dramatic breakthrough in world peace that Maharishi had predicted. On July 23, Reuters, Britain's international news service, carried a story with the headline, "Peace Breaking Out All Over the World." The story began by stating that "1988 appears to be shaping up as the year that peace broke out in some of the world's hottest trouble spots."

On July 29, *The Wall Street Journal* reported: "In trouble spots across the globe, some of the bitterest enemies, exhausted by their wars, suddenly are suing for peace." On July 30, *The Economist* had as its headline, "Oh, What a Peaceful World," and proclaimed, "Peace, you might say, is breaking out all over. . . . The Gulf war [between Iran and Iraq] is ending, Mr. Gorbachev's soldiers are pulling out of Afghanistan, a peace agreement seems likely in Angola, and maybe even one in Kampuchea, too. That is a fair chunk of the past decade's conflicts on the way to settlement." And on August 20, the world press announced that the cease-fire in the eight-year-old Iran-Iraq war had officially begun.

Prior to this, terrorism was already diminishing. In December, 1987, *Time* magazine reported: "Unless the situation suddenly

In the summer of 1988, the world press began to document the dramatic breakthrough in world peace that Maharishi had predicted.

Summary of the Results

NUMBER OF EXPERTS IN THE MAHARISHI TECHNOLOGY OF THE UNIFIED FIELD

Beginning on December 17, the size of the coherence creating group at MIU increased to over 6855, the square root of one percent of the world's population. *On January 6, the Taste of Utopia Assembly ended and the number of experts participating in the collective performance of the Maharishi Technology of the Unified Field fell far below the number needed to maintain coherence and positivity in world consciousness.*

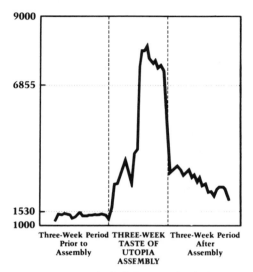

SOURCE: Capital of the Age of Enlightenment

INCREASED POSITIVITY OF EVENTS IN SITUATIONS OF INTERNATIONAL CONFLICT
Percent of Total Events as Rated for Degree of Conflict

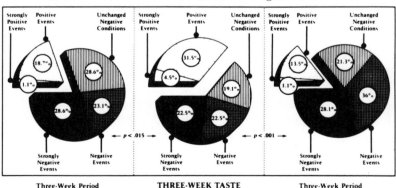

SOURCE: Content Analysis of *New York Times*

During the three-week period of the Taste of Utopia Assembly the balance of negativity to positivity in events pertaining to international conflicts in the trouble-spot areas of the world shifted significantly towards increased positivity. *After the Assembly the balance of events reverted towards increased negativity.*

■ **Figure 18.** This group of charts summarizes the results of 7000 people collectively practicing the TM-Sidhi program during the Taste of Utopia assembly.

of the Taste of Utopia Assembly

DECREASED TRAFFIC FATALITIES PER MILES DRIVEN—U.S.A.

Traffic Fatalities per Billion Miles Driven per Day over Christmas and New Year's Weekends

Traffic fatalities per day were at an all-time low over the Christmas and New Year's weekends during the Taste of Utopia Assembly, even though miles driven per day were at an all-time high, eliminating the possibility that the decrease was a consequence of fewer miles driven due to cold weather.

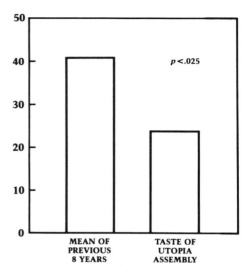

$p < .025$

MEAN OF PREVIOUS 8 YEARS

TASTE OF UTOPIA ASSEMBLY

SOURCE: National Safety Council, USA

INCREASED VITALITY AND POSITIVITY OF HEADS OF STATE
Percent of Events with Prior Negative Trends Rated for Reversal or Non-Reversal of Trend

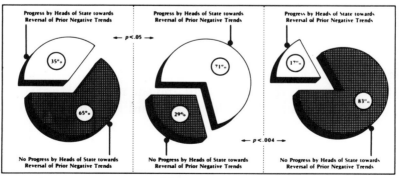

Progress by Heads of State towards Reversal of Prior Negative Trends

$\leftarrow p < .05 \rightarrow$

$\leftarrow p < .004 \rightarrow$

No Progress by Heads of State towards Reversal of Prior Negative Trends

| Three-Week Period Prior to Assembly | THREE-WEEK TASTE OF UTOPIA ASSEMBLY | Three-Week Period After Assembly |

SOURCE: Content Analysis of *New York Times*

According to Maharishi's Absolute Theory of Government, government is the innocent mirror of the nation and the head of state reflects by his speech and actions the quality of national consciousness. During the Taste of Utopia Assembly, coherence increased in world consciousness as exhibited by more positive, evolutionary statements and actions of heads of state of nations throughout the world, and by more national and international support for their policies and leadership. *After the Assembly the quality of the statements and actions of heads of state and of the support they received reverted towards less positivity.*

changes, this year will go down as the safest from state-sponsored terrorism in more than 20 years."

Many experts agree that this sudden upsurge of world peace was a direct result of improved relations between the United States and the Soviet Union, epitomized by the success of the superpower summit in Moscow in June, 1988. At this historic event, President Reagan and General Secretary Gorbachev signed landmark agreements on arms control and several other key issues.[18] The spirit of the time was captured in President Reagan's request to Soviet officials to "tell the people of the deep feelings of friendship felt by us and by the people of our country towards them."

Maharishi explained that this sudden upsurge of harmony and peace in the world occurred because of the rise of the "nourishing power of natural law" in world consciousness as a result of the group practice of the Transcendental Meditation and TM-Sidhi program.[19]

The peaceful and progressive trend of world events in 1988 continued and increased in 1989. The friendly relationship between the superpowers grew steadily, with a growing emphasis on arms reductions; localized conflicts in many other areas continued to abate. President Bush's inaugural address called for a "kinder, gentler America," and he noted that a "fresh breeze" of freedom was blowing around the world. This was especially apparent in the extraordinary changes in attitude in the leadership of the Soviet Union, which have fostered growing economic and political freedoms for its citizens, and also in that country's relationships with the countries of Eastern Europe. The most dramatic evidence of growing freedom in the world was the dismantling of the Berlin Wall and the move toward the reunification of East and West Germany. Another sign of growing world consciousness was the increasing global focus on the quality of the environment. All these developments reflect the continuing rise in world consciousness as a result of large groups practicing the TM and TM-Sidhi program around the world.

Knowledge of the Total Potential of Natural Law Through Maharishi's Unified Field Based Education

Maharishi says, "The knowledge of today is the world of tomorrow. We need new knowledge to create a new world."[20] The

"The knowledge of today is the world of tomorrow. We need new knowledge to create a new world."
— Maharishi

knowledge of the unified field of natural law not only improves the life of the individual but, as we have seen in this chapter, promotes world peace. This knowledge of how life can be lived in accord with the total potential of natural law, provided by Maharishi's Unified Field Based Education, is the new knowledge that is now creating a new world.

Current education, which is based on modern science, focuses exclusively on the objects of knowledge, and thus provides only partial knowledge of natural law. This partial knowledge, for example of only the electronic and nuclear levels of nature's functioning, has improved the outer quality of life but has brought neither greater happiness to the individual nor harmony to the family of nations.

Today, the failure of modern science based education to provide knowledge of the total potential of natural law has created a dangerous imbalance in life. For the individual, this can make life seem meaningless and undirected, and constantly threatened by the destructive capability of modern technology. The proverb "a little knowledge is a dangerous thing" is an appropriate commentary on this situation: partial knowledge of natural law has given us the means for our own destruction at the same time as it has given us the means to explore the stars.

The laws of nature govern all progress and evolution. According to Maharishi, when people do not act in accord with natural law, progress is restricted and stress accumulates in the collective consciousness of society, the nation, and the world. This build-up of stress in collective consciousness is the cause of all problems in society, including social unrest, terrorism, and national and international conflicts. When stress builds up to an extreme degree, it inevitably bursts out in violence and conflict.[21] Maharishi states that because the whole world's population has continued to violate the laws of nature, tension and conflict have been common for thousands of years of recorded history.[22]

Why do people violate natural law? Only because of lack of knowledge — knowledge of the total potential of natural law. It is the responsibility of the educational system to train students to think and act spontaneously in accord with natural law so that at least they do not cause problems for themselves or for others. Because the current systems of education have not included the

"**Now that the self-interaction of the unified field has been discovered as the most fundamental activity in nature, it is time for a new basis to education.**"
— **Maharishi**

knowledge and experience of the unified field of natural law in their curricula, the individual has inevitably continued to violate natural law, resulting in the accumulation of stress in society.

Traditionally, education has incorporated the latest discoveries of modern science so that students can gain the most up-to-date knowledge. Now that modern science has glimpsed the total potential of natural law in the unified field, and now that Maharishi has provided the complete knowledge and direct experience of the unified field, education can fulfill its responsibility of producing individuals able to fulfill their own desires without making mistakes or causing suffering to others.

Maharishi declares that now is the time for modern science based education to be raised to Unified Field Based Education so every student can live in accord with the total potential of natural law:

> Education is always progressive. When any new discovery about nature's functioning is gained through modern science, it is immediately incorporated in education. This has been the basis of progress in every generation. Now that the self-interaction of the unified field has been discovered as the most fundamental activity in nature, it is time for a new basis to education. The discovery of the unified field is an immensely important area of scientific research that opens a new gate to life, to society and its administration, to economics, to all aspects of man's life everywhere. It is time for science-based education to become Unified Field Based Education.[23]

In Chapter Nine, we will see how Maharishi's Unified Field Based Education is implemented in higher education at Maharishi International University. We will discuss how the system of education at MIU produces graduates who are not only specialists in their fields, but who are simultaneously living the wholeness of life, life in accord with the total potential of natural law. We will also examine in more detail how MIU's Super Radiance is playing a key role in creating coherence in world consciousness.

C H A P T E R   N I N E

Maharishi International University: Higher Education for Higher Consciousness

The success of Maharishi International University will be measured by its direct and indirect effects on the quality of life everywhere. We will count ourselves successful only when the problems of today's world are substantially reduced and eventually eliminated and the educational institutions of every country are capable of producing fully developed citizens.[1] —*Maharishi*

THE 181 GRADUATES OF MAHARISHI INTERNATIONAL UNIversity, in white and gold caps and gowns, file onto the stage in the Maharishi Patanjali Golden Dome of Pure Knowledge to receive their bachelor's, master's and doctoral diplomas in 15 different fields of study. The students taking part in this 14th commencement radiate an inner self-confidence and glow that reflect their years of one-pointed dedication to their studies, to gaining enlightenment, and to creating world peace. This graduating class is truly international — over half the students come from foreign countries, including Australia, Germany, France, Israel, Panama, Barbados, and Hong Kong.

By all accounts this class can be considered extraordinary. Not only have these students excelled in their academic work and made great strides in their personal development, but they have accomplished something that no other graduating class can claim, declares the commencement speaker, Dr. Robert Keith Wallace, Trustee and Founding President of MIU. "No other graduating class can claim that it was the underlying force

■ Maharishi International University (MIU) occupies a 262-acre campus in Fairfield, Iowa. MIU is accredited by the North Central Association of Colleges and Schools and offers 16 undergraduate, 10 master's and 6 doctoral degree programs.

responsible for the greatest breakthrough in international relations at this most crucial time in history."

The commencement took place only weeks after the historic summit between President Reagan and General Secretary Gorbachev in Moscow in June 1988, and Dr. Wallace was referring to the new spirit of goodwill between the United States and the Soviet Union. He said that Maharishi attributed this turn of events to the increased coherence in national and world consciousness resulting from the Super Radiance program at MIU.

The same point was also made by MIU president Dr. Bevan

Morris, in his July 1988 President's Report:

> Maharishi has attributed this change in global relationships — perhaps the most historic in living memory — to the indomitable influence of positivity, harmony, and coherence created by the more than 2,500 TM-Sidhi Yogic Flyers living in the MIU community, through their group practice of the Transcendental Meditation and TM-Sidhi program in MIU's Golden Domes.[2]

■ Through the MIU Super Radiance Program — the collective practice of the Transcendental Meditation and TM-Sidhi program — the graduates of MIU, representing more than 50 countries, have participated in achieving world peace.

Maharishi International University occupies a 262-acre campus in Fairfield, Iowa. It is accredited by the North Central Association of Colleges and Schools and offers 16 undergraduate majors in a wide range of subjects, including physics, chemistry, mathematics, business administration, computer science, electronic engineering, literature, art and the Science of Creative Intelligence. MIU's Graduate School offers 10 master's and 6 doctoral degrees in such areas as physics, physiology, psychology, professional writing, teacher education, fine arts, business administration, and the Science of Creative Intelligence. The MIU curriculum provides the leading edge of knowledge from each discipline in the light of the knowledge of the unified field, preparing students for doctoral level work and successful professional careers. MIU graduates have been accepted to Harvard, Yale, the University of Chicago, Columbia University, and Johns Hopkins, among others.

When you visit the MIU campus, you see something that immediately sets MIU well apart from all other universities, large or small, private or public: the large Golden Domes in the center of the campus. What goes on in these domes represents not only the heart of the university's curriculum but the heart of its mission in the world.

At MIU, all students practice Maharishi's Transcendental Meditation technique, and most practice the advanced TM-Sidhi program (students who do not already participate in the TM-Sidhi program upon enrollment usually learn it as part of a special course during their first year or two). Together with the faculty and staff, they practice this program twice daily as a large group in the Golden Domes. In fact, concurrently with their other courses, all MIU students are automatically enrolled in an ongoing course called Research in Consciousness, for which they receive academic credit; their twice-daily practice in the Golden Domes constitutes the "work" for this course.

This course represents the "laboratory component" for all other courses offered at the university. It is the laboratory component because it gives direct experience of the field of pure intelligence, the unified field of natural law, supplementing the theoretical study of Maharishi's Science of Creative Intelligence. As we have seen in previous chapters, Maharishi's Transcendental Meditation technique improves students' ability to learn and develops their creative potential. And as we saw in Chapter Eight, students at MIU and Maharishi Upper School participate in Maharishi's Transcendental Meditation and TM-Sidhi program for more than personal reasons — they do so to create world peace. Through the Super Radiance program (the collective practice of the TM and TM-Sidhi program), they are directly participating in Maharishi's Program to Create World Peace. By doing little more than going about the ordinary business of being students, they are helping to achieve a goal that not even the greatest leaders in modern history have been able to achieve.

In this chapter, we will examine MIU's success in promoting student development and the quality of life of society. In the first part, we will discuss how MIU is unfolding students' full potential through Unified Field Based Education. Then we will see how the collective practice of Maharishi's Transcendental Meditation and TM-Sidhi program is improving the quality of life of the United States and the world. The founding goals of MIU will also be discussed, showing how MIU is bringing enlightenment and fulfillment to all areas of society around the world. Then, in the final chapter, we will present Maharishi's supreme target for humanity — the creation of Heaven on Earth.

Producing Fully Developed Individuals

Most educators agree that the main purpose of higher education should be to develop the student as a full human being. Professor Allan Bloom, author of the recent best-selling book on higher education, *The Closing of the American Mind*, states: "These are the charmed years when [the student] can, if he so chooses, become anything he wishes and when he has the opportunity to survey his alternatives, not merely those current in his time or provided by careers, but those available to him as a human being. . . . In looking at him we are forced to reflect on what he should learn if he is to be called educated; we must speculate on what the human potential to be fulfilled is."[3]

However, even with their good intentions, today's educators have not been successful in developing the student as a full human being. Professor Bloom explains that the student who says, "I am a whole human being. Help me to form myself in wholeness and let me develop my real potential," is the one to whom the universities "have nothing to say." He emphasizes that higher education today fails to nurture the self-knowledge that is the basis for serious, humane learning.[4]

At the basis of MIU's approach to education is what is missing from higher education today — complete knowledge of the knower. The essential nature of the knower is not his or her physical body or changing thoughts and attitudes. The student's essential nature is pure consciousness, which is experienced during the practice of Maharishi's Transcendental Meditation technique. In discussing the nature of the knower in an address to the American Association for Higher Education, Maharishi stated:

> When we say "knower" we mean consciousness, one's consciousness, the Self within, or the awareness. Whatever knowledge we gain, through perception, through action, through hearing, all these impulses of information enter our senses and reach somewhere deep within us on the level of our awareness, on the level of our conscious mind, on the level where the emotions fall — in short, on the level of consciousness. That is how the knower gains knowledge. The TM technique brings one's awareness to that level of consciousness, so one may know in totality what the knower is. This direct experience of

the knower eliminates the ignorance of the knower and eliminates the lack of basis of all knowledge.[5]

Higher education has not been successful in giving students
complete knowledge of their own essential nature. In the process of studying the various academic fields of knowledge —
physics, biology, literature, etc. — students are left unaware of
the basis of these seemingly diverse disciplines, the field of pure
intelligence, pure consciousness. Maharishi explains:

> The arts, the sciences, the humanities — all have a place — but
> acquiring information about different fields does not open to
> conscious awareness the full value of the knower, which alone
> is the basis of all knowledge. . . . The essential characteristic of
> the knower is pure intelligence, and it is that unmanifest field
> of pure creative intelligence which alone is the fountainhead
> of all knowledge."[6]

The strength of the educational system at MIU is that the entire 44-week school year (about two months longer than most other
colleges) is directed toward developing higher states of consciousness in every student. In each course at MIU, starting with the first-
year core curriculum and continuing throughout the student's academic major and on into the graduate programs, every lesson is
structured to enliven the student's self-referral state of consciousness, which is the basis for unfolding full human potential.

The First-Year Core Curriculum: A Vision of All Disciplines in Light of Maharishi's Science of Creative Intelligence

In their freshman year, all students begin by taking a four-
week course in Maharishi's Science of Creative Intelligence,
consisting of 33 videotaped lectures by Maharishi. The course
examines in detail the principles that promote the development
of creative intelligence in the life of the student and in society.[7]
Like all other courses at MIU, the SCI course is offered on a
block system, whereby students focus on one course at a time.

Following this course, all first-year students take a sequence
of 24 core courses that integrate the most profound principles of
each academic discipline with the knowledge of Maharishi's
Science of Creative Intelligence. As with all MIU courses, the
central aim of these core courses is the personal development of

**"The arts, the sciences, the humanities — all have a place — but acquiring information about different fields does not open to conscious awareness the full value of the knower, which alone is the basis of all knowledge."
— Maharishi**

the student. Maharishi explains that this is practically achieved by giving students in their first year of college a vision of all the disciplines of science, art, and the humanities and showing every discipline as emerging from the unified field, which they experience as their self-referral state of consciousness during the practice of Transcendental Meditation.[8]

Through this integrated approach to knowledge, Maharishi emphasizes that "every discipline becomes a means to develop the creative potential of the conscious mind, to enliven the Self":

> Whatever the students study in the process of gaining specific knowledge of different subjects, they grow in the awareness that the center of all knowledge is present within themselves. This means that if they study 30 different disciplines, then 30 times the Self is connected with the discipline, and with this, all the knowledge remains connected with the knower.
>
> Since the Self is the unified field of all the laws of nature, the intellect becomes more and more surcharged with the totality of knowledge. The conscious mind becomes fully alert and lively in creative intelligence, more familiar with the total potential of natural law. . . .[9]

Instead of being lost in the wilderness of knowledge, as most first-year students are at other colleges, MIU students are becoming more "at home" with all knowledge. At the same time they are also experiencing the growing connection between the various streams of knowledge and their own Self. The result of this fully integrated approach is that the first-year students immediately begin to enjoy the fruit of all knowledge — the ability to accomplish anything, and spontaneously to think and act free from mistakes.[10]

Because of the importance placed upon this first-year core curriculum, the senior faculty are responsible for teaching these courses. During the core courses, the faculty teach the most profound, up-to-date principles of their field, and connect them to the unified field of natural law, the field of pure consciousness. For example, in the core course "Literature and SCI: Expressions of the Unified Field," Dr. Rhoda Orme-Johnson discusses how the writer's level of consciousness, as viewed from the perspective of Maharishi's seven states of consciousness, determines the quality of what is written, its universality, and its

**"Whatever the students study in the process of gaining specific knowledge of different subjects, they grow in the awareness that the center of all knowledge is present within themselves."
— Maharishi**

range of influence. She also examines how the various literary techniques affect the reader's consciousness and physiology.

In Dr. Bruce Lester's course "Computers and SCI: Full Awakening of the Cosmic Computer," students learn how the principles of computer science reflect the dynamical properties of the unified field of natural law. He expands the traditional focus of computer science to include not only electronic computing, but all computational processes in nature. Nature's cosmic computer is the unified field, which computes all activity in the universe in the most orderly and perfect manner. Relating this to the student, Dr. Lester explains that the hardware of the cosmic computer is the human brain, which, when properly cultured by Maharishi's TM and TM-Sidhi program, gains access to the cosmic computer and thus can accomplish anything. Following are the titles of some of the other first-year core courses:

- Physics and SCI: The Unified Field of Natural Law
- Astronomy and SCI: The Range of the Universe: from Point to Infinity
- Writing and SCI: Discovering and Expressing Knowledge in the Field of Language
- Education and SCI: Unifying Knower, Known, and Process of Knowing
- Mathematics and SCI: Locating the Foundation of Mathematics in the Field of Pure Intelligence
- Art and SCI: Images of Consciousness
- Neurophysiology and SCI: The Neurophysiology of Enlightenment
- Music and SCI: The Dynamics of Wholeness

"I have become so much stronger since coming to MIU — physically, mentally, and emotionally — because the whole program is centered around inner development."
— MIU student

Students have commented on the effectiveness of the first-year program in promoting their personal growth. "I have become so much stronger since coming to MIU — physically, mentally, and emotionally," one student says, "because the whole program is centered around inner development." Students report that they feel more "at home" with knowledge, perceive more of a unified basis to knowledge, and see the knowledge they learn as personally relevant. "One often sees everything in life as separate, but SCI demonstrates that there is a unity," says another student. "It shows that there is something inside us that relates to every area of life."

An MIU Education: The Interrelationship of the Unity and Diversity of Knowledge

It is common for universities to offer an array of majors in the sciences, arts, humanities, and vocational training. Over the past two decades, there has been a substantial increase in the number of majors, due primarily to the expansion in vocational training. According to a recent report by the Association of American Colleges, this proliferation of majors especially in the vocational and technical fields "has blinded institutions and students to the ephemeral nature of much that is contained in the new majors. In the meantime, students are being short-changed, denied the intellectual experiences that will enable them to comprehend their world and to live in it freely, courageously, happily, and responsibly."[11]

With the emphasis today on developing specialized knowledge and skills, universities are failing to give students a coherent and unified view of knowledge. This, according to Professor Bloom, is the main reason we now experience a crisis in higher education:

> The crisis in liberal education is a reflection of a crisis at the peaks of learning, an incoherence and incompatibility among the first principles with which we interpret the world, an intellectual crisis of the greatest magnitude, which constitutes the crisis of our civilization. . . . Liberal education flourished when it prepared the way for discussion of a unified view of nature and man's place in it, which the best minds debated on the highest level. It decayed when what lay beyond it were only specialities, the premises of which do not lead to any such vision.[12]

Unlike other universities, which are experiencing the crisis that Bloom describes, MIU gives its students a thorough education in the traditional academic disciplines *along with* the direct experience and complete intellectual understanding of the unified state of knowledge—the unified field of all the laws of nature. With the intellectual knowledge of Maharishi's Science of Creative Intelligence, students know how unity transforms itself into diversity through the mechanics of self-referral, the first principle of nature's functioning.

They see how all the diversified knowledge contained in the academic disciplines is just the expression of one fundamental, field—the unified field—which is the source of both nature's

With the intellectual knowledge of Maharishi's Science of Creative Intelligence, students know how unity transforms itself into diversity through the mechanics of self-referral, the first principle of nature's functioning.

activity and human thought and behavior. And through the practice of Maharishi's Transcendental Meditation technique, students directly experience the unified field of all the laws of nature, which they find to be nothing other than their own self-referral state of consciousness. Through the knowledge and experience of the unified field, MIU students structure the home of all knowledge in their awareness while learning the specialized knowledge of their academic majors.

In MIU's undergraduate and graduate courses — usually taught in four-week blocks — the MIU faculty use the same SCI-based teaching methods used at Maharishi School (see Chapter Four). This serves to connect the specialized knowledge of each discipline to the unified source of all knowledge. By emphasizing this connection, MIU has set an example of what a university should be.

While specialized knowledge is certainly a necessity in our age, it is also important to give students a framework that unifies all aspects of knowledge.

While specialized knowledge is certainly a necessity in our age, it is also important to give students a framework that unifies all aspects of knowledge. The theoretical and practical aspects of Maharishi's Science of Creative Intelligence establish an intimate connection between knower and knowledge — structuring the home of all knowledge in each student's awareness.

The original MIU catalogue states:

> At MIU all fields of knowledge are viewed as expressions of the basic field of existence, pure creative intelligence. By developing within each student the subjective field of pure creative intelligence and by conceptually locating pure creative intelligence as the basis of all fields of knowledge, the curri-culum at MIU provides a bridge, an intimate connection, between the knower and knowledge. This establishes the home of all knowledge on the level of the student's awareness, and for such a student no knowledge can be alien. It is by advancing the knowledge of the field of pure creative intelligence [the unified field] in all areas of thought, and at the same time providing that field as a concrete experience to all students, that the Science of Creative Intelligence fulfills the most necessary requirement of education sought by the world's great thinkers and provides the most significant ingredient of the word *university* — the continuous inter-relationship of unity and diversity.[13]

As a result of its unified field based integrated approach, MIU has gained a reputation in higher education as a leader in academic excellence and in developing higher states of consciousness. Dr. Louis Albert, Director of Special Projects for the American Association for Higher Education, observes:

> As a visitor to MIU, I have been impressed with the growth of the students. They go through a remarkable transformation. One is forced to ask, 'How do the students get to be this way?' MIU provides a rich traditional academic program like other schools, but what makes the difference at MIU is the unified field based approach.[14]

In commenting on the value of their own MIU education, graduates typically describe how it has contributed to their personal development. A graduating psychology major from Malaysia says: "Completing my psychology degree at MIU has given sufficient insight into human behavior to prepare me for a career in human resource management. I have understood and experienced that human consciousness is the fundamental resource of any enterprise." An elementary school teacher in Pennsylvania who graduated from MIU comments: "MIU has changed my life dramatically and shaped me gently into the person I am today. All aspects of my life have grown and prospered." Another MIU graduate, employed at a computer products marketing firm in New Jersey, says: "The single most important thing I gained at MIU was growth of consciousness. Generally, I have gained stability, happiness, a feeling of being at home in any situation."

The results of a recent alumni survey conducted by MIU's Office of Evaluation showed that 92 percent feel that their education has contributed markedly to their physical and mental health (compared to the norm of 26 percent). Also 80 percent reported that it has contributed to their working cooperatively in a group (compared to the norm of 40 percent); 71 percent that it has helped them develop leadership skills (compared to the norm of 35 percent); 73 percent that it has promoted their understanding of scientific principles and methods (compared to the norm of 29 percent); 79 percent that it is has enriched their understanding of different philosophies and cultures (compared to the norm of 36 percent) and 87 percent that it has contributed to their understanding of the interaction of man and his environment (compared to the norm of 27 percent).[15]

Research studies further indicate how MIU fosters student

"As a visitor to MIU, I have been impressed with the growth of the students. They go through a remarkable transformation. One is forced to ask, 'How do the students get to be this way?'"
— Visiting educator

■ Figure 19.
Significant increases
in both intellectual
ability and field
independence — an
indication of broader
comprehension and an
improved ability to
focus — were found in
MIU students during
their undergraduate
education

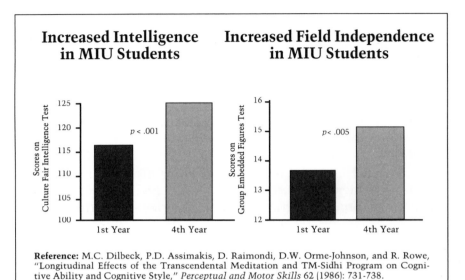

Reference: M.C. Dilbeck, P.D. Assimakis, D. Raimondi, D.W. Orme-Johnson, and R. Rowe, "Longitudinal Effects of the Transcendental Meditation and TM-Sidhi Program on Cognitive Ability and Cognitive Style," *Perceptual and Motor Skills* 62 (1986): 731-738.

development. MIU students exhibit higher levels of moral reasoning ability, and greater psychological well-being compared to students from other colleges. They also show significant increases in intelligence, field independence, social maturity, and psychological health during the four years of their undergraduate training. Other research shows that MIU students who learn Maharishi's TM-Sidhi program display improved concept learning ability, increased flexibility of the central nervous system, and increased orderliness of brain functioning over the course of a few months.[16]

Dr. Bevan Morris summarizes the success of MIU's system of education:

> At MIU all traditional disciplines are studied in the light of SCI. This holistic science gives students the knowledge that all the impulses of natural law are structured in the unified unmanifest nonchanging field of consciousness, and gives students the direct experience of this unified field as the simplest, least excited state of their own awareness.
>
> With the addition of this knowledge to the traditional curriculum, our students have achieved not only outstanding academic success but have grown in the qualities of enlightenment — greater happiness, integrity, creativity, inner freedom, and more

ideal social behavior. Their lives are marked by greater vigor, balance, harmony, and responsibility. They have fulfilled the ideal of education in the experience of complete knowledge of the knower — pure consciousness — the Self.[17]

As we mentioned at the beginning of the chapter, the heart of MIU's curriculum is the experience of the unified field of natural law, the self-referral state of consciousness, through the student's practice of Maharishi's Transcendental Meditation and TM-Sidhi program. Together with the intellectual knowledge of how the unified field gives rise to all the diversified values of natural law throughout creation, the TM and TM-Sidhi program promotes the development of higher states of consciousness in students.

The goal of this development is the state of unity consciousness, in which the gulf between the knower and the object of knowing has been bridged. At this highest level of human development, every aspect of knowledge and every element of creation is perceived to be an expression of one's own Self.

Maharishi's Transcendental Meditation and TM-Sidhi program not only develops the student's full potential — when practiced collectively in large groups, it enriches the quality of life throughout the whole society.

Maharishi's Super Radiance Program: MIU as the Center of Organizing Power for the Nation and the World

The success of any government, explains Maharishi in his Absolute Theory of Government, depends on the degree of coherence in collective consciousness. "The government of any country, irrespective of its system — whether capitalist, communist, or any system — is governed by the collective consciousness of the nation," he says. "Whatever the quality of national consciousness, that will always be the quality of national government and national law. Therefore, it is the national consciousness that has to be made more coherent."[18]

Maharishi's Absolute Theory of Government further explains how a nation is governed by its collective consciousness:

National consciousness governs the activity of every nation in the same way that the consciousness of the individual governs the activity of the individual. Since national consciousness is the collective consciousness of all the individuals of the nation,

"With the addition of this knowledge to the traditional curriculum, our students have achieved not only outstanding academic success but have grown in the qualities of enlightenment — greater happiness, integrity, creativity, inner freedom, and more ideal social behavior."

— Dr. Bevan Morris, President of MIU

Maharishi explains that by collectively practicing the Transcendental Meditation and TM-Sidhi program, students can increase coherence in national consciousness and help create a more powerful and successful government.

it is ultimately the consciousness of the individual which is the prime mover of the nation and shapes its destiny. Every decision of government is the expression of national consciousness. Government is the pure and innocent mirror of the nation, faithfully reflecting whatever is presented to it.[19]

Maharishi explains that by collectively practicing the Transcendental Meditation and TM-Sidhi program, students can increase coherence in national consciousness and help create a more powerful and successful government: "The truth is that the well-being and progress of a nation depend upon the government, which in turn depends upon the quality of collective consciousness." By practicing the TM and TM-Sidhi program in their classes, he says, "students can radiate a powerful influence of coherence in national consciousness, which will create a powerful and successful government. Seen from this angle, the students are the basis of their government. While in the process of gaining knowledge, they can really create a powerful nation."[20] This is what is being accomplished at MIU.

In 1979, MIU started a program to create immediate, positive changes in the collective consciousness of the U.S. Since then, all MIU students, faculty, and staff, as well as the TM-Sidhas living in the surrounding community, have been participating in MIU's Super Radiance program — twice daily collective practice of the Transcendental Meditation and TM-Sidhi program.

The original goal of the Super Radiance program was to have at least 1600 people — approximately the square root of one percent of the U.S. population — practicing Maharishi's TM and TM-Sidhi program together in one place every day. As we described in Chapter Eight, this is the formula to increase the coherence in national consciousness. It was expected that this program would give a strong impetus to permanent world peace, and recent world events show that it has.

Effect of the MIU Super Radiance Program on the Actions of The Head of State, The Reflector of National Consciousness

Maharishi explains that the head of state of any government, as the leader of the nation, reflects national consciousness. We can see how coherent national consciousness is by looking at the leader's interactions with other leaders and his statements to the press.

In the last several years of his administration, President Reagan's statements about the Soviet Union became more cordial. Words of distrust and enmity were replaced by words of cooperation and friendship. This trend has continued in the Bush administration. These improved relations between the superpowers led to a marked decrease in regional and national conflicts throughout the world. The President's increasing cordiality to the Soviet Union was a direct reflection of growing coherence in collective consciousness in the United States through MIU's Super Radiance program.

To show more clearly the relationship between the number of participants in MIU's Super Radiance program and the quality of relations between the U.S. and the U.S.S.R., MIU Professor Paul Gelderloos and a team of researchers systematically analyzed the content of President Reagan's public statements towards the Soviet Union from April 4, 1985, to September 23, 1987. A total of 347 statements were prepared for content analysis from speeches, statements, interviews, proclamations, radio addresses, and remarks published in the *Weekly Compilation of Presidential Documents* by the Office of the Federal Register of the National Archives and Records Administration. (Content analysis is an objective approach to assessing written and spoken texts.) The results of their study indicate that there is a significant, positive relationship between large numbers of participants in the MIU Super Radiance program and improved relations between the superpowers, as reflected by the statements of President Reagan. Analysis showed that the number of MIU Super Radiance participants "led in time"— preceded — the improvements in U.S.-U.S.S.R. relations, suggesting a causal relationship.[21]

MIU Super Radiance Improves the Overall Quality of Life of the Nation

The increased coherence in collective consciousness resulting from collective practice of Maharishi's Transcendental Meditation and TM-Sidhi program at MIU is reflected in the results of other studies on the overall quality of life of the nation.

Figure 20 shows that after the MIU Super Radiance program began in 1979 there was a corresponding increase in the overall quality of life of the nation. The top figure shows that the U.S. quality of life, as measured by an index of 12 variables, was declining

■ Figure 20. The top figure shows that the U.S. quality of life, as measured by an index of 12 variables, was declining throughout the 1960s and early 1970s (dark line). The Maharishi Effect Index (light line) reflects the percentage of TM meditators in the U.S., and the group practice of the TM and TM-Sidhi program at MIU which comprised the MIU Super Radiance program. The declining trend in the U.S. quality of life began to reverse in 1975 after a large increase in the number (225,000) of people practicing the TM technique in the United States. After MIU started its Super Radiance program in 1979, the improvement in the quality of life began to accelerate to an unprecedented rate of improvement.

The bottom figure shows that the improvement in quality of life was even more striking in Iowa, the state in which the MIU Super Radiance program is located, compared to improvements in the U.S. as a whole.

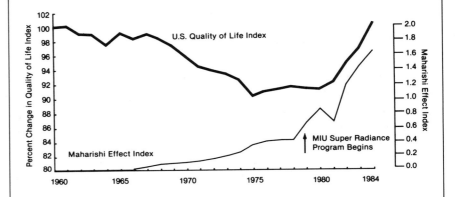

Reference: D.W. Orme-Johnson and P. Gelderloos, "The Long-term Effects of the Maharishi Technology of the Unified Field on the Quality of Life of the United States (1960 to 1983)," in *Scientific Research on the Transcendental Meditation and TM-Sidhi Programme: Collected Papers,* Vol. 3, eds. R.A. Chalmers, G. Clements, H. Schenkluhn, and M. Weinless (Vlodrop, The Netherlands: Maharishi European Research University Press), in press.

throughout the 1960s and early 1970s (dark line). The Maharishi Effect Index (light line) reflects the percentage of TM meditators in the U.S., and the number of people participating in the MIU Super Radiance program. The declining trend in the U.S. quality of life began to reverse in 1975 after a large increase in the number of TM meditators (225,000) in the United States. After MIU started its Super Radiance program in 1979, the improvement in national quality of life began to accelerate at an unprecedented rate.[22]

A closer look at the graph reveals that the largest improvement in the quality of national life occurred in 1982, 1983, and 1984, coinciding with a sharp rise in the number of TM-Sidhas collectively practicing the TM and TM-Sidhi program at MIU. The lower figure shows that the improvement in quality of life was even more striking in Iowa, the state in which the MIU Super Radiance program is located, compared to improvements in the U.S. as a whole.

Research conducted by Dr. Kenneth Cavanaugh also shows that the economic "misery index" — defined as the sum of the monthly inflation rate and unemployment rate — substantially decreased in the United States between 1979 and 1987.[23] Figure 21 shows the largest decreases in the misery index for both the United States and Canada when the Super Radiance numbers in MIU's Golden Domes were greater than 1700 (approximately the square root of one percent of the combined population of the U.S. and Canada). The misery index also decreased dramatically when only 1500 to 1700 people participated in the Super Radiance program. Smaller, although still statistically significant, decreases in the misery index occurred when the numbers were between 1100 and 1500. This study shows that reduced inflation and unemployment in the United States and even in Canada were associated with an increase in the size of the Super Radiance group at MIU.

Using time-series analysis of monthly data, other studies show that the leading economic indicators increased and notifiable diseases, auto fatalities, and homicides decreased when the MIU Super Radiance program exceeded the square root of one percent of the nation's population.[24] These studies show that many of the improvements in the quality of life in the United States were related to times when there were high numbers in

■ Figure 21. During the period from April 1979 to January 1987, the sum of the monthly inflation rate and unemployment rate (the "misery" index) substantially decreased in the U.S. and Canada during and following months when more than 1500 people participated in the group practice of the TM and TM-Sidhi program.

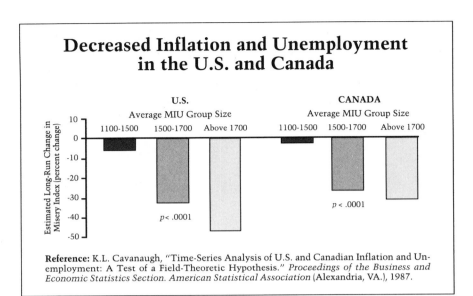

Decreased Inflation and Unemployment in the U.S. and Canada

Reference: K.L. Cavanaugh, "Time-Series Analysis of U.S. and Canadian Inflation and Unemployment: A Test of a Field-Theoretic Hypothesis." *Proceedings of the Business and Economic Statistics Section. American Statistical Association* (Alexandria, VA.), 1987.

the MIU Super Radiance program.[25]

The above research illustrates the principle that by directly enlivening the total potential of nature's functioning at the level of the unified field through the collective practice of Maharishi's TM and TM-Sidhi program, it is possible to successfully handle the collective consciousness of the nation and the whole world. MIU's target is now to establish a permanent community of 7000 TM-Sidhas — the square root of one percent of the *world's* population — to accelerate and stabilize the growth of coherence in national and world consciousness.

The Seven Goals of MIU

Maharishi founded MIU to offer the knowledge that will create a new world — a Heaven on Earth. According to Dr. Robert Keith Wallace, MIU's founding president, seven "admittedly ambitious but necessary and now attainable goals" were established to guide the activities of MIU and accomplish this purpose.[26] These goals are:

1. To develop the full potential of the individual.
2. To realize the highest ideal of education.
3. To improve governmental achievements.

4. To solve the age-old problem of crime and all behavior that brings unhappiness to the family of man.
5. To bring fulfillment to the economic aspirations of individuals and society.
6. To maximize the intelligent use of the environment.
7. To achieve the spiritual goals of mankind in this generation.

As you can see, MIU has come far in achieving these goals. Its educational system has been shown to be effective in developing the full potential of the student. And through its Super Radiance program, MIU has dramatically increased the level of coherence in national and world consciousness. Crime and accident rates have dropped significantly, economic conditions have improved, and trust in our government has increased. Most importantly for the security of the world, relations between the two superpowers have improved dramatically.

In addition to these accomplishments, new breakthroughs in knowledge are being achieved by the MIU faculty that are helping to create a better world. During the past several years, MIU faculty members have made major research discoveries in such areas as biochemistry, neuroscience, physics, laser optics, sociology, psychology, preventive health, and computer science. They have been awarded major government and large foundation grants for cancer-related research in molecular biology and for research in developmental neurobiology and hypertension.

By investigating the deep structures of natural law through their scientific research and connecting the fundamental theories of their disciplines to the unified field of natural law, MIU faculty are creating new knowledge that will bring fulfillment to every area of life. Through their scholarly and professional activities, the MIU faculty are creating the ground for all human suffering to be eliminated and for life to be lived in peace and happiness. The MIU faculty's research is being published in leading journals in every field and in MIU's interdisciplinary journal, *Modern Science and Vedic Science*. The faculty have also recently been developing curricula for all disciplines, professions, and trades to bring perfection to every area of society through the application of the Science and Technology of the Unified Field.

By incorporating the practice of Maharishi's Transcendental Meditation and TM-Sidhi program and the knowledge of SCI into their curricula, all educational institutions can become capable of producing fully-developed citizens, while at the same time radiating coherence throughout the nation and world. MIU offers a model for how a university can simultaneously develop higher states of consciousness in its students, promote academic excellence, and improve the quality of life in society.

Dr. Morris summarizes the role that higher education should play in developing enlightened students and creating Heaven on Earth:

> Higher education should be for higher consciousness. Higher education should not be dedicated only to some fragmented knowledge of the laws of nature, such as that offered by the traditional scientific disciplines, but to enlightenment, the permanently established experience of that universal state of consciousness from which all the laws of nature arise. Truly educated people cease to violate the laws of nature, and thus cease to create problems and suffering for themselves and their surroundings. Gaining the support of natural law for their every endeavor, they are a joy to themselves and a joy to their environment. At MIU we are educating such individuals to go out to be the lighthouses of enlightenment for the whole society.[27]

C H A P T E R   T E N

Education for Creating Heaven on Earth

The heavenly life enjoyed at Maharishi International University and Maharishi School of the Age of Enlightenment in Fairfield has been a major source of inspiration for Maharishi in his inauguration of the Master Plan to Create Heaven on Earth. The MIU community is increasingly enjoying a life of heavenly bliss, and possesses all the amenities for life to be heavenly in every respect.[1]
— *Dr. Bevan Morris, President*
of Maharishi International University

AS WE HAVE SEEN THROUGHOUT THIS BOOK, THE STUdents at Maharishi School of the Age of Enlightenment and Maharishi International University are unique in the world today. They are receiving an education that is rapidly developing their consciousness and providing a basis for their success and achievement at all levels of their lives. In their thinking and behavior they are developing a high degree of self-confidence, self-reliance, and organizing power. In their relations with others, they are expressing the higher human values of compassion, kindness, love, and responsibility.

Most importantly, through their group practice of Maharishi's Transcendental Meditation and TM-Sidhi program, these students are creating increased coherence in national and world consciousness, which is resulting in an upsurge of peace and harmony among the family of nations.

"Through Proper Education We Can Accomplish Anything"

For Maharishi, the ultimate purpose of education is to create perfection in individual life and a heavenly quality of life for the

Maharishi has added something to education that even the most idealistic and far-reaching thinkers and educators in the past have lacked — a technology of consciousness that works from the most fundamental level of human life, nourishing life from its source and setting life in accord with natural law.

whole society. For centuries, wise men and women have dreamed of creating a better world. A rare few have envisioned an ideal world. But although many communities and even nations have been founded with the hope of creating a better life for their citizens, none has succeeded in fulfilling the idealistic vision at its basis.

Yet, as Maharishi says, "Through proper education we can accomplish anything." Maharishi has added something to education that even the most idealistic and far-reaching thinkers and educators in the past have lacked — a technology of consciousness that works from the most fundamental level of human life, nourishing life from its source and setting life in accord with natural law. On this basis, Heaven on Earth becomes not only possible, but inevitable.

Throughout the ages, "Heaven" has signified life in its most exalted, ideal state. Many cultures and religions have their own conceptions of heavenly life. The exact expressions may differ, but to everyone the word "Heaven" means "all good everywhere and non-good nowhere," to use Maharishi's words.[2]

Maharishi explains: "Transcendental consciousness, pure consciousness — that is the field of Heaven. It's eternal bliss, immortality, perfect health, and that experience will create Heaven on Earth."[3]

Maharishi has described Heaven on Earth as it pertains to both the individual and society. For the individual, Heaven on Earth means "perfect health, long life in bliss, and the ability to fulfill one's desires." For society, Heaven on Earth "will be characterized by an indomitable influence of positivity, harmony, and peace on all levels of collective life — family, community, nation, and the world."[4]

Maharishi explains that by educating students and individuals in all fields of life to think and act according to natural law, Heaven on Earth — perfection in life — can be achieved:

> What is Heaven on Earth? It is perfect health, a perfect way of thinking, a perfect way of doing. A perfect way of thinking means every thought will be appropriate for the thinker and his surroundings, and appropriate thought results in appropriate action and appropriate behavior. We have that knowledge to train the whole of mankind to think spontaneously in accord with natural law, in favor of the evolution of life. When

thinking is always spontaneously evolutionary then there is Heaven for everyone. We have only to educate a man in the art of thinking and the science of behaving with the support of natural law. With the support of natural law, there is nothing which cannot be accomplished.[5]

According to Maharishi, education now has the knowledge necessary to create Heaven on Earth. This knowledge, Maharishi explains, "has its basis in the very nature of life, which is bliss eternal, and the nature of pure knowledge, which is ever lively in the self-referral state of everyone's consciousness."[6] Maharishi further explains that the "liveliness of the total potential of natural law is inscribed in the pure consciousness of everyone and easily available to everyone through Transcendental Meditation."[7]

As we saw in Chapter Eight, it is on the basis of enlivening the total potential of natural law through the TM and TM-Sidhi program that world peace has been achieved. And it is also through this educational technology of consciousness that Heaven on Earth will be created. Maharishi says, "World peace is the first step to creating Heaven on Earth, and having achieved quite a lot of the first step we are now making a supreme target — Heaven on Earth for all mankind."[8]

Maharishi's Master Plan to Create Heaven on Earth

On January 12, 1988, Maharishi inaugurated his Master Plan to Create Heaven on Earth. Maharishi's plan includes two main approaches for reconstructing the whole world — the glorification of inner and outer life. Maharishi's Master Plan to Create Heaven on Earth has its basis in the World Plan, which was inaugurated by Maharishi in 1972 to eliminate the age-old problems of mankind in this generation through teaching Transcendental Meditation and SCI throughout the world.[9] The goals of the World Plan are the same as the goals of MIU, given at the end of Chapter Nine. The global activities of Maharishi's World Plan have resulted in practical programs for the fulfillment of every area of society, including education, business, health, government, retired people, agriculture, law and rehabilitation, and defense. Dr. Morris, who has worked closely with Maharishi in preparing the Master Plan, explains that "the World Plan has created

"World peace is the first step to creating Heaven on Earth, and having achieved quite a lot of the first step we are now making a supreme target — Heaven on Earth for all mankind."
— Maharishi

To create Heaven on Earth, Maharishi has revived the precious technologies of ancient Vedic Science in their completeness.

waves of achievement year after year, culminating in the experience of bliss 24 hours a day. This experience has demonstrated to Maha-rishi the practicality of creating Heaven on Earth."[10]

The following chart summarizes at a glance Maharishi's Master Plan to Create Heaven on Earth through the inner and outer glorification of life.

The inner glorification of life is accomplished through Maharishi's Vedic Science. The practice of Maharishi's Transcendental Meditation technique, described in detail in Chapter Two, and the TM-Sidhi program, described in Chapter Eight, develop higher states of consciousness in the individual. "Higher states of consciousness" means a permanent state of bliss consciousness, so that, as Maharishi says, wherever one may be on earth one will always be in heaven.[11] Maharishi's Vedic Science also includes other techniques for glorifying inner life, some of which are described below.

To glorify outer life, Maharishi's Master Plan has two aspects. The first is constructing Maharishi Cities of Immortals and Ideal Villages. These will provide ideal living and working environments, free from noise, pollution, stress, and crime. They include not only all the amenities traditionally associated with the best planned communities, but also those necessary to live Heaven on Earth — Maharishi Schools of the Age of Enlightenment, offering ideal education; Maharishi Ayur-Ved Prevention Centers, for long life in bliss and perfect health; and Maharishi Festival Halls, with facilities for social, cultural, and educational programs. The second aspect is developing new economic and agricultural programs to create self-sufficiency for every nation and balance in global trade.[12]

Additional Technologies of Maharishi's Vedic Science to Create Heaven on Earth

To create Heaven on Earth, Maharishi has revived the precious technologies of ancient Vedic Science in their completeness. In addition to the Transcendental Meditation and TM-Sidhi program, Maharishi has also brought out other applied aspects of his Vedic Science, including Maharishi Ayur-Ved, the complete science of perfect health, and Maharishi Gandharva-Ved, the "eternal music of nature" that restores balance and harmony in the mind, body,

Maharishi's Master Plan To Create
Heaven On Earth
Reconstruction of the Whole World

 INNER   **OUTER**

GLORIFICATION OF INNER LIFE

- Development of higher states of consciousness
- Blossoming of noble qualities and bliss
- Gaining support of nature from within — happiness, peace, and fulfilling progress through

MAHARISHI'S TRANSCENDENTAL MEDITATION and TM-SIDHI PROGRAM
the Practical Aspect of
MAHARISHI'S VEDIC SCIENCE

which develops all the seven states of consciousness in the individual, and develops a perfect man with the ability to employ natural law to work for him and achieve anything he wants.

The seven states of consciousness are:

- Waking — *Jagrat Chetna*
- Dreaming — *Swapn Chetna*
- Sleeping — *Sushupti Chetna*
- Transcendental Consciousness — *Turya Chetna*
- Cosmic Consciousness — *Turyateet Chetna*
- God Consciousness — *Bhagavat Chetna*
- Unity Consciousness — *Brahmi Chetna* — awakening of the pure nature of consciousness to its own self-referral reality — the unified reality of the diversified universe — which renders individual life to be a lively field of all possibilities — infinite organizing power of the unified field of natural law spontaneously upholding individual life.

GLORIFICATION OF OUTER LIFE

- **Building Ideal Villages, Towns, and Cities** based on **Maharishi Sthapatya-Ved** — the science of building in accord with natural law — to create a beautiful and healthy environment free of pollution, noise, and stress so that everyone feels, "I am living in Heaven."
- **Creating Global Green Revolution** — farming all the unfarmed lands in the world using the scientific principles of **Maharishi Vedic Farming** to produce naturally grown, healthy food to achieve food **self-sufficiency** in every country.
- **Achieving global eradication of poverty** and acheiving economic self-sufficiency in every nation through Maharishi's programs to develop agriculture, forestry, mining, and industry in every country.
- **Realizing Global Rural Development and Urban Renewal** — providing better living conditions for an integrated life for the rich and poor throughout the world.
- **Achieving economic balance** in the world family through **Maharishi Global Trading.**
- **Achieving ideal education** through **Maharishi's Vedic Science**, which offers the **fruit of all knowledge** to everyone — life free from mistakes and suffering.
- **Achieving perfect health** for everyone and every nation through prevention-oriented **Maharishi Ayur-Ved.**
- **Achieving coherence, harmony, and balance in nature** for everyone and every nation through **Maharishi Gandharva-Ved.**
- Achieving **invincible defense** for every nation through**Maharishi Dhanur-Ved**, which will disallow the birth of an enemy.
- **Achieving perfect government** in every country modeled on nature's government, which silently governs through natural law from the unified level of all the laws of nature — the common basis of all creation, the unseen, prime mover of life, eternally fully awake within itself and available to everyone on the level of one's own self-referral consciousness — transcendental consciousness.
- **Achieving the rise of a supremely nourishing power in the world**, which will unrestrictedly uphold the power of evolution in nature, eliminating all destructive tendencies and negative trends in the world. As a result, every nation will lovingly own every other nation and all the nations together will nourish every nation — everyone and every nation in the world will enjoy Heaven on Earth.

This is a summary of the 1,500-page book, *Maharishi's Master Plan to Create Heaven on Earth*.

"Ayur-Ved, being
an aspect of the
total science of
life, is the
scientific means
for prevention of
disease, preserva-
tion of health,
and promotion
of longevity."
— Maharishi

behavior, and environment. These technologies complement and support the benefits of Maharishi's TM and TM-Sidhi program.

Maharishi Ayur-Ved

The goal of Maharishi Ayur-Ved is to restore mind and body to a state of wholeness and perfect health. The goal of Ayur-Ved, the world's oldest scientific system of natural medicine, is to preserve health and promote longevity. Working with the world's foremost experts in Ayur-Ved, Maharishi has revived Ayur-Ved as a complete science of health. According to Maharishi:

> Ayur-Ved is an aspect of Ved, an aspect of that science which is holistic in nature and which alone in the world is competent to deal with the holistic value of life. Ayur-Ved, being an aspect of the total science of life, is the scientific means for prevention of disease, preservation of health, and promotion of longevity.
>
> Ayur-Ved achieves these purposes through knowledge of the impulses of intelligence or consciousness which have taken some material form. Through knowledge of the infinitely balancing impulses of intelligence . . ., Ayur-Ved provides a cure for any imbalance that has developed in the body. . . .
>
> The knowledge contained in Ayur-Ved of restoring balance to an imbalanced state is from that absolute state of knowledge about how self-referral consciousness assumes material form. In Ayur-Ved this total knowledge of life is made practical for the sake of maintaining health.[13]

Dr. Deepak Chopra, President of the Maharishi Ayur-Ved Association of America and former Chief of Staff at New England Memorial Hospital, explains the value of Maharishi Ayur-Ved for promoting health and longevity:

> It should be possible to maintain the body indefinitely in a youthful, disease-free condition. We simply need to rewrite the blueprint or program through which the body is created. If we can operate from that finest level of consciousness, where consciousness separates into Rishi [knower], Devata [process of knowing], and Chhandas [known], we can do anything with the body, because at this level we experience nature's elementary particles as impulses of our consciousness. We can revitalize it, reenergize it, recreate it it, renew it.[14]

In total, there are 20 approaches of Maharishi Ayur-Ved that work on the levels of consciousness, physiology, behavior, and environment to create and maintain perfect health. These 20 approaches include Maharishi's Transcendental Meditation and TM-Sidhi program, individually prescribed dietary programs, herbal supplements that help restore balance in the mind and body (*rasayanas*); neuromuscular integration and neurorespiratory programs; and the Maharishi Ayur-Ved Panchakarma program (physiotherapeutic treatments that help eliminate impurities from the body).[15] Dr. Deepak Chopra's new best-selling book, *Perfect Health* (published by Harmony Books, a division of Crown Publishers, Inc.) provides a useful guide to Maharishi Ayur-Ved programs.

Research indicates that participants in Maharishi Ayur-Ved programs enjoy better health, including increased energy, stamina, memory, and intelligence, and decreased anxiety, depression, and fatigue. Preliminary studies suggest that Maharishi Amrit Kalash — the *rasayana* said to have brought about a high standard of health in the ancient Vedic civilization — leads to fewer headaches, backaches, digestive problems, colds, and reduced sinus congestion, and to greater immunity to allergies and improved neurophysiological efficiency. Dr. Hari Sharma of Ohio State University has found that Maharishi Amrit Kalash increases the

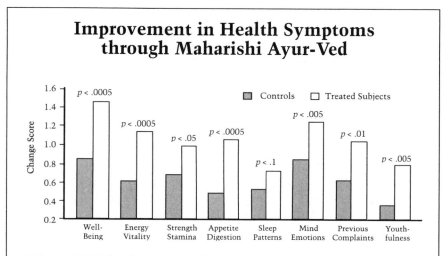

Improvement in Health Symptoms through Maharishi Ayur-Ved

Reference: R.H. Schneider, K. Cavanaugh, S. Rothenberg, R. Averbach, and R.K. Wallace, "Improvements in Health with the Maharishi Ayurveda Prevention Program," paper presented at the International College of Psychosomatic Medicine, Eighth World Congress (Chicago, Ill.), September 1985.

■ Figure 22. People who participated in a one-week Maharishi Ayur-Ved physiological purification program called *panchakarma* showed significant improvements in a wide range of factors including well-being, vitality, digestion, and sleep patterns.

"Gandharva music is that eternal melody of nature which is ever lively in transcendental consciousness. From there it reverberates and constructs different levels of creation."
— Maharishi

immune response and prevents chemically-induced cancer in laboratory animals.[16]

In Maharishi's *Science of Being and Art of Living* the potential benefits of Maharishi Ayur-Ved are described:

> The motto of Maharishi Ayur-Ved is *Ayur-Ved Amritanam* — Ayur-Ved is for immortality — starting from immortality in the self-referral state of consciousness progressing to unfold the full potential of immortality in daily life.
>
> Maharishi Ayur-Ved offers perfect health for the individual and perfect collective health for society, the nation, and for all of humanity — world health, which necessarily includes world peace, prosperity, happiness, and an ideal family of nations.[17]

Maharishi Gandharva-Ved

Maharishi Gandharva-Ved, another discipline of Maharishi's Vedic Science, is being introduced around the globe to create "harmony within oneself, one's family, one's city, one's country, and the whole world."[18] Gandharva music is the classical music of the ancient Vedic civilization, which Maharishi says enjoyed Heaven on Earth. Maharishi explains that:

> Gandharva music is that eternal melody of nature which is ever lively in transcendental consciousness. From there it reverberates and constructs different levels of creation. Gandharva music is the basis of all order and harmony in nature; therefore it has that most harmonizing, most integrating influence.[19]

During the past several years, Gandharva-Ved musicians have toured the world performing in hundreds of cities, from Beijing to New York, as part of Maharishi's Festival of Music for World Peace and Heaven on Earth. One of the musicians, Professor Devabrata Chaudhuri, Dean of the Faculty of Music and Fine Arts and Chairman of the Department of Music at Delhi University, India, explains that Gandharva music "is music in alliance with natural law. It upholds the natural rhythms that prevail at different times throughout the day and night."[20] Because of this, Gandharva music spontaneously creates increased balance and harmony in the environment and greater bliss within the individual.

In Maharishi's words, "From morning to morning the melody of nature is changing. Gandharva-Ved music goes with the time, setting its melodies according to the changing nature. It sets forth those melodies that match with the process of evolution, providing a powerful harmonizing influence in the whole atmosphere to balance the imbalances in nature."[21]

People who attend performances of Gandharva-Ved music report that it has a profound effect on their consciousness and physiology:

> I experienced continued pulses of blissful energy — wave after wave surging through my whole body. (New York City)

> The performance had a deep healing and purifying effect on my physiology. A beautiful feeling of energy and warmth was flowing through my body. (Washington, D.C.)

> I felt most moved by the vocal part of the performance. It seemed as if I were hearing an aspect of eternity. (Vancouver)[22]

In addition to Gandharva-Ved concerts held world-wide audiotapes of Gandharva music are being played in homes and on several radio stations to produce a soothing influence of coherence in the environment 24 hours a day. To hasten the creation of Heaven on Earth, Maharishi's Master Plan calls for establishing Maharishi Schools of Gandharva-Ved throughout the world. Videotaped courses in Gandharva-Ved are currently being prepared to present the knowledge of this beautiful science and art of creating balance in nature.

Over the past few years Maharishi School has been systematically incorporating the knowledge of Maharishi Ayur-Ved and Maharishi Gandharva-Ved into its curriculum. Initial reports indicate that these programs enliven bliss, clarity of thinking, and balance in the lives of the students.

MIU Rising to Become Heaven on Earth

By basing their curricula on Maharishi's knowledge of Vedic Science and its applied technologies, MIU and Maharishi School are rapidly rising to become a complete Heaven on Earth community. According to Dr. Morris:

> The goal of the MIU community is that our University and School, and the surrounding community, will be [a] complete Heaven on Earth, ... where everyone is living bliss. ... Our goal is for every faculty member, every student, every staff member, and everyone in the community to feel always that

"The goal of the MIU community is that our University and School, and the surrounding community, will be complete Heaven on Earth, ... where everyone is living bliss."
— Dr. Bevan Morris, President of MIU

"Higher principles of life are emerging which are enabling mankind to live life in happiness, success, prosperity, and fulfillment, free from the historical tradition of suffering, problems, and weakness."

— Maharishi

"the world is my family," and "I am living in Heaven. . . ."

MIU will continue its world-leading role in unfolding the complete understanding of Maharishi's Vedic Science, and demonstrating through scientific research and through the application of Maharishi's knowledge in education, health, and other areas, the enormous effect that this supreme knowledge of life has produced.[23]

Most importantly, through its Super Radiance program the students, staff, and faculty at MIU and Maharishi School, together with the rest of the meditators and TM-Sidhas in the MIU community, are enlivening coherence in national and world consciousness and creating a lively basis for Heaven on Earth everywhere.

New Principles Arising to Guide Life in Accord with Natural Law

With the rise of coherence in world consciousness, new principles of life are arising in every area of society. These new principles are based on the knowledge of life in accord with natural law — life in perfect harmony with the evolutionary direction of nature. Applying these higher principles of life to every area of society will enable humanity to live in happiness, peace, and prosperity. Maharishi explains:

A radically new time is arising in the Age Enlightenment, brought about by individuals who are spontaneously incapable of making mistakes against the laws of nature. It is natural that this should bring with it completely opposite principles of life from those that prevailed during the previous age of ignorance, where the established rules were, "To err is human," and "Life is a struggle."

Due to the global influence of coherence and harmony, brought about by the [three] million people in the world practicing the Transcendental Meditation program, stress is being released from world consciousness. As a result, higher principles of life are emerging which are enabling mankind to live life in happiness, success, prosperity, and fulfillment, free from the historical tradition of suffering, problems, and weakness.[24]

In the past, principles of living have been based upon the partial, fragmented knowledge of natural law provided by modern science. While the goal of modern science is to uncover knowledge that will benefit everyone, the application of this partial knowledge of natural law has negative side-effects and even threatens our very existence. It is time for new knowledge and new principles to give a new direction to human destiny. Fortunately, Maharishi is fulfilling this great need with his Vedic Science and Technology, which is creating coherence in world consciousness and transforming the trends of time. Maharishi's Master Plan to Create Heaven on Earth calls for introducing programs based on his Vedic Science in every area of society, so that each area can function fully in accord with natural law, and thus fulfill all of its goals.

Here are a few examples from Maharishi's Master Plan of the new principles arising to guide life in different areas of society:

- By adding the knowledge of Maharishi's Vedic Science to government training programs in every country, "coherence will be created in national consciousness and governments will employ the skills of nature in administering society and will thereby raise their administration to that supreme level of efficiency of the government of nature which administers the universe with perfect orderliness."
- In defense, through the knowledge of Maharishi's Vedic Science "every military will be able to prevent the birth of an enemy and this will eliminate the very basis of suspicion, doubts, fear, and controversies which lead to conflict and war."
- In agriculture, Maharishi's Vedic Science will produce "a high level of productivity of the seed and soil, ideal weather conditions and higher consciousness of the farmer, with the ability to spontaneously command natural law and produce abundant harvests for society."[25]

As people in all walks of life in all parts of the world begin to enjoy life more in accord with natural law, the cultural integrity of each nation will be strengthened. Strengthening collective consciousness in one country will not impede the progress of other countries and cultures. According to Maharishi, "No culture will overshadow any other culture. With Heaven on Earth, life will be lived spontaneously in accord with the natural law of the land. . . . The whole world family will be a beautiful mosaic of different cultures [and] with the full blossoming of every culture on earth, civilization will be perfect."[26]

Education plays a key role in creating Heaven on Earth — it

As people in all walks of life in all parts of the world begin to enjoy life spontaneously in accord with natural law, the cultural integrity of each nation will be strengthened.

provides the knowledge that will bring fulfillment to every area of society. The educational programs of Maharishi's Master Plan will train the whole population to live spontaneously in accord with natural law. By introducing Maharishi's Unified Field Based Education into every level of education — primary, secondary, and postsecondary — every nation can give its youth the fruit of all knowledge — the ability to know anything, do anything, and accomplish anything.

Ten Thousand to Create Heaven on Earth

Maharishi's Master Plan to Create Heaven on Earth also calls for establishing large, permanent groups of TM-Sidhas in every city, nation, and continent. As we saw in Chapters Eight and Nine, the collective practice of Maharishi's Transcendental Meditation and TM-Sidhi program by approximately the square root of one percent of the population enlivens the evolutionary power of nature, creating increased coherence, harmony, and peace throughout society.

Through the growing number of people collectively practicing the Transcendental Meditation and TM-Sidhi program in MIU's Golden Domes of Pure Knowledge, the MIU community is playing a key role in fulfilling the requirement of Maharishi's Master Plan for a group of at least 7000 TM-Sidhas on every continent to create a heavenly state of life for the whole world.

The number of students, staff, faculty, and parents at Maharishi School and in the MIU community is quickly growing. At present there are 2,500 TM-Sidhas in the community creating coherence in national and world consciousness. The goal of the MIU community is 10,000 TM-Sidhas living in Fairfield so that there will always be at least 7,000 practicing the TM-Sidhi program together each day in MIU's Golden Domes of Pure Knowledge. This will help satisfy the requirement of Maharishi's Master Plan to have a group of at least 7,000 TM-Sidhas — the square root of one percent of the world's population — on every continent to create a heavenly state of life for the whole world.

By establishing these large, permanent coherence-creating groups throughout the world, Maharishi feels confident that life will be lived in waves of fulfillment, free from problems and suffering, generation after generation. "In every generation," Maharishi explains, these groups "will enliven the unified field of natural law at the basis of creation in the collective consciousness of the population. This will ensure that the trends and tendencies of the life of the people are always positive, peaceful and progressive, supported by the evolutionary power of natural law."[27]

In summarizing his Master Plan to Create Heaven on Earth, Maharishi states:

> The practical program to create Heaven on Earth is to create a strong, indomitable influence of positivity and harmony in world consciousness, an integrated national consciousness in every country, and raise higher states of consciousness in the individual.
>
> The practical means to achieve this is the simple, natural, effortless program to develop bliss consciousness and stabilize it so that no matter where one may be on earth, one will always be in Heaven. . . .
>
> The practicality of creating Heaven on Earth has been verified through the growing experiences of heavenly life on earth by millions of people throughout the world today, through the evidence of the growing Maharishi Effect — increasing coherence in world consciousness year after year — and through a wide range of research on the Transcendental Meditation and TM-Sidhi program. . . .
>
> The world has already moved quite a lot in the direction of Heaven, and Heaven has moved quite a lot towards the earth.

> *—from Maharishi's Master Plan
> to Create Heaven on Earth,
> January 12, 1988*

"**The practical program to create Heaven on Earth is to create a strong, indomitable influence of positivity and harmony in world consciousness, an integrated national consciousness in every country, and raise higher states of consciousness in the individual. "**
— Maharishi

C O N C L U S I O N

THROUGHOUT HISTORY, SOCIETY HAS PLACED ITS TRUST in the power of education to improve life. As Thomas Jefferson said, "No other sure foundation can be devised for the preservation of freedom and happiness."[1] In the two hundred years since Jefferson, however, confidence in education has declined.

"In recent decades," states former Secretary of Education William Bennett, "our schools have too often failed to accomplish what Americans rightly expect of them. Though our allegiance to quality education remains firm, our confidence in the ability of our schools to realize that ideal has been battered by signs of decline: falling test scores, weakened curricula, classroom disorder, and student drug use."[2]

No educator today would contend that education has been completely successful. Although education has produced impressive technological progress, it has not produced individuals who are capable of fulfilling all their own desires while promoting the total well-being of society. The result of our current system of education is that "our nation is at risk," morally, economically, and spiritually.

Modern science based education offers only the objective approach to gaining knowledge, which can impart knowledge only of the outer aspects of life. But life, Maharishi explains, is not only objective — life is subjective and objective both together. Education that offers only the objective knowledge of life will never satisfy students. To be fulfilling, education must be holistic — it must impart knowledge of the complete range of life, from subjective to objective. To do this, education should incorporate Maharishi's unified field based approach.

Throughout this book, we have seen how Maharishi's Unified Field Based Education integrates the knower, known, and process of knowing, bringing fulfillment to students as they gain deeper understanding of their fields of study. Instead of making students pursue a fruitless search for knowledge, Maharishi's Unified Field Based Education gives the "fruit of all knowledge while the tree of knowledge is still growing." Maharishi explains that through Unified Field Based Education, students quickly rise to fulfillment and "grow in the ability to be at home with everything while they are still learning." (See Maharishi's Absolute Theory of Education in Appendix B.)

With the rise of Unified Field Based Education, the "old principles" of science based education are becoming outmoded and are being replaced by more enlightened "new principles," which promote the complete fulfillment of every area of students' lives. The following chart contrasts the current science based approach to education with Unified Field Based Education.

Comparison of Principles of Modern Science Based Education with Maharishi's Unified Field Based Education

Old Principles of Science Based Education	New Principles of Unified Field Based Education
• Utilizes objective approach to gaining knowledge only	• Utilizes objective and subjective approaches to gaining knowledge simultaneously
• Provides knowledge of the known only	• Provides knowledge of the knower, known, and process of knowing
• Provides knowledge of only one state of consciousness — the waking state	• Provides knowledge of all seven states of consciousness — waking, dreaming, sleeping, transcendental consciousness, cosmic consciousness, God consciousness, and unity consciousness
• Develops limited creativity and intelligence	• Develops full creativity and intelligence in everyone
• Makes knowledge available in a campus	• Makes all knowledge lively in every human brain
• Provides incomplete and fragmented knowledge of natural law, resulting in the	• Provides complete and holistic knowledge of natural law, bringing life in accord with natural law,

continuous violation of natural law which impedes progress and damages life*	resulting in fulfilling progress for everyone
• Leads to life lived on the basis of incomplete knowledge — ignorance and lack of fulfillment in life	• Leads to life lived on the basis of complete knowledge — enlightenment and fulfillment in life
• Does not provide the source and goal of knowledge	• Makes the source, course, and goal of all knowledge lively in everyone
• Puts one on a never-ending pursuit of knowledge which does not satisfy the thirst for knowledge, thus leading to perpetual dissatisfaction, frustration, and stress in life	• Delivers the fruit of all knowledge to everyone — life in fulfillment in the state of unity consciousness, with the ability to know anything, do anything, and accomplish anything
• Provides only intellectual understanding of natural law; as a result, one continually violates the laws of nature	• Enlivens the unified field of all the laws of nature in human awareness, resulting in thought and action spontaneously in accord with natural law
• Makes one a slave of the partial laws of nature — a slave to one's own creation, a slave to machines	• Makes one a master of natural law
• Creates imperfect individuals who make mistakes and create problems and suffering for themselves and others	• Creates perfect individuals who do not make mistakes and do not create problems and suffering for themselves or others
• Results in everyone having to struggle to accomplish even a little in life	• Develops the ability to fulfill desires by mere intention
• Creates a society characterized by problems, crime, stress, sickness, unhappiness, and disharmony	• Creates a problem-free, crime-free, disease-free, happy, harmonious society
• Has created the urgent necessity to create Heaven on Earth	• Offers to create Heaven on Earth

*For example, the harmful side effects of modern medicine, pollution of air, water, and food by industry and chemical technology promoted by modern science, and the destructive power of electronic and nuclear technologies have all affirmed the truth, "A little knowledge is a dangerous thing."

Maharishi's Unified Field Based Education goes beyond national boundaries and ideologies. It raises all existing educational systems to fulfillment. The knowledge presented is not mere intellectual knowledge — it directly unfolds students' full creative potential, contributing to success in their own lives and enriching society.

Maharishi School of the Age of Enlightenment and Maharishi International University are models of Unified Field Based Education from preschool through Ph.D. Their success has inspired schools worldwide to implement Unified Field Based Education.

In Sri Lanka, over 5000 students in 22 schools learned Maharishi's TM program. After five months, a survey showed that 96 percent of the students reported personal benefits, including better health, less tiredness, easier learning, and more regular attendance at school. Ninety-four percent also noticed positive effects in their friends. They perceived their friends as being better students, happier, better behaved, more friendly, and less worried after beginning Maharishi's TM technique. A survey of the teachers indicated that the students were less tired, more alert, better disciplined, and more settled in class.[3]

Students attending a large secondary school in Madras, India, have attained top academic honors since Maharishi's TM program was implemented. Mrs. Y.G. Parthasarathy, principal of Padma Seshadri Bala Bhavan Senior Secondary School, where 5000 students and teachers have been practicing Maharishi's Transcendental Meditation since 1980, reviews the success of the TM program in her school:

> When I heard that the TM technique improved alertness, memory, and concentration in students, and that it would improve their performance in classes, I decided that all my students and teachers should learn. Right away I noticed that discipline improved tremendously in all classes, and the students seemed brighter and happier. Then the results on their public exams showed they scored in the top 10 percent of the nation. More students in the upper grades of our school have achieved national academic honors than any other non-governmental school in India.[4]

As we approach the 21st century, it is becoming clear that we need new knowledge — knowledge that will produce happy,

healthy, and prosperous people. Modern science, through its objective approach to gaining knowledge, has glimpsed the unified
field and taken us to the shore of this new knowledge. What is
needed now is for all students to enliven this unbounded source of
intelligence, creativity, and energy in their own awareness. This
is now possible with Maharishi's Unified Field Based Education.

Maharishi's Unified Field Based Education comes at a time
when the problems in education and society are greatest. Our
real hope to bring peace and fulfillment to our nation and the
world is through knowledge. Maharishi explains that only wisdom will bring world peace. By incorporating the knowledge
and technology of the unified field of natural law into their curricula, schools can help awaken the hidden genius in every
child and create a world free from problems and suffering.

Implementing Unified Field Based Education in schools is
easy. It involves no major changes in the school's administra-
tive structure or basic curriculum. All that is required is to incorporate a core course in Maharishi's Science of Creative Intelligence for one period per day (or even one period a week), along
with the use of Unified Field Charts for only one minute per
period in every class. Doing this will give every child the same
opportunity that the students at Maharishi School have to gain
the fruit of all knowledge — the ability to fulfill their own desires and not cause suffering to others.

All parents dream of their children living completely happy
and productive lives, free from restrictions and problems. This
dream is coming true for the parents of children at Maharishi
School of the Age of Enlightenment. This is the first generation
of children with the opportunity to create a heavenly state of
life for themselves and their world. They are the first generation not to know the meaning of suffering, for whom the words
"enlightenment" and "perfection" have a practical meaning.

In this unified field based school, ideal education is an everyday reality, not a fanciful idea. Maharishi's Unified Field
Based Education offers to humanity the solution to all problems
and the promise to create Heaven on Earth.[5] Maharishi summarizes the goal of Unified Field Based Education as follows:

> Throughout the world for the last few years there has been a de-
> mand for some change in education. We are very happy today to

present to the world an ideal system of education where not only will the intellect be fed and satisfied, but the source and basis of life will be fully realized by everyone. The result will be a life that is not baseless but that has a profound basis on the lively field of all possibilities. This is unified field based life, and for that we have Unified Field Based Education.[6]

A P P E N D I X   A

What You Can Do Now

THIS BOOK DEMONSTRATES WHAT CAN BE ACCOMPLISHED in education through Maharishi's Science of Creative Intelligence and its applied technology, the Transcendental Meditation technique. We encourage you to take advantage of this knowledge yourselves — in your schools and in your own lives. It's easy to do.

■ Learn the Transcendental Meditation technique yourself

The TM technique is the heart of the Maharishi Unified Field Based Integrated System of Education. It gives direct experience of pure consciousness — the unified field of all the laws of nature. Research has shown that practicing the Transcendental Meditation technique for fifteen to twenty minutes twice a day develops one's mental potential, improves health, produces more ideal social behavior, and creates world peace. TM is taught worldwide and is practiced by people of all cultures. The seven-step course includes:

1. *Introductory Lecture*: A vision of the possibilities through the Transcendental Meditation program (1 hour)

2. *Preparatory Lecture*: The mechanics and origin of the Transcendental Meditation technique (1 hour)

3. *Personal Interview* with a qualified teacher of the Transcendental Meditation program (15 minutes)

4. *Personal Instruction*: Learning the technique (1 hour)

5. *Verification and Validation of Experiences*: Verifying the correctness of the practice (90 minutes)

6. *Verification and Validation of Experiences*: Understanding the mechanics of stabilizing the benefits of the Transcendental Meditation technique (90 minutes)

7. *Verification and Validation of Experiences*: Understanding the mechanics of the development of higher states of consciousness through the Transcendental Meditation technique (90 minutes)

To learn the TM technique, please call your local Maharishi City Capital of the Age of Enlightenment (Transcendental Meditation Center) — there are TM centers in every major city in North America and throughout the world. For more information, you can also contact:

National Capital of the Age of Enlightenment
5000 14th Street, NW
Washington, DC 20011
Telephone: 202–723–9111

Maharishi International University
Fairfield, Iowa 52556
Telephone: 515–472–1166

■ Visit Maharishi School in Fairfield

To arrange a visit to Maharishi School of the Age of Enlightenment in Fairfield, Iowa, please write or call:

Maharishi School of the Age of Enlightenment
Fairfield, Iowa 52556
Telephone: 515–472–1174,1172.

There are also Maharishi Schools of the Age of Enlightenment in Washington, D.C., Texas, and in many countries around the world. Please contact Maharishi School in Fairfield for further information.

■ Visit Maharishi International University

For more information about Maharishi International University, including visitors' weekends, conferences, and special events, please contact:

Office of Admissions
Maharishi International University
Fairfield, Iowa 52556
Telephone: 515–472–1166

■ **If you are a professional educator, upgrade your knowledge and skills through in-service courses on TM and Unified Field Based Education.**

The American Association for Ideal Education offers special in-service courses for professional educators on the Transcendental Meditation program and its application to education. These courses include instruction in the Transcendental Meditation technique and training in how to use the special unified field based teaching methods in the classroom.

Many school teachers and principals have learned the Transcendental Meditation technique and have attested to its benefits.

The Transcendental Meditation program is the most effective stress management technique available. It is the single most important preparation I do before class. It clears my mind and relieves the stress and tension that accumulates in teaching. It helps prepare my mind for more creative lesson planning.

—Dr. Ronald Zigler, Secondary
school social studies teacher,
Prince George's County, Maryland

Transcendental Meditation is the answer to stress. It produces a calm and settling influence, so that one doesn't get so enmeshed in problems but can approach them with a clear mind, a broad perspective, and an even sense of humor. With a collected mind my energy is less scattered, I get more done, and I can focus in on things more quickly. Also my health has improved — I don't get colds since I learned TM. It is simple to practice; it just takes the decision that you're going to do it twice a day. I recommend it highly to teachers, administrators, and board members."

—Dr. Norman Brust, Principal
Garfield High School
St. Louis, Missouri

For further information about these in-service courses, please contact:

American Association for Ideal Education
Attention: Dr. Susan Dillbeck
MIU Campus
Fairfield, Iowa 52556
Telephone: 515–472–6507

■ **Introduce Maharishi's Science of Creative Intelligence into your own school**

One need not start a new Maharishi School to take advantage of this knowledge — it can be easily incorporated into any existing school or curriculum. Consultants from Maharishi School would be happy to consult with you and your school. For more information, please contact:

> American Association for Ideal Education
> Attention: Dr. Susan Dillbeck
> MIU Campus
> Fairfield, Iowa 52556
> Telephone: 515–472–6507

■ **Help start a Maharishi School of the Age of Enlightenment in your area**

Maharishi Schools of the Age of Enlightenment are being established in many cities in countries around the world. If you are interested in starting a Maharishi School in your own community at either the preschool, elementary, or secondary level, or if you are interested in teaching at a Maharishi School, please contact:

> Maharishi School of the Age of Enlightenment
> Attention: Dr. Robin Rowe
> MIU
> Fairfield, Iowa 52556
> Telephone: 515–472–1174

■ **Take advantage of Maharishi Ayur-Ved for prevention of disease and promotion of health**

Further information on Maharishi Ayur-Ved may be obtained by contacting:

> Maharishi Ayur-Ved Health Center
> 679 Georgehill Road
> Post Office Box 344
> Lancaster, Massachusetts 01523
> 617–365–4549

■ **Read about the applications of Maharishi's knowledge to all areas of society**

Maharishi International University Press offers a quarterly journal, a videotape subscription series, and a wide variety of books on how Maharishi's knowledge has been applied in other areas of society. For a free copy of the MIU Press Catalogue, please call 515–472–1101 or write MIU Press, MIU Box 1115, Fairfield, Iowa 52556.

A P P E N D I X   B

Maharishi's Absolute Theory of Education

Maharishi's Absolute Theory of Education can be summarized as follows:

1. The philosophy of education has its beginnings before creation when the unmanifest Absolute, in its state of eternal continuum, could not hold itself back from knowing its own nature.

2. In the process of knowing itself, the Absolute divided into knowledge and knower, and thus provided the ideal of education—full knowledge of the knower within himself.

3. Full knowledge of the knower is essential for education because it alone provides the stable reference point for the unrestricted flow of knowledge. It gives a common basis to all disciplines and integrates all fields of knowledge.

4. Knowledge is structured in consciousness. The process of education takes place in the field of consciousness; the prerequisite to complete education is therefore the full development of consciousness.

5. An individual whose consciousness is fully developed is said to be enlightened. Knowledge is not the basis of enlightenment, enlightenment is the basis of knowledge.

6. Ideal education is capable of providing the fruits of all knowledge while the tree of knowledge is still growing: the student is fulfilled, and grows in the ability of being at home with everything while he is still in the process of learning.

7. By providing the means to gain enlightenment through the full development of consciousness, the Transcendental Meditation technique brings about an ideal educational system in every culture.

8. An ideal educational system should develop wholeness in the life of the learner. The Transcendental Meditation technique strengthens and integrates the physical, mental, and social aspects of life by developing their common basis, pure consciousness. This creates a wholeness of awareness, the expression of a truly integrated life in which all the material and spiritual aspects of life are fulfilled.

9. When individual awareness is established in pure consciousness, the home of all the laws of nature, thinking is free from weakness and action is free from mistakes. In this state of enlightenment the individual meets with no resistance in achieving his goals; problems and failures are foreign to his life.

10. A few fully educated, or enlightened, individuals are sufficient to give a new direction to the life of their community and by their very presence bring about an enlightened society.

Every man of knowledge knows what an inspiration it is to be in the company of the wise, where every expression shines with the light of knowledge. In the past this opportunity was scarce, and was available only in the presence of highly educated and experienced scholars. The time has now come to have this joy even in the company of the young with the growth of higher states of consciousness. Enlightenment is now going to be a common feature of the youth of the Age of Enlightenment in every country.

C H A P T E R   N O T E S

PREFACE

1. National Commission on Excellence in Education, *A Nation At Risk: The Imperative for Educational Reform* (Washington, DC: U.S. Government Printing Office, 1983).
2. William Bennett, *American Education: Making It Work* (Washington, DC: U.S. Government Printing Office, 1988).
3. Ernest Boyer, *High School: A Report on Secondary Education in America, The Carnegie Foundation for the Advancement of Teaching* (New York: Harper and Row, 1983), p. 6.
4. Boyer, *High School*, p. 56.
5. See, for example, Allan Bloom, *The Closing of the American Mind: How Higher Education Has Failed Democracy and Improverished the Souls of Today's Students* (New York: Simon and Schuster, 1987), pp. 344–345.
   E.D. Hirsch, Jr., *Cultural Literacy: What Every American Needs to Know* (Boston: Houghton Mifflin Co., 1987).
6. Maharishi Mahesh Yogi, *Enlightenment and Invincibility* (Rheinweiler, West Germany: Maharishi European Research University Press, 1978), p. 148.
7. Maharishi Mahesh Yogi, *Thirty Years Around the World: Dawn of the Age of Enlightenment, Vol. 1, 1957–1964.* (The Netherlands: Maharishi Vedic University Press, 1986).

CHAPTER ONE

1. Faculty children now comprise only about 15 percent of the students attending Maharishi School of the Age of Enlightenment although most children do come from families where at least one parent holds a B.A. degree. While most children are from white middle class backgrounds, a number of children come from single parent families, various minority and religious groups, and several non-Western cultures.
2. Maharishi Mahesh Yogi, "Keynote Address," Lecture presented at the annual meeting of the American Association for Higher Education (Chicago, Illinois, March 1973).
3. See John S. Hagelin, "Is Consciousness the Unified Field? A Field Theorist's Perspective," *Modern Science and Vedic Science*, Vol. 1, 1987, pp. 29–87.
   Daniel Freedman and P. Van Nieuwenhuizen, "Supergravity and the unification of the laws of the physics," *Scientific American*, Vol. 238(2), 1978, pp. 126–143.
4. See Hagelin, "Is Consciousness the Unified Field? A Field Theorist's Perspective."
5. Ibid.

6. Personal communication with John S. Hagelin, October 17, 1988.

7. Robert Roth, *TM: Transcendental Meditation: A New Introduction to Maharishi's Easy, Effective and Scientifically Proven Technique for Promoting Better Health, Unfolding Your Creative Potential — and Creating Peace in the World* (New York: Donald I. Fine, Inc, 1987), p. 24.

8. Maharish Mahesh Yogi, *Life Supported by Natural Law* (Washington, DC: Age of Enlightenment Press, 1986), p. 29.

9. Lecture by Maharishi Mahesh Yogi, February 10, 1988.

10. David Orme-Johnson and John Farrow (eds.), *Scientific Research on the Transcendental Meditation Program: Collected Papers Vol. 1* (Rheinweiler, W. Germany: Maharishi European University Press, 1977).

   Robert Keith Wallace, *The Neurophysiology of Enlightenment,*(Fairfield, Iowa: Maharishi International University Press, 1989).

   Susan Dillbeck and Michael Dillbeck, "The Maharishi Technology of the Unified Field in Education," *Modern Science and Vedic Science*, Vol. 1, 1987, pp. 383–432.

11. The names of Maharishi School students have been changed to protect their privacy. This statement by a 12th-grade student first appeared in Roth, *TM*, introductory section.

12. Maharishi International University, *Scientific Research on the Maharishi Technology of the Unified Field: The Transcendental Meditation and TM-Sidhi Program — One Program to Develop All Areas of Life* (Fairfield, Iowa: Maharishi International University Press, 1987), p. 1.

13. See Maharishi Mahesh Yogi, *Enlightenment and Invincibility*, p. 150.

14. See Francis M. Cornford (trans.), *The Republic of Plato* (New York: Oxford University Press, 1967) for Plato's views on education.

   Abraham H. Maslow, *The Farther Reaches of Human Nature* (New York: Viking Press, Inc., 1971), pp. 168–169.

CHAPTER TWO

1. See Maharishi International University, *Scientific Research on the Maharishi Technology of the Unified Field*, p. 1.

2. Robert Keith Wallace, Herbert Benson, and Archie Wilson, "A Wakeful Hypometabolic Physiologic State, *American Journal of Physiology*, Vol. 221, 1971, pp. 795–799.

   Wallace, *The Neurophysiology of Enlightenment*, pp. 52–95.

3. Maharishi Mahesh Yogi, "Keynote Address," Lecture presented at the annual meeting of the American Association for Higher Education.

4. George B. Leonard, *Education and Ecstasy* (New York: Dell Publishing Co., 1968).

5. Maharishi Mahesh Yogi, "Keynote Address," Lecture presented at the annual meeting of the American Association for Higher Education.

6. Maharishi Mahesh Yogi, "The Nature of the Mind as Revealed by the Practice of SCI." In *Science of Creative Intelligence: Knowledge and Experience, Lessons 1–33* [Syllabus of videotaped course] (Los Angeles, CA: Maharishi International University Press), pp. 19–4 to 19–5.

7. Sanford Nidich and Randi Nidich, "Holistic Student Development at Maharishi School of the Age of Enlightenment," *Modern Science and Vedic Science*, Vol. 1, 1987, pp. 433–470.

Stuart Appelle, and Lawrence Oswald, "Simple Reaction as a Function of Alertness and Prior Mental Activity," *Perceptual and Motor Skills*, Vol. 38, 1974, pp. 1263–1268.

Ken Rowe, Joseph Neuschatz, and Sanford Nidich, "Effect of the Transcendental Meditation and TM-Sidhi Program on Reaction Time," Paper presented at the meeting of the American Psychological Association, Montreal, Canada, August 1980.

Kenneth Pelletier, "Influence of Transcendental Meditation Upon Autokinetic Perception," *Perceptual and Motor Skills*, Vol. 39, 1974, pp. 1031–1034.

R. Martinetti, "Influence of Transcendental Meditation on Perceptual Illusion: A Pilot Study," *Perceptual and Motor Skills*, Vol. 43, 1976 p. 822.

Charles Alexander, Robert Boyer, and Victoria Alexander, "Higher States of Consciousness in the Vedic Psychology of Maharishi Mahesh Yogi: A Theoretical Introduction and Research Review," *Modern Science and Vedic Science*, Vol. 1, 1987, pp. 89–126.

Michael Dillbeck, "Meditation and Flexibility of Visual Perception and Verbal Problem Solving," *Memory and Cognition*, Vol. 10, 1982, pp. 207–215.

Willem Berg and Bert van den Mulder, "Psychological Research on the Effects of the Transcendental Meditation Technique on a Number of Personality Variables, *Gedrag: Tijdschrift voor Psychologie* [Behavior: Journal of Psychology] Vol. 4, 1976, pp. 206–218.

Larry Hjelle, "Transcendental Meditation and Psychological Health," *Perceptual and Motor Skills*, Vol. 39, 1974, pp. 623–628.

William Seeman, Sanford Nidich, and Thomas Banta, "Influence of Transcendental Meditation on a Measure of Self-Actualization," *Journal of Counseling Psychology*, Vol. 19, 1972, pp. 184–187.

Charles Alexander, "Ego Development,Personality, and Behavioral Change in Inmates Practicing the Transcendental Meditation Technique or Participating in Other Programs: A Cross Sectional and Longitudinal Study," *Dissertation Abstracts International*, Vol. 43, 1982, p. 539B.

8. David Orme-Johnson, "The Cosmic Psyche as the Unified Source of Creation," *Modern Science and Vedic Science*, Vol. 2, 1988, pp. 165–221.

9. Maharishi Mahesh Yogi, "The Seven States of Consciousness." In *Science of Creative Intelligence: Knowledge and Experience*, pp. 23–4 to 23–5.

10. Ibid., pp. 23–6 to 23–7.

11. Ibid., p. 23–9.

12. See Maharishi Mahesh Yogi, *Creating An Ideal Society* (U.S.A.: Age of Enlightenment Press, 1987), pp. 77–82.

CHAPTER THREE

1. Maharishi International University, *Science of Creative Intelligence for Secondary Education: Three-Year Curriculum* (Livingston Manor, New York: Maharishi International University Press, 1974), p. 85.

2. The Science of Creative Intelligence (SCI) is taught as six-week block courses in the Upper School. During this time, students study SCI for about an hour and fifteen minutes each day. During an entire school year, students will take six blocks of SCI.

3. Maharishi International University Department of Education and Maharishi School of the Age of Enlightenment, *Maharishi's Principles of Teaching*: *Guiding Life Toward Enlightenment* [unpublished].

4. Ibid.

5. Ibid.

6. Maharishi International University, *Science of Creative Intelligence for Secondary Education: Three-Year Curriculum*, p. 57.

7. Maharishi International University, *Science of Creative Intelligence for Secondary Education: First-Year Course* (W. Germany: Maharishi International University Press, 1975), p. 10.

8. Ibid., p. 10.

9. Maharishi Mahesh Yogi, "Creative Intelligence as the Basis of All Knowledge." *In Science of Creative Intelligence*: *Knowledge and Experience, Lessons 1–33*, pp. 9–3 to 9–4.

10. Maharishi International University, *Science of Creative Intelligence for Secondary Education: Three-Year Curriculum*.

11. Ibid., p. 132.

12. Ibid., p. 132.

CHAPTER FOUR

1. Lecture by Maharishi Mahesh Yogi, August 1, 1986, cited in Dillbeck and Dillbeck, "The Maharishi Technology of the Unified Field in Education," p. 339.

2. National Commission on Excellence in Education. *A Nation at Risk*: *The Imperative for Educational Reform*.

3. Maharishi Mahesh Yogi. Lecture presented at The International Symposium on the Applications of Modern Science and Natural Law: To Promote Higher States of Consciousness and the Evolution of an Ideal Society (Luxembourg, March 1982).

4. Maharishi Mahesh Yogi, *Life Supported by Natural Law*, pp. 164–165.

5. Julie Hane, Ashley Deans, and Kurt Kleinschnitz, "Teaching the Unified Field In High School Physics Courses," Paper presented at the meeting of the American Association of Physics Teachers (San Francisco, CA, January 1987).

6. Robert Keith Wallace, Michael Dillbeck, E. Jacobe, and B. Harrington, "The Effects of the Transcendental Meditation and TM-Sidhi program on the Aging Process," *International Journal of Neuroscience*, Vol. 16, 1982, pp. 53–58.

7. Dillbeck and Dillbeck, "The Maharishi Technology of the Unified Field in Education," p. 399.

8. Ibid., pp. 402–403.

9. See, for example, John Bransford, *Human Cognition* (Belmont, CA.: Wadsworth, 1979).

CHAPTER FIVE

1. The Associated Press article dated August 31, 1985, stated that every class at the school, with the exception of the fourth and sixth grades, scored in the 99th percentile on the 1985 Iowa Tests of Basic Skills and the Iowa Tests of Educational Development. The fourth-grade class placed in the 96th percentile and the sixth grade in the 97th percentile.

2. Class percentile ranks and student percentile ranks constitute different units of analysis. To obtain a class percentile rank, the average percentile rank for an entire class is first derived and then compared to all other classes of the same grade level in all other schools. A class percentile rank of 99 does not mean that the average student in a class has scored at the 99th percentile. It simply means that the class average ranks in the 99th percentile compared to the class average of other schools. Nonetheless, Table 1 does indicate that as a whole, students in the Maharishi Upper School exhibit an exceptionally high level of academic achievement compared to other schools across the country.

3. Sanford Nidich, Randi Nidich, and Maxwell Rainforth, "School Effectiveness: Achievement Gains at Maharishi School of the Age of Enlightenment," *Education*, Vol. 107, 1986, pp. 49–54. This study involved 75 students in grades 3 to 8 who took the ITBS both in the fall and in the spring of the same academic year. Of the 75 students who took the ITBS both times during the same school year, 37 of the students were new to the school, and 38 were continuing students. It was found that both new and continuing students exhibited significant improvement in overall (composite) academic achievement over the course of the school year. The new students showed a median score increase of 15 percentile ranks on overall academic achievement (Wilcoxon $T=93.5$, $z=3.89$, $p<.001$). These students also showed significant improvements in mathematics ($T=124$, $z=3.43$, $p<.001$), reading ($T=176.5$, $z=2.64$, $p<.01$), language ($T=156$, $z=2.95$, $p<.01$), and work-study skills ($T=203.5$, $z=2.23$, $p<.01$). The continuing students showed significant gains on overall academic achievement ($T=168.5$, $z=2.93$, $p<.01$), language ($T=192$, $z=2.59$, $p<.01$), and work-study skills ($T=185.5$, $z=2.68$, $p<.05$). This study and all other studies reporting student academic achievement gains are based on Iowa percentile ranks.

4. Sanford Nidich and Randi Nidich, "Increased Academic Achievement at Maharishi School of the Age of Enlightenment: A Replication Study," *Education*, Vol. 109, 1989, pp. 302–304. A total of 42 new students, 21 entering grades 3–7 and 21 entering 9–11 were included in this study. Results showed significant increases in overall achievement during a one-year period of time as measured by composite achievement scales of the ITBS and ITED (Wilcoxon $T=141$, $p<.01$). The students in grades 3–7 also showed significant increases on the reading ($T=50.5$, $p<.05$), vocabulary ($T=60$, $p<.10$), work-study skills ($T=60$, $p<.10$), and language skills ($T=67$, $p=.10$) scales of the ITBS. The new Lower School students showed an improvement of 8 percentile ranks, increasing form 58 to 66 on overall (composite) academic achievement.

5. Continuing students in grades 3 to 8 showed a median score increase of 7 percentile ranks on overall academic achievement, improving from a median score of 70 to 77. They also showed increases of 9.5 percentile ranks in language and 4.5 percentile ranks in work-study skills. See chapter note 3 above.

6. The 21 new Upper School students, included in the replication study cited in chapter note 4 above, showed significant increases in overall academic achievement (Wiloxon T=25.2, p<.02), knowledge of literary materials (T=33, p<.02), social studies (T=48, p<.10), reading (T=48, p<.10), and quantitative thinking (T=64.5, p<.10). Students showed a median score increase of 7 percentile ranks on overall academic achievement, increasing from a median percentile rank of 63 to a percentile rank of 70. In comparing the percentile ranks of new students in grades 3 to 8 to new students in grades in grades 9 to 11, new students in the Upper School tended to exhibit a higher level of academic achievement on their first testing.

7. The number of years students had been practicing Transcendental Meditation was significantly correlated with their overall academic achievement scores on the ITBS and ITED (r=.414, p<.05). Length of time practicing the TM technique was also found to significantly add to the prediction of academic achievement beyond that which could be accounted for by IQ scores alone (t=2.079, p<.05). This study was conducted with 31 students in grades 7 through 12. See Nidich and Nidich, "Holistic Student Development at Maharishi School of the Age of Enlightenment," p. 444.

8. John Muehlman, Sanford Nidich, Bea Reilly, and Catharine Cole, "Relationship of the Practice of the Transcendental Meditation Technique to Academic Achievement." Paper presented to the meeting of the Midwest Educational Research Association, (Chicago, Illinois, October 1988).

9. Robert Kory and Patricia Hufnagel, "The Effect of the Science of Creative Intelligence Course on High School Students: A Preliminary Report." In *Scientific Research on the Transcendental Meditation Program: Collected Papers Vol. 1*, pp. 400–402.

   Roy Collier, "The Effect of the Transcendental Meditation Program Upon University Academic Attainment." In *Scientific Research on the Transcendental Meditation Program: Collected Papers Vol. 1*, pp. 393–395.

   Dennis Heaton and David Orme-Johnson, "The Transcendental Meditation Program and Academic Achievement," pp. 396–399. In *Scientific Research on the Transcendental Meditation Program: Collected Papers Vol. 1*, pp. 396–399.

   P. Kember, "The Transcendental Meditation Technique and Postgraduate Academic Performance," *British Journal of Educational Psychology*, Vol. 55, 1985, pp. 164–166.

10. See, for example, Benjamin Bloom, *Human Characteristics and School Learning* (New York: McGraw Hill, 1976).

    Benjamin Bloom, "The New Direction in Educational Research: Alterable

Variables," *The State of Research on Selected Alterable Variables in Learning* (Chicago: Department of Education, University of Chicago, 1980).

Norman Sprinthall and Richard Sprinthall, *Educational Psychology: A Developmental Approach* (New York: Random House, 1987).

11. See, for example, Nidich and Nidich, "Holistic Student Development at Maharishi School of the Age of Enlightenment," pp. 444–447.

David Orme-Johnson and John Farrow (eds.), *Scientific Research on the Transcendental Meditation Program: Collected Papers Vol. 1*, pp. 361–410.

Paul Williams and Michael West, "EEG Responses to Photic Stimulation in Persons Experienced in Meditation," *Electroencephalography and Clinical Neurophysiology*, Vol. 39, 1975, pp. 519–522.

Andre Tjoa, "Increased Intelligence and Reduced Neuroticism Through the Transcendental Meditation Program," *Gedrag: Tijdschrift voor Psychologie* [Behavior: Journal of Psychology], Vol. 3, 1975, 167–182.

Fred Travis, "The Transcendental Meditation Technique and Creativity: A Longitudinal Study of Cornell University Undergraduates," *The Journal of Creative Behavior*, Vol. 13, 1979, pp. 169–180.

M. Nystul and M. Garde, "Comparison of Self-concepts of Transcendental Meditators and Nonmeditators," *Psychological Reports*, Vol. 4, 1977, pp. 303–306.

12. Howard Shecter, "A Psychological Investigation into the Source of the Effect of the Transcendental Meditation Technique," *Dissertation Abstracts International*, Vol. 38, 7–B, 1978, pp. 3372–3373.

13. Charles Matthews, "Lesson-related Behavior of Students at Maharishi School of the Age of Enlightenment." Lecture presented to the World Assembly on Vedic Science, (Washington, DC, July 1985).

14. This study on IQ included 27 new students in grades 4 to 11. Students increased from an average score of 114 (SD=12.45) to an average score of 119 (SD= 13.46, t=2.15, p<.05). Nidich and Nidich, "Holistic Student Development at Maharishi School of the Age of Enlightenment," p. 447.

15. Tifra Warner, "Transcendental Meditation and Developmental Advancement: Mediating Abilities and Conservation Performance." Doctoral dissertation, (Toronto, Canada: Department of Psychology, York University, 1986).

16. The mean creativity score for the Maharishi School 5th grade students was 110 (n=14, SD=32) compared to 61 for the controls (n=14, SD=16), who were selected from Torrance's data bank. Mean creativity scores for Maharishi School 6th-grade students was 111 (n=15, SD=28) compared to 63 for the controls (n=15, SD=16). Mean creativity scores for Maharishi School 7th-grade students was 111 (n=15, SD=27) compared to 78 for the controls (n=15, SD=18). Mean creativity scores for Maharishi School 8th-grade students was 100 (N=8, SD=18) compared to 74 for the controls (N=8, SD=26; t-values ranged from 2.352, p<.05, to 5.777, p<.001). Nidich and Nidich, "Holistic Student Development at Maharishi School of the Age of Enlightenment," p. 447.

17. Twenty-six students in grades 11 and 12 were given a modified version of the self-concept scale used in Goodlad's, "A Study of Schooling." A four-point Likert-type scale was initially used for student responses. For the purpose of reporting the data in a concise manner, the strongly and mildly "agree" categories were combined into one category with the strongly and mildly "disagree" categories also being combined into a single category. Only one student in the sample gave a "strongly disagree" response and that was to the statement: "I am able to do schoolwork at least as well as others." Nidich and Nidich," Holistic Student Development at Maharishi School of the Age of Enlightenment," p. 447.

18. Personal communication with Richard Beall, principal of Maharishi Upper School, March 1988.

19. Maharishi Mahesh Yogi, "Inaugural Address," Global Celebration for World Peace Day [Satellite Broadcast] (Maharishi Nagar, India, January 12, 1988).

20. Maharishi Mahesh Yogi, *Invitation to Action: Maharishi's Program to Create World Peace* [pamphlet] (Fairfield, Iowa: Maharishi International University Press, 1987), p. 2.

21. Ibid., p. 2.

22. Maharishi Mahesh Yogi, *Maharishi's Master Plan to Create Heaven on Earth* [unpublished pamphlet], p. 7.

23. Maharishi Mahesh Yogi, *Enlightenment and Invincibility*, pp. 151–152.

CHAPTER SIX

1. Gerald Grant, "The Character of Education and the Education of Character," *Daedalus*, 1981, pp. 135–149.

2. John Raven, as quoted in John Goodlad, *A Place Called School: Prospects for the Future* (New York: McGraw Hill, 1984), p. 15.

3. See National Commission on Excellence in Education, *A Nation at Risk* for a more detailed discussion of the problems faced by education today.

4. This study originally appeared in Randi Nidich and Sanford Nidich, "An Empirical Study of the Moral Atmosphere of Maharishi International University High School [Maharishi School of the Age of Enlightenment]." Paper presented at the meeting of the American Educational Research Association, (Chicago, Illinois, April 1985).

5. We wish to thank Ann Higgins and the late Lawrence Kohlberg of the Center for Moral Education at Harvard University for generously sharing their data with us on their Just Community Schools. They had interviewed 15 students in the Just Community School near Boston and 18 students in the Just Community School outside of New York City. For a more detailed presentation of Just Community Schools, see Ann Higgins, Clark Power, and Lawrence Kohlberg, "A Study of Moral Atmosphere." Paper presented at the International Conference on Morality and Moral Development, Florida International University, Miami, Florida, 1981.

6. The percentage of students responding in a prosocial manner to *all* of the dilemmas including the issue of trust were as follows:

	Maharishi School	JCS#1	JCS#2
Prosocial choice for self	71%	60%	50%
Prosocial behavior for self	79%	44%	47%
Prosocial choice for others	83%	60%	67%
Prosocial behavior for others	83%	33%	50%

The *chi* square statistical values showing significant differences between Maharishi School and the Just Community School student responses on prosocial behavior for self and others ranged from 4.39 to 10.03.

Since these figures reflect the number of instances where the same student responded prosocially to all of the dilemmas, these figures would naturally tend to be lower than those in Table 2, which gives the total percentage of prosocial responses of all students for each dilemma.

Due to the very high level of prosocial responses and reasoning ability of JCS students, no statistically significant differences were found on the other scales comprising the Moral Atmosphere Interview, including the prosocial choice categories and the sense-of-community valuing scale.

7. See, for example, P.F. Grimm, Lawrence Kohlberg, and Sheldon White, "Some Relationships between Conscience and Attentional Process," *Journal of Personality and Social Psychology*, Vol. 8, 1968, pp. 239–252.

R. Krebs, "Relations between Attention, Moral Judgment, and Moral Action." Doctoral Dissertation, University of Chicago, 1967.

Lawrence Kohlberg and Dan Candee, "The Relationship Between Moral Judgment and Moral Action." Paper presented to the International Conference on Morality and Moral Development, (Florida International University, Miami, 1981).

M.R. Yarrow, R. Scott, and C.Z. Waxler, "Learning Concern for Others," *Developmental Psychology*, Vol. 8, 1973, pp. 240–260.

8. Kenneth Rowe, Joseph Neuschatz, and Sanford Nidich, "Effect of the Transcendental Meditation and TM-Sidhi Program on Reaction Time." In R. Chalmers, G. Clements, H. Schenkluhn, and M. Weinless (eds.), *Scientific Research on the TM and TM-Sidhi Programme: Collected Papers, Vol. 3*, in press.

Pelletier, "Influence of Transcendental Meditation Upon Autokinetic Perception."

9. Paul Gelderloos, Randy Lockie, and Sooneeta Chuttoorgoon, "Field Independence of Students at Maharishi School of the Age of Enlightenment and a Montessori School," *Perceptual and Motors Skills*, Vol. 65, 1987, pp. 613–614.

10. Sanford Nidich, "A Study of the Relationship of the Transcendental Meditation Program to Kohlberg's Stages of Moral Reasoning," *Dissertation Abstracts International*, Vol. 36, 1975, pp. 4361A–4362A.

Sanford Nidich, and Randi Nidich, "The Transcendental Meditation and TM-Sidhi Program and Moral Development." In R. Chalmers, G. Clements, H. Schenkluhn, and M. Weinless (eds.), *Scientific Research on the Transcendental Meditation and TM-Sidhi Programme: Collected Papers*

Vol. 3, in press.

11. S. Griggs, "A Preliminary Study into the Effect of Transcendental Meditation on Empathy." In R. Chalmers, G. Clements, H. Schenkluhn, and M. Weinless (eds.), *Scientific Research on the Transcendental Meditation and TM-Sidhi Programme: Collected Papers Vol. 2*, in press.

    Nystul and Garde, "Comparison of Self-concepts of Transcendental Meditators and Nonmeditators," pp. 303–306.

    Shecter, "A Psychological Investigation into the Source of the Effect of the Transcendental Meditation Technique."

12. Sanford Nidich, Robert Ryncarz, Allan Abrams, David Orme-Johnson, and Robert K. Wallace, "Kohlbergian Cosmic Perspective Responses, EEG Coherence, and the Transcendental Meditation and TM-Sidhi Program," *Journal of Moral Education*, Vol. 12, 1983, pp. 166–173.

    Sanford Nidich, Randi Nidich, David Orme-Johnson, Allan Abrams, and Robert Keith Wallace, "Frontal Lobe Functioning: EEG Coherence as a Predictor of Highly Prosocial Behavior in Subjects Practicing the Transcendental Meditation and TM-Sidhi Program." In *Scientific Research on the Transcendental Meditation and TM-Sidhi Programme: Collected Papers Vol. 3*, in press.

13. John Farrow, "Physiological Changes Associated with Transcendental Consciousness, the Least Excited State of Consciousness." In *Scientific Research on the Transcendental Meditation Program: Collected Papers Vol. 1*, pp. 108–133.

    David Orme-Johnson and Chris Haynes, "EEG Phase Coherence, Pure Consciousness, and TM-Sidhi Experiences," *International Journal of Neuroscience*, Vol. 13, 1981, pp. 211–217.

    Michael Dillbeck and E.C. Bronson, "Short-term Longitudinal Effects of the Transcendental Meditation Technique on EEG Power and Coherence," *International Journal of Neuroscience*, Vol. 14, 1981, pp. 147–151.

14. Maharishi Mahesh Yogi, "Inaugural Address." In *First World Assembly on Law, Justice, and Rehabilitation* (Rheinweiler, W. Germany: Maharishi European University Press, 1977), p. 25. English translation of *Rig Veda* I.164.39 by Maharishi.

15. See Maharishi Mahesh Yogi, "Inaugural Address." In *First World Assembly on Law, Justice, and Rehabilitation*, p. 25.

16. See Maharishi Mahesh Yogi, *Creating an Ideal Society*, pp. 76–85.

17. Maharishi Mahesh Yogi, *Life Supported by Natural Law*, p. 34.

CHAPTER SEVEN

1. Edgar Kelley, *Improving School Climate* (Reston, Virginia: National Association of School Principals, 1980), p. 17.

2. Michael Rutter, Barbara Maughan, Peter Mortimore, and Janet Ouston, *Fifteen Thousand Hours: Secondary Schools and Their Effects on Children* (Cambridge, MA.: Harvard University Press, 1982), p. 179.

3. Kurt Lewin, *Field Theory in Social Science* (New York: Harper and Row, 1951), p. 44.

4. Emile Durkheim, *Moral Education: A Study in the Theory and Application in the Sociology of Education* (New York: Free Press, 1961), pp. 310–319.
5. Questionnaires used to access teacher responses to school climate were based on forms used in John Goodlad's "Study of Schooling." Seventeen (57 percent) of the elementary and secondary school teachers at the time of the study filled out the questionnaires. Dr. Goodlad's *A Place Called School: Prospects for the Future* (New York: McGraw Hill, 1984) summarizes the results of his "Study of Schooling."
6. See, for example, Wilbur Brookover and others, "Elementary School Climate and School Achievement,"*American Educational Research Journal,* Vol. 15, 1978, pp. 301–318.
7. This poem first appeared in Norman Zierold, "The MSAE Teachers: One For All and All for One," *The Fairfield Source,* Vol. 4, June 1987, p. 15.
8. Goodlad, *A Place Called School,* p. 178. Also see J. Nwankwo, "The School Climate as a Factor in Students' Conflict in Nigeria," *Educational Studies,* Vol. 10, 1979, pp. 267–279.
9. Thirty-seven Maharishi School teachers, who were administered the Maslach Burnout Inventory, showed less teacher stress than norms, as indicated by lower levels of emotional exhaustion $(t=2.92, p<.01)$ and depersonalization $(t=8.28, p<.001)$, and a greater sense of personal accomplishment $(t=8.60, p<.001)$.
10. Edward Wynne, *Looking at Schools: Good, Bad, and Indifferent* (Lexington, MA.: D.C. Heath and Co., 1980).
11. Goodlad, *A Place Called School,* p. 255.
12. See David Orme-Johnson and Michael Dillbeck, "Maharishi's Program to Create World Peace," *Modern Science and Vedic Science,* Vol. 1, 1987, pp. 207–259.
13. Ibid., pp. 207–259.
   Michael Dillbeck, Kenneth Cavanaugh, Tom Glenn, David Orme-Johnson, and V. Mittlefehldt, "Consciousness as a Field: The Transcendental Meditation and TM-Sidhi Program and Changes in Social Indicators," *The Journal of Mind and Behavior,* Vol. 8, 1987, pp. 67–104.

CHAPTER EIGHT

1. Maharishi Mahesh Yogi, *Invitation to Action: Maharishi's Program to Create World Peace* [pamphlet] (Fairfield, Iowa: Maharishi International University Press, 1987), p. 1.
2. Ibid., p. 1.
3. Maharishi International University. *Scientific Research on the Maharishi Technology of the Unified Field: The Transcendental Meditation and TM-Sidhi Program* (Fairfield, Iowa: Maharishi International University Press, 1988), p. 5.
   Orme-Johnson and Dillbeck, "Maharishi's Program to Create World Peace," *Modern Science and Vedic Science,* Vol. 1, 1987, pp. 206–259.
4. Maharishi Mahesh Yogi, *Enlightenment and Invincibility,* p. 27.

Maharishi International University, *Scientific Research on the Maharishi Technology of the Unified Field*, p. 65.

5. Maharishi International University, *Scientific Research on the Maharishi Technology of the Unified Field*, pp. 70–71.

6. Maharishi Mahesh Yogi, *Maharishi's Programme to Create World Peace: Global Inauguration* (Vlodrop, Holland: Maharishi European University Press, 1987), p. vii.

7. Maharishi International University, *Scientific Research on the Maharishi Technology of the Unified Field*, p. 70.

8. John Hagelin, as quoted in Paul Gelderloos, "Book Review: Maharishi's Programme to Create World Peace: Global Inauguration," *Modern Science and Vedic Science*, Vol. 1, 1987, p. 261.

9. Maharishi Mahesh Yogi, as quoted in Paul Gelderloos, "Book Review: Maharishi's Programme to Create World Peace," p. 262.

10. Michael Dillbeck, Garland Landrith III, and David Orme-Johnson, "The Transcendental Meditation Program and Crime Changes in a Sample of Forty-Eight Cities," *Journal of Crime and Justice*, Vol. 4, 1981, pp. 25–45.

11. Orme-Johnson and Dillbeck, "Maharishi's Program to Create World Peace," pp. 206–259.

12. International Association for the Advancement of the Science of Creative Intelligence, *World Government News*, Nov./Dec., 1979, p. 41.

13. David Orme-Johnson, Charles Alexander, and John Davies, "Peace Project in the Middle East: Effects of the Maharishi Technology of the Unified Field on Conflict and Quality of Life in Israel and Lebanon." Paper presented at the Annual Conference of the Midwestern Psychological Association, (Chicago, Illinois, May 1987).

14. Orme-Johnson and Dillbeck, "Maharishi's Program to Create World Peace," pp. 241–249.

15. Ibid., pp. 230–249.
Dillbeck and others, "Consciousness as a Field," pp. 67–104.
John Davies, as part of his 1988 dissertation at MIU, studied the effects of coherence-creating groups in different parts of the world during 821 days of the conflict in Lebanon. He found that on those days when the groups were above the predicted threshold to create an influence on Lebanon, there was a 66 percent increase in cooperative events, a 48 percent reduction in the level of armed conflict, a 71 percent reduction in war deaths, and a 68 percent reduction in war injuries. The statistical significance of these findings was extraordinary. On a global measure, all the seven assemblies that occurred during this period created an effect which was significant at the level of 1×10^{-19}, indicating that the probability of this effect being due to chance was less than one in ten million trillion.

16. Maharishi Mahesh Yogi, *Life Supported by Natural Law*, pp. 163–164.

17. Maharishi Mahesh Yogi, *Invitation to Action: Maharishi's Program to Create World Peace*, p. 4.

18. We are indebted to Dr. Vinton Tompkins for the research on the rise of world peace, as reported by the world press.

19. "Maharishi's Programme to Create World Peace: Global Inauguration."
20. Bevan Morris, *President's Report* (Fairfield Iowa: Maharishi International University Press, 1988), p. 4.
21. For a more detailed discussion, see Orme-Johnson and Dillbeck, "Maharishi's Program to Create World Peace," pp. 241–249.
22. All means employed to achieve world peace have failed. Since 1000 B.C. there have been over 8,000 peace treaties, and each one has lasted on average no more than nine years. Since the United Nations was established there have been approximately 150 major wars. See *Maharishi's Programme to Create World Peace: Global Inauguration* .
23. American Association for Ideal Education, *The Maharishi Unified Field Based Integrated System of Education: Unfolding the Creative Genius of Every Student and Teacher* (Washington, DC: Age of Enlightenment Press, 1985), p. 6.

CHAPTER NINE

1. *Maharishi International University Catalogue 1974/75* (Los Angeles, CA.: Maharishi International University Press), pp. xiii.
2. Bevan Morris, *President's Report*, pp. 3–4.
3. Allan Bloom, *The Closing of the American Mind*, p. 336.
4. Ibid., p. 339.
5. Maharishi Mahesh Yogi, "Keynote Address," lecture presented at the annual meeting of the American Association for Higher Education.
6. Maharishi Mahesh Yogi, "SCI and Interdisciplinary Studies." In *Science of Creative Intelligence: Knowledge and Experience*, p. 28–6.
7. *Maharishi International University Catalogue*, 1974/75, p. 132.
8. Maharishi Mahesh Yogi, "Maharishi's Philosophy of Education," [Printed in several newspapers in Manila, Philippines, October 1984].
9. Maharishi Mahesh Yogi, as quoted in Dillbeck and Dillbeck, "The Maharishi Technology of the Unified Field in Education," p. 405.
10. American Association for Ideal Education, *The Maharishi Unified Field Based Integrated System of Education: Unfolding the Creative Genius of Every Student and Teacher*, p. 5.
11. American Association of Colleges, as quoted in Dillbeck and Dillbeck, "The Maharishi Technology of the Unified Field in Education," p. 417.
12. Allan Bloom, *The Closing of the American Mind*, pp. 346–347.
13. *Maharishi International University Catalogue*, 1974/75, pp. 139–140.
14. American Association for Ideal Education, *The Maharishi Unified Field Based Integrated System of Education: Unfolding the Creative Genius of Every Student and Teacher*, p. 20.
15. Office of Institutional Research, *Maharishi International University Fact Book*, 1987–1988, pp. II–45, II–46.
16. Sanford Nidich, "A Study of the Relationship of the Transcendental Meditation Program to Kohlberg's Stages of Moral Reasoning," *Dissertation Abstracts International*, 36, pp. 4361A–4362A.
    Paul Gelderloos, "Psychological Health and Development of Students at

Maharishi International University: A Controlled Longitudinal Study," *Modern Science and Vedic Science*, Vol. 1, 1987, pp. 470–487.

Michael Dillbeck, Dennis Raimondi, P.D. Assimakis, Robin Rowe, and David Orme-Johnson, "Longitudinal Effects of the TM and TM-Sidhi Program on Cognitive Ability and Cognitive Style," *Perceptual and Motor Skills*, Vol. 62, 1986, pp. 731–738.

Art Aron, David Orme-Johnson, and Paul Brubaker "The Transcendental Meditation Program in the College Curriculum: A Four-year Longitudinal Study of Effects on Cognitive and Affective Functioning," *College Student Journal*, Vol. 15, 1981, pp. 140–146.

Michael Dillbeck, David Orme-Johnson, and Robert K. Wallace, "Frontal EEG Coherence, H-reflex Recovery, Concept Learning, and the TM-Sidhi Program," *International Journal of Neuroscience*, Vol. 15, 1981, pp. 151–157.

Dillbeck and Dillbeck, "The Maharishi Technology of the Unified Field in Education," pp. 409–410.

17. Maharishi International University, *Education for Enlightenment* (Fairfield, Iowa: Maharishi International University Press, 1981), p. 7.

18. Maharishi Mahesh Yogi, *Life Supported by Natural Law*, p. 80.

19. Ibid., p. 81.

20. Maharishi Mahesh Yogi, "Maharishi's Philosophy of Education."

21. Paul Gelderloos, Martin Frid, Phil Goddard, Xiaoping Xue, and Sarah Loliger, "Creating World Peace through Collective Practice of the Maharishi Technology of the Unified Field: Improved U.S.–Soviet Relations." Paper presented at the Second Midwest Social Science Conference (Chicago, Illinois, March 1988).

22. David Orme-Johnson and Paul Gelderloos, "The Long-term Effects of the Maharishi Technology of the Unified Field on the Quality of Life of the United States," (1960 to 1983). In *Scientific Research on the Transcendental Meditation and TM-Sidhi Programme: Collected Papers Vol. 3*, in press.

23. Kenneth Cavanaugh, "Time-Series Analysis of U.S. and Canada Inflation and Unemployment: A Test of a Field-Theoretic Hypothesis." Paper presented at the meeting of the American Statistical Association Alexandria, VA., 1987.

24. Michael Dillbeck, Wallace Larimore, and Robert Keith Wallace, "A Time Series Analysis of the Effect of the Maharishi Technology of the Unified Field: Reduction of Traffic Fatalities in the United States." In R. Chalmers, G. Clements, H. Schenkluhn, and M. Weinless (eds.), *Scientific Research on the Transcendental Meditation and TM-Sidhi Programme: Collected Papers Vol. 4*, in press.

Audrey Lanford, Carol Dixon, and D.L. Reeks, "A Reduction in Homicide in the United States through the Maharishi Technology of the Unified Field, 1980–1983: A Time Series Analysis." (Washington, DC: Maharishi International University College of Natural Law, 1984).

25. Orme-Johnson and Dillbeck, "Maharishi's Program to Create World Peace," p. 238.

26. *Maharishi International University Catalogue 1974/75*, p. xv.

27. Maharishi International University, *Education for Enlightenment*, p. 7.

CHAPTER TEN

1. Morris, *President's Report*, p. 2.
2. *Age of Enlightenment News*, "Maharishi Inaugurates Master Plan to Create Heaven on Earth," Summer, 1988, p. 1.
3. Ibid. p. 1.
4. *Maharishi's Master Plan to Create Heaven on Earth* [unpublished pamphet] p. 3.
5. *Age of Enlightenment News*, "Maharishi Inaugurates Master Plan to Create Heaven on Earth," p. 1.
6. *Maharishi's Master Plan to Create Heaven on Earth*, p. 8.
7. Ibid. p. 8.
8. Ibid., p. 1.
9. Morris, *President's Report*, p. 1.
10. Ibid., p. 2.
11. Ibid., p. 2.
12. Ibid., pp. 2–3.
13. Maharishi Mahesh Yogi, *Life Supported by Natural Law*, pp. 46–47.
14. *Age of Enlightenment News*, "Maharishi Ayur-Veda and the Quantum Mechanical Body," Summer, 1988, p. 13.
15. Jay L. Glaser, "Maharishi Ayur-Veda: An Introduction to Recent Research," *Modern Science and Vedic Science*, Vol. 2, No. 1, 1988, pp. 89–108.
16. Ibid., pp. 89–108.
17. Maharishi Mahesh Yogi, *Science of Being and Art of Living: Transcendental Meditation* (New York: Signet, 1988), pp. 326–327.
18. Maharishi Mahesh Yogi, "Maharishi's Festival of Music to Create World Peace," 1987 [pamphlet].
19. Ibid.
20. *Age of Enlightenment News*, "Maharishi's Festival of Music for World Peace — 1988: The First Step Towards Heaven on Earth," Summer, 1988, p. 9.
21. "Maharishi's Festival of Music for World Peace," 1988 [pamphlet].
22. Age of Enlightenment News "Maharishi's Festival of Music for World Peace — 1988. "The First Step Towards Heaven on Earth," p. 9.
23. Morris, *President's Report*, p. 4.
24. *World Government News*, "The Global Maharishi Effect: New Principles of Life Taking Over in the Dawning Age of Enlightenment," August, 1978, pp. 4–5.
25. *Maharishi's Master Plan to Create Heaven on Earth*, pp. 16–18.
26. Ibid., p. 6.
27. Ibid., p. 19.

CONCLUSION

1. William Bennett, *American Education: Making It Work*, text quoted in *The Chronicle of Higher Education*, May 4, 1988, p. A29.
2. Ibid., p. A29.

3. David Orme-Johnson, D.W., E. Isen, B. Brown, and G. Woollcombe, *Effects of Practicing the Transcendental Meditation Program in 22 Schools in Sri Lanka* (Fairfield, Iowa: Department of Psychology, Maharishi International University, 1986).
4. Y.G. Parthasarathy, as quoted in Dillbeck and Dillbeck, "The Maharishi Technology of the Unified Field in Education," p. 415.
5. See Maharishi Mahesh Yogi, *Maharishi's Master Plan to Create Heaven on Earth* [unpublished pamphlet], pp. 9–13.
6. Maharishi Mahesh Yogi, *"Inaugural Address of His Holiness Maharishi Mahesh Yogi." Maharishi Vedic University Inauguration (Washington, DC: Age of Enlightenment Press, 1985)*, pp. 61–62.

S E L E C T E D
B I B L I O G R A P H Y

Abrams, A.I. 1977. Paired-associate learning and recall: A pilot study of the Transcendental Meditation program. In D.W. Orme-Johnson and J.T. Farrow, eds., *Scientific research on the Transcendental Meditation program: Collected papers, vol. 1.* Rheinweiler, W. Germany: Maharishi European Research University Press, 377–381.

Alexander, C.N. 1982. Ego development, personality, and behavioral change in inmates practicing the Transcendental Meditation technique or participating in other programs: A cross sectional and longitudinal study. *Dissertation Abstracts International* 43:539B.

Alexander, C.N., R.W. Boyer, and V.K. Alexander. 1987. Higher states of consciousness in the Vedic Psychology of Maharishi Mahesh Yogi: A theoretical introduction and research review. *Modern Science and Vedic Science* 1:89–126.

Alexander, C.N., S.C. Kurth, F. Travis, T. Warner, and V.K. Alexander. In press. Cognitive stage development in children practicing the Transcendental Meditation program: Acquisition and consolidation of conservation. In R.A. Chalmers, G. Clements, H. Schenkluhn, and M. Weinless, eds., *Scientific research on the Transcendental Meditation and TM-Sidhi programme: Collected papers, vol. 4.* Vlodrop, The Netherlands: Maharishi International University Press.

Alexander, C.N., G. Swanson, M. Rainforth, T. Carlisle, and C. Todd. 1987, March. *The effects of the Transcendental Meditation program on stress reduction, job performance, and health in two business settings.* Paper presented at the National Conference of the Center for Management Research, Maharishi International University, Fairfield, IA.

American Association for Ideal Education. 1985. *The Maharishi Unified Field Based Integrated System of Education: Unfolding the creative genius of every student and teacher.* Washington, DC: Age of Enlightenment Press.

Appelle, S. and L.E. Oswald. 1974. Simple reaction as a function of alertness and prior mental activity. *Perceptual and Motor Skills* 38:1263–1268.

Aron, A., D.W. Orme-Johnson, and P. Brubaker. 1981. The Transcendental Meditation program in the college curriculum: A four year longitudinal study of effects on cognitive and affective functioning. *College Student Journal* 15:140–146.

Bennett, W. 1988. *American education: Making it work.* Washington, DC: U.S. Government Printing Office.

Berg, W.P. van den and B. Mulder. 1976. Psychological research on the effects of the Transcendental Meditation technique on a number of personality variables. *Gedrag: Tijdschrift voor Psychologie* [Behavior: Journal of Psychology] 4:20–218.

Bloom, A. 1987. *The closing of the American mind: How higher education has failed democracy and improverished the souls of today's students.* New York: Simon and Schuster.

Bloom, B.S. 1976. *Human characteristics and school learning.* New York: McGraw-Hill.

———. 1980. The new direction in educational research: Alterable variables. In *The state of research on selected alterable variables in learning.* Chicago: Department of Education, University of Chicago.

Boyer, E. 1983. *High school: A report on secondary education in America, The Carnegie Foundation for the Advancement of Teaching.* New York: Harper and Row.

Bransford, J.D. 1979. *Human cognition.* Belmont, CA: Wadsworth.

Cavanaugh, K. 1987. Time-series analysis of U.S. and Canada inflation and unemployment: A test of a field-theoretic hypothesis. Paper presented at the meeting of the American Statistical Association, Alexandria, VA.

Chandler, K. 1987. Modern science and Vedic Science: An introduction. *Modern Science and Vedic Science* 1:5–26.

Coleman, J., T. Hoffer, and S. Kilgore. 1981. *Public and private schools: An analysis of high school and beyond, a national longitudinal study for the 1980s.* Washington, DC: National Center for Education Statistics.

Collier, R.W. 1977. The effect of the Transcendental Meditation program upon university academic attainment. In D.W. Orme-Johnson and J.T. Farrow, eds., *Scientific research on the Transcendental Meditation program: Collected papers, vol. 1.* Rheinweiler, W. Germany: Maharishi European Research University Press, 393–395.

Cornford, F.M., trans. 1967. *The republic of Plato.* New York: Oxford University Press.

Cranson, R.W. 1989. *Intelligence and the growth of intelligence in Maharishi's Vedic Psychology and twentieth century psychology. Dissertation Abstracts International* 50.

Davies, J.L. 1988. Alleviating political violence through enhancing coherence in collective consciousness: Impact assessment analysis of the Lebanon war. *Dissertation Abstracts International* 49:2381A.

Dillbeck, M.C. 1977. The effect of the Transcendental Meditation technique on anxiety level. *Journal of Clinical Psychology* 33: 1076–1078.

Dillbeck, M.C., P.D. Assimakis, D. Raimondi, D.W. Orme-Johnson, and R. Rowe. 1986. Longitudinal Effects of the Transcendental Meditation and TM-Sidhi Program on Cognitive Ability and Cognitive Style, *Perceptual and Motor Skills* 62:731–738.

Dillbeck, M.C. 1982. Meditation and flexibility of visual perception and verbal problem solving. *Memory and Cognition* 10:207–215.

Dillbeck, M.C. and E.C. Bronson. 1981. Short-term longitudinal effects of the Transcendental Meditation technique on EEG power and coherence

International Journal of Neuroscience 14:147–151.

Dillbeck, M.C., K. Cavanaugh, T. Glenn, D.W. Orme-Johnson, and V. Mittle-fehldt. 1987. Consciousness as a field: The Transcendental Meditation and TM-Sidhi program and changes in social indicators. *The Journal of Mind and Behavior* 8:67–104.

Dillbeck, M.C., G. Landrith III, and D.W. Orme-Johnson. The TM-Sidhi program and crime rate in forty-eight cities. *Journal of Crime and Justice* 4:25–45.

Dillbeck, M.C., W. Larimore, and R.K. Wallace. In press. A time series analysis of the effect of the Maharishi Technology of the Unified Field: Reduction of traffic fatalities in the United States. In Chalmers, Clements, Schenkluhn, and Weinless, eds., *Scientific research on the Transcendental Meditation and TM-Sidhi Programme: Collected papers, vol. 4.* Vlodrop, The Netherlands: Maharishi International University Press.

Dillbeck, M.C. and D.W. Orme-Johnson. 1987. Physiological differences between Transcendental Meditation and rest. *American Psychologist* 42:879–881.

Dillbeck, M.C., D.W. Orme-Johnson, and R.K. Wallace. 1981. Frontal EEG coherence, H-reflex recovery, concept learning, and the TM-Sidhi program. *International Journal of Neuroscience* 15:151–157.

Dillbeck, M.C., D. Raimondi, P.D. Assimakis, R. Rowe, and D.W. Orme-Johnson. 1986. Longitudinal effects of the TM and TM-Sidhi program on cognitive ability and cognitive style. *Perceptual and Motor Skills* 62:731–738.

Dillbeck, S. and M.C. Dillbeck. 1987. The Maharishi Technology of the Unified Field in education: Principles, practice, and research. *Modern Science and Vedic Science* 1:383–432.

Dixon, C. 1989. Consciousness and cognitive development. A six-month longitudinal study of four year-olds practicing the children's TM technique. *Dissertation Abstracts International* 50.

Durkheim, E. 1961. *Moral education: A study in the theory and application in the sociology of education.* New York: Free Press.

Farrow, J.T. 1977. Physiological changes associated with transcendental consciousness, the least excited state of consciousness. In D.W. Orme-Johnson and J.T. Farrow, eds., *Scientific research on the Transcendental Meditation program: Collected papers, vol. 1.* Rheinweiler, W. Germany: Maharishi European Research University Press, pp. 108–133.

Ferguson, P.C., and J.C. Gowan, 1976. TM: Some preliminary findings. *Journal of Humanistic Psychology* 16:51–60.

Freedman, D.Z. and P. Van Nieuwenhuizen. 1978. Supergravity and the unification of the laws of the physics. *Scientific American* 238: 126–143.

Gardner, H. 1982. *Developmental psychology.* Boston: Little, Brown and Co.

Gelderloos, P. 1987. Psychological health and development of students at Maharishi International University: A controlled longitudinal study. *Modern Science and Vedic Science* 1:470–487.

———. 1987. Book review: Maharishi's programme to create world peace: Global inauguration. *Modern Science and Vedic Science* 2:261.

Gelderloos, P., M. Frid, P. Goddard, X. Xue, and S. Loliger. 1988, March. Creating world peace through collective practice of the Maharishi Technology of the Unified Field: Improved U.S.–Soviet relations. Paper presented at the Second Midwest Social Science Conference, Chicago, Illinois.

Gelderloos, P., R. Lockie, and S. Chuttoorgoon. 1987. Field independence of students at Maharishi School of the Age of Enlightenment and a Montessori School. *Perceptual and Motor Skills* 65:613–614.

Georgi, H. 1981. *A unified theory of elementary particles and forces. Scientific American* 244:48–63.

Glaser, J.L. 1988. Maharishi Ayur-Veda: An introduction to recent research. *Modern Science and Vedic Science* 2:89–108.

Goodlad, J. 1984. *A place called school: Prospects for the future.* New York: McGraw Hill.

Grant, G. 1981. The character of education and the education of character. *Daedalus.* pp. 135–149.

Griggs, S.T. In press. A preliminary study into the effect of Transcendental Meditation on empathy. In R.A. Chalmers, G. Clements, H. Schenkluhn, and M. Weinless, eds., *Scientific research on the Transcendental Meditation and TM-Sidhi programme: Collected papers, vol. 2.* Vlodrop, The Netherlands: Maharishi European Research University Press.

Grimm, P.F., L. Kohlberg, and S.H. White. 1968. Some relationships between conscience and attentional processes. *Journal of Personality and Social Psychology* 8:239–252.

Hagelin, J. 1987. Is consciousness the unified field: A field theorist's perspective. *Modern Science and Vedic Science* 1:29–88.

Hane, J., A. Deans, and K. Kleinschnitz. 1987, January. Teaching the unified field in high school physics courses. Paper presented to the meeting of the American Association of Physics Teachers, San Francisco, CA.

Heaton, D. and D.W. Orme-Johnson. 1977. The Transcendental Meditation program and academic achievement. In D.W. Orme-Johnson and J.T. Farrow, eds., *Scientific research on the Transcendental Meditation program: Collected papers, vol. 1.* Rheinweiler, W. Germany: Maharishi European Research University Press, 396–399.

Higgins, A., C. Power, and L. Kohlberg. 1981. A study of moral atmosphere. Paper presented to the International Conference on Morality and Moral Development, Florida International University, Miami, Florida.

Hirsch, E.D., Jr. 1987. *Cultural literacy: What every American needs to know.* Boston: Houghton Mifflin Co..

Hjelle, L.A. 1974. Transcendental Meditation and psychological health. *Perceptual and Motor Skills* 39:623–628.

International Association for the Advancement of the Science of Creative Intelligence. 1978, August. The global Maharishi Effect: New principles of life taking over in the dawning age of enlightenment. *World Government News*, pp. 4–5.

———. 1987. *Maharishi festival for world peace — 1987* [pamphlet]. Washington, DC: Age of Enlightenment Press.

———. 1988. *Vedic Science — Fulfilment of Modern Science.* Holland: Maharishi Vedic University Press.

Jevning, R., A.F. Wilson, and J.D. Davidson. 1978. Adrenocortical Activity During Meditation, *Hormones and Behavior* 10:54–60.

Kelley, E. 1980. *Improving school climate.* Reston, Virginia: National Association of School Principals.

Kember, P. 1985. The Transcendental Meditation technique and postgraduate academic performance. *British Journal of Educational Psychology* 55:164–166.

Kesterson, J.B. 1986. *Changes in respiratory control pattern during the practice of the Transcendental Meditation technique. Dissertation Abstracts International* 47:4337B.

Kohlberg, L. and D. Candee. 1981. The relationship between moral judgment and moral action. Paper presented to the International Conference on Morality and Moral Development, Florida International University, Miami, Florida.

Kory, R. and P. Hufnagel. 1977. The effect of the Science of Creative Intelligence course on high school students: A preliminary report. In D.W. Orme-Johnson and J.T. Farrow, eds., *Scientific research on the Transcendental Meditation program: Collected papers, vol. 1.* Rheinweiler, W. Germany: Maharishi European Research University Press, pp. 400–402.

Kotchabhakdi, N.J., S. Pipatveravat, N. Kotchabhakdi, P. Tapanya, and S. Pornpathkul. 1982, February. Improvement of intelligence, learning ability and moral judgment through the practice of the Transcendental Meditation technique. In *Proceedings of the Second Asian Workshop on Child and Adolescent Development*, Bangkok and Bangsaen, Thailand. Bangkok: Sri Nakharinwirot University.

Krebs, R. 1967. *Relations between attention, moral judgment and moral action.* Doctoral dissertation, University of Chicago, Chicago, Illinois.

Lanford, A., C. Dixon, and D.L. Reeks. 1984. *A reduction in homicide in the United States through the Maharishi Technology of the Unified Field, 1980–1983: A time series analysis.* Washington, DC: Maharishi International University College of Natural Law.

Leonard, G.B. 1968. *Education and ecstasy.* New York: Dell Publishing Co..

Levine, P. 1976. The Coherence Spectral Array (COSPAR) and its Application to the Study of Spatial Ordering in the EEG. *Proceedings of the San Diego Biomedical Symposium* 15.

Lewin, K. 1951. *Field theory in social science.* New York: Harper and Row.

Maharishi International University. 1974. *Catalog 74–75.* Los Angeles, CA.: Maharishi International University Press.

———. 1974. *Science of Creative Intelligence for secondary education: Three year curriculum.* Livingston Manor, New York: Maharishi International University Press.

———. 1975. Science of Creative Intelligence for secondary education: First year course. West Germany: Maharishi International University Press.

———. 1981. *Education for Enlightenment.* Fairfield, Iowa: Maharishi International University Press.

————. 1988. *Scientific research on the Maharishi Technology of the Unified Field: The Transcendental Meditation and TM-Sidhi Program — One program to develop all areas of life*. Fairfield, Iowa: Maharishi Interna-tional University Press.

Maharishi Mahesh Yogi. 1969. *Maharishi Mahesh Yogi on the Bhagavad-Gita: A translation and commentary, Chapters 1–6*. Baltimore: Penguin.

————. 1972. Science of Creative Intelligence: Knowledge and experience, Lessons 1–33 [syllabus of videotaped course]. Los Angeles: Maharishi International University Press.

————. 1973, March. Address to the American Association for Higher Education, Chicago, Illionis.

————. 1976. *Creating an ideal society: a global undertaking*. Los Angeles: Age of Enlightenment Press.

————. 1977. *First world assembly on law, justice, and rehabilitation*. W. Germany: Maharishi European Research University Press.

————. 1978. *Enlightenment to every individual and invincibility to every nation*. Rheinweiler, W. Germany: Maharishi European Research University Press.

————. 1985. Inaugural address of His Holiness Maharishi Mahesh Yogi. *Maharishi Vedic University Inauguration*. Washington, DC: Age of Enlightenment Press.

————. 1986. *Life supported by natural law*. Washington, DC: Age of Enlightenment Press.

————. 1986. *Thirty years around the world: Dawn of the Age of Enlightenment*. The Netherlands: Maharishi Vedic University Press.

————. 1987. *Invitation to action: Maharishi's program to create world peace*. Fairfield, Iowa: Maharishi International University Press.

————. 1987. *Maharishi's programme to create world peace: Global inauguration*. Vlodrop, Holland: Maharishi European University Press.

————. 1988. *Science of being and art of living: Transcendental Meditation*. New York: Signet.

Martinetti, R.F. 1976. Influence of Transcendental Meditation on perceptual illusion: A pilot study. *Perceptual and Motor Skills* 43:822.

Maslow, A.H. 1971. *The farther reaches of human nature*. New York: Viking Press, Inc..

Miskiman, D.E. 1977. The effect of the Transcendental Meditation program on the organization of thinking and recall (secondary organization). In D.W. Orme-Johnson and J.T. Farrow, eds., *Scientific research on the Transcendental Meditation program: Collected papers, vol. 1*. Rheinweiler, W. Germany: Maharishi European Research University Press, pp. 385–392.

Morris, B. 1988, July. *President's Report*. Fairfield, Iowa: Maharishi International University Press.

Muehlman, J.M., S. Nidich, B. Reilly, and C. Cole. 1988, October. Relationship of the practice of the Transcendental Meditation technique to academic achievement. Paper presented to the meeting of the Midwest Educational

Research Association, Chicago, Illinois.

National Commission on Excellence in Education. 1983. *A nation at risk: The imperative for educational reform.* Washington, DC: U.S. Government Printing Office.

Nidich, R. and S. Nidich. 1985, April. An empirical study of the moral atmosphere of Maharishi International University High School. Paper presented at the meeting of the American Educational Research Association, Chicago, Illinois.

———. 1988, October. Improving the social climate of a Philippine secondary school through the practice of the Transcendental Meditation program. Paper presented to the Midwest Educational Research Association, Chicago, Illinois.

Nidich, S. 1975. A study of the relationship of the Transcendental Meditation program to Kohlberg's stages of moral reasoning. *Dissertation Abstracts International* 36:4361A–4362A.

Nidich, S. and R. Nidich. 1986, October. Student academic development at Maharishi School of the Age of Enlightenment. Paper presented at the meeting of the Midwest Educational Research Association, Chicago, Illinois.

———. 1987. Holistic student development at Maharishi School of the Age of Enlightenment: Theory and research. *Modern Science and Vedic Science* 1:433–470.

———. 1989. Increased academic achievement at Maharishi School of the Age of Enlightenment: A replication study. *Education* 109:302–304.

———. In press. The Transcendental Meditation and TM-Sidhi program and moral development. In R.A. Chalmers, G. Clements, H. Schenkluhn, and M. Weinless, eds., *Scientific research on the Transcendental Meditation and TM-Sidhi programme: Collected papers, vol. 3.* Vlodrop, The Netherlands: Maharishi International University Press.

Nidich, S., R. Nidich, A. Abrams, D.W. Orme-Johnson, and R.K. Wallace. In press. Frontal lobe functioning: EEG coherence as a predictor of highly prosocial behavior in subjects practicing the Transcendental Meditation and TM-Sidhi program. In R.A. Chalmers, G. Clements, H. Schenkluhn, and M. Weinless, eds., *Scientific research on the Transcendental Meditation and TM-Sidhi programme: Collected papers, vol. 3.* Vlodrop, The Netherlands: Maharishi European Research University Press.

Nidich, S., R. Nidich, and M. Rainforth. 1986. School effectiveness: Achievement gains at the Maharishi School of the Age of Enlightenment. *Education* 107:49–54.

Nidich, S., R. Ryncarz, A. Abrams, D.W. Orme-Johnson, and R.K. Wallace. 1983. Kohlbergian cosmic perspective responses, EEG coherence, and the Transcendental Meditation and TM-Sidhi program. *Journal of Moral Education* 12:199–173.

Nidich, S., W. Seeman, and T. Dreskin. 1973. Influence of Transcendental Meditation: A replication. *Journal of Counseling Psychology* 20:565–566.

Nwankwo, J. 1979. The school climate as a factor in students' conflict in Nigeria. *Educational Studies* 10: 267–279.

Nystul, M.S. and M. Garde. 1977. Comparison of self-concepts of Transcendental Meditators and nonmeditators. *Psychological Reports* 4:303–306.

Orme-Johnson, D.W. 1987, June. Conflict Resolution and Improved Quality of Life Through the Maharishi Technology of the Unified Field, given as part of a presentation on Maharishi's Program to Create World Peace at Dag Hammarskjold Auditorium, United Nations, New York, N.Y.

Orme-Johnson, D.W. 1987. Medical care utilization and the Transcendental Meditation program. *Psychosomatic Medicine* 49:493–507.

Orme-Johnson, D.W. 1988 The cosmic psyche as the unified source of creation. *Modern Science and Vedic Science* 2:164–221

Orme-Johnson, D.W., C. Alexander, and J. Davies. 1987, May. International Peace project in the Middle East: Effects of the Maharishi Technology of the Unified Field on conflict and quality of life in Israel and Lebanon. Paper presented at the Annual Conference of the Midwestern Psychological Association, Chicago, Illinois.

Orme-Johnson, D.W., C.N. Alexander, J. Davies, H.M. Chandler, and W.E. Larimore. 1988. International Peace Project in the Middle East: The Effects of the Maharishi Technology of the Unified Field, *Journal of Conflict Resolution* 32:776–812.

Orme-Johnson, D.W. and M.C. Dillbeck. 1987. Maharishi's program to create world peace: Theory and research. *Modern Science and Vedic Science* 1:207–259.

Orme-Johnson, D.W. and J.T. Farrow, eds. 1977. *Scientific research on the Transcendental Meditation program: Collected papers, vol. 1.* Rheinweiler, W. Germany: Maharishi European Research University Press.

Orme-Johnson, D.W., P. Gelderloos, and M.C. Dillbeck. 1988. The effects of the Maharishi Technology of the Unified Field on the U.S. quality of life (1960–1984). *Social Science Perspectives Journal* 2:127–146.

Orme-Johnson, D.W. and B. Granieri. 1977. The effect of the Age of Enlightenment Governor Training Course on field independence, creativity, intelligence, and behavioral flexibility. In D.W. Orme-Johnson and J.T. Farrow, eds., *Scientific research on the Transcendental Meditation program: Collected papers, vol. 1.* Rheinweiler, W. Germany: Maharishi European Research University Press, pp. 713–718.

Orme-Johnson, D.W. and C. Haynes. 1981. EEG phase coherence, pure consciousness, creativity, and TM-Sidhi experiences. *International Journal of Neuroscience* 13:211–217.

Orme-Johnson, D.W., E. Isen, B. Brown, and G. Woollcombe. 1986. Effects of practicing the Transcendental Meditation program in 22 schools in Sri Lanka. Maharishi International University, Department of Psychology, Fairfield, Iowa.

Pelletier, K. R. 1974. Influence of Transcendental Meditation upon autokinetic perception. *Perceptual and Motor Skills* 39:1031–1034.

Roth, R. 1987. *Maharishi Mahesh Yogi's Transcendental Meditation.* New York: Donald I. Fine, Inc.

Rowe, K.C., J. Neuschatz, and S. Nidich. 1980, August. Effect of the Transcendental Meditation and TM-Sidhi program on reaction time. Paper presented at the meeting of the American Psychological Association, Montreal, Canada.

Rutter, M., B. Maughan, P. Mortimore, and J. Ouston. 1982. *Fifteen thousand hours*: *Secondary schools and their effects on children*. Cambridge, MA.: Harvard University Press.

Schilling, P. 1977. The effect of the regular practice of the Transcendental Meditation technique on behavior and personality. In D.W. Orme-Johnson and J.T. Farrow, eds., *Scientific research on the Transcendental Meditation program*: *Collected papers, vol. 1*. Rheinweiler, W. Germany: Maharishi European Research University Press, pp. 453–461.

Schneider, R.H., K. Cavanaugh, S. Rothenberg, R. Averbach, and R.K. Wallace. 1985. Improvements in health with the Maharishi Ayurveda Prevention Program. Paper presented at the International College of Psychosomatic Medicine, Eighth World Congress. Chicago, Ill.

Schwartzschild, B.M. 1985. Anomaly cancellation launches bandwagon for superstring theory of everything. *Physics Today* 38:17–20.

Seeman, W., S. Nidich, and T. Banta. 1972. Influence of Transcendental Meditation on a measure of self-actualization. *Journal of Counseling Psychology* 19:184–187.

Shaw, R. and D. Kolb. 1977. Reaction time following the Transcendental Meditation technique. In D.W. Orme-Johnson and J.T. Farrow, eds. *Scientific research on the Transcendental Meditation program*: *Collected papers, vol. 1*. Rheinweiler, W. Germany: Maharishi European Research University Press, pp. 309–311.

Shecter, H. 1978. A psychological investigation into the source of the effect of the Transcendental Meditation technique. *Dissertation Abstracts International* 38, 7B:3372–3373.

Sprinthal, N. and R. Sprinthall. 1987. *Educational psychology*: *A developmental approach*. New York: Random House.

Tjoa, A. 1975. Increased intelligence and reduced neuroticism through the Transcendental Meditation program. *Gedrag*: *Tijdschrift voor Psychologie* [Behavior: Journal of Psychology] 3:167–182.

Travis, F. 1979. The Transcendental Meditation technique and creativity: A longitudinal study of Cornell University undergraduates. *The Journal of Creative Behavior* 13:169–180.

Wallace, R.K. 1970. Physiological effects of Transcendental Meditation. *Science* 167:1751–1754.

———. 1989. *The neurophysiology of enlightenment*. Fairfield, IA: Maharishi International University Press.

Wallace, R.K., H. Benson, and A.F. Wilson. 1971. A wakeful hypometabolic physiologic state. *American Journal of Physiology* 221:795–799.

Wallace, R.K., M.C. Dillbeck, E. Jacobe, and B. Harrington. 1982. The effects of the Transcendental Meditation and TM-Sidhi program on the aging process. *International Journal of Neuroscience* 16:53–58.

Warner, T. 1986. *Transcendental Meditation and developmental advancement: Mediating abilities and conservation performance.* Doctoral dissertation, York University, Department of Psychology, Toronto, Canada.

Williams, P. and M. West. 1975. EEG responses to photic stimulation in persons experienced in meditation. *Electroencephalography and Clinical Neurophysiology* 39:519–522.

Wynne, E. 1980. *Looking at schools: Good, bad, and indifferent.* Lexington, MA.: DC Health and Co.

Yarrow, M.R., R. Scott, and C.Z. Waxler. 1973. Learning concern for others. *Developmental Psychology* 8:240–26

Zierold, N. 1987, June. The MSAE teachers: One for all and all for one. *The Fairfield Source* 4:15.

I N D E X